Education an

Education and Schooling

W. Kenneth Richmond

Methuen & Co Ltd
11 New Fetter Lane, London EC4P 4EE

First published 1975 by Methuen & Co Ltd
11 New Fetter Lane London EC4P 4EE
© *1975 W. Kenneth Richmond*
Printed in Great Britain by
Cox & Wyman Ltd, Fakenham, Norfolk

ISBN (hardbound) 0 416 78760 6
ISBN (paperback) 0 416 78770 3

Distributed in the USA by
HARPER & ROW PUBLISHERS INC.
BARNES & NOBLE IMPORT DIVISION

Contents

Acknowledgements

The author and publishers would like to thank Macmillan Ltd for permission to reproduce Figure 5, 'Educational expenditure at different levels' from F. Edding, *The Economics of Education,* ed. E. A. Robinson and J. E. Vaizey, and Malmberg/Westermann for permission to reproduce Figure 6, 'Distribution of teacher-centred (favourable) and discursive metaphors in four official publications' from P. H. Taylor, 'New frontiers in educational research' in *Guidance and Assessment in European Education* (Paedogogica Europaea).

1 Introduction

Faced with a world energy crisis which looks like being unresolved in the immediate future, we are obliged to reflect on the pros and cons of power cuts in the education industry. That some hefty cuts are inevitable is probable; that they may actually be desirable seems, on the face of it, highly contentious. To suggest that as standards of living rise so the quality of life declines is to invite incredulity; and to argue that the steady expansion of the educational services which has been taking place since 1870 has now reached the point where it can be seen as a form of cultural pollution that needs to be checked is to risk being called a fool.

Significantly, however, anyone who adopts this line of argument need not be unduly depressed when it meets with stiff resistance, as it is sure to do, for he finds himself in good company nowadays. Although they may disagree in other respects, some of the best minds in the business now share a sense of profound disillusion with the established system of education and all it stands for. As yet they remain a minority (conceivably a creative minority), but it is only a matter of time before others awaken from the intellectual torpor which addiction to the educational services provided for us has induced. The disavowal of ideas and assumptions whose validity was taken for granted until quite recently is bound to be disconcerting, as when Adam Curle declares that 'Education enslaves: men and women become free through their own efforts',[1] or when Jerome Bruner acknowledges that the school may itself be part of the problem of curriculum reform, *not* a solution to it[2] – or, again, when the National Children's Bureau report *Born to Fail* finds that 'school compounds rather than eases the difficulties of the disadvantaged child'.[3] The disavowal manifests itself in unexpected places and at all levels – in professors of education who vacate their chairs because they can no longer keep up the pretence that education in terms of normal school provision is necessarily a Good Thing, as well as in the million and more truants who daily show their contempt for it. While it may be true that the deschoolers have shot their bolt in the sense that any wholesale dismantling of the school system cannot really be entertained and would almost certainly do more harm than good, the *spirit* of deschooling informs our thinking today to an extent undreamed of in the philosophy of the 1960s. Not that the influence of radical extremists like Ivan Illich, Paul Goodman, Jonathan Kozol and John Holt is primarily responsible for what looks like a U-turn in educational thought: the reversal of century-old convictions which have hardened into dogmas stems from a variety of causes, not least those as yet dimly understood as the 'information revolution'.

Inevitably, the suddenness of this reversal looks like a betrayal. Until 1970 the annual increase in the educational budget and the progressive lengthening of the learner's school life were regarded as a cause for congratulation, part and parcel of an improvident philosophy of perpetual economic growth. As a secular substitute for religion, education was universally held to be the indispensable means of achieving the good life. As a commodity, it was impossible to have too much of it and only dyed-in-the-wool reactionaries could dream of protesting that 'More means worse' (a dictum which still sounds curiously wrong-headed in the context in which it was first uttered). Living in a precariously affluent society, most of us remained blind to the extent to which conspicuous consumption was giving way to conspicuous waste, indifferent to the fact that the escalation of costs was yielding something like a nil return. In the USA this has led such influential bodies as the Ford Foundation and the Rand Corporation to recommend radical, immediate and far-reaching revisions of current school finance policies. After reviewing the available research evidence, both concluded that schooling was largely ineffective and that the massive resources devoted to it needed to be deployed in other directions.

In this situation the immediate reaction tends to be one of panic. Like motorists who have come to be dependent on a plentiful supply of petrol, the thought of having to go without luxuries which have come to be regarded as necessities – and which we can no longer afford – fills us with alarm. The trouble is that we are as dependent on the educational services as we are on public transport, electricity supply and all the other services on which any industrial society relies. 'Doing your own thing' may be the motto of an ascendant counter-culture which embraces austerity among other unfashionable virtues, but hardly one that is calculated to appeal to the vast majority conditioned by an education based through and through on competitive materialism.

While it would be naïve to suppose that the connection between policies of educational expansion and economic growth is one of cause and effect, or vice versa, it is evident that the one is implicated in the other. As a subsystem, the education industry is geared to the same set of assumptions, values and objectives as the wider economic system. Once this is recognized two of the most carefully cherished myths in educational theory are exposed as essentially fraudulent.

* The first is the myth of education as an agent for people-processing, the theory (which has never worked in practice) that human beings, like raw materials in any industrial process, can and need to be converted into finished products by being subjected to graded treatment in special institutions designed for that purpose. On this reckoning, schools are to the education industry as factories are to industry at large.

* The second myth, which feeds upon the first, is the one which sees education as the means of achieving equality of opportunity. The assurance that there is always room at the top and that the way to it is open to anyone who cares to scale the educational ladder has kept theorists happy since the days of Plato. Equality of opportunity is a *sine qua non* for any policymaking aimed at social justice, but there is no longer any excuse for clinging to the illusion that education is the route leading to this highly desirable state of affairs. Sociological analyses reveal what common sense should have told us all along, that *all* education systems, even those which pride themselves on

being egalitarian, serve to promote and safeguard the interests of a dominant élite. Thus, in Bruner's latest judgement,

> Both the American and the British experience show that equal opportunity to be educated does *not* overcome the effect produced by unequal access to power and well-being determined by class or race or religion. Children start school in the American system with matching I.Q.s, and end up after a decade of schooling with the black child or the poor child ten or more points down.[4]

Of the two myths, the first is by far the more insidious. In the first place, it has led to education becoming confused in the popular mind with schooling. Thanks to this, learning in the classroom has come to enjoy a prestige and legitimacy out of all proportion to its educational importance. Moreover, it has monopolized the available resources of manpower and finance. Operating as a closed shop, the teaching profession has consistently failed, if it has not actually refused, to exploit resources for learning in the community or to recognize any kinds of learning other than those which fall within its own arbitrary classifications and pedagogical frames of reference. Even today, when the school system in several of our larger cities is perilously close to breaking down altogether, the more adventurous RSLA schemes, schools without walls, truancy centres and other moves towards breaking or bending the laws of compulsory attendance are eyed with official disfavour. So deep-rooted is the conviction that the proper place for adolescents is the classroom that any suggestion that school-bound experience is precisely what many of them do *not* need if they are to fulfil themselves is more often than not brushed aside. Against all the evidence, the authorities continue to insist that only an insignificant minority are disaffected. Public opinion, moreover, is not disposed to give much credence to research findings which demonstrate that full-time five-day school attendance makes relatively little difference to eventual educational achievement and may, to that extent, be reckoned very largely a waste of time and money.

Worst of all are the effects of a protracted school life on teenagers who are not cut out for academic studies. Quite apart from the all-too-frequent news items reporting unruliness, hooliganism and acts of violence on and off the premises of secondary schools, there is increasing evidence that a law of diminishing returns sets in around the age of thirteen to fourteen. The restiveness of the young who are legally compelled to remain *in statu pupillari* is of course an international phenomenon; and the danger is that, in the absence of any major shift in their outlook, the authorities will seek to contain it, as they have done in the past and for the most part are still doing, by imposing more rigorous bureaucratic controls. But to pretend that the system must be maintained at all costs is futile when the costs are as prohibitive as they are and when the returns are so minimal.

In the US James Coleman notes, as many educationists have already done, that the student role of young persons has become so enlarged as to constitute the major portion of their youth. The parts formerly played by the family, the workplace, the peer group and the community have gradually been ousted as the school has taken over more and more of the responsibilities – and more and more of the time – for their upbringing. In general, adolescents have been relegated to a passive role, always in preparation for action, rarely or never acting. 'They are shielded from responsibility, and they become irresponsible,' Coleman says. 'They are held in dependent status, and they come to act as dependents; they are kept away from productive work, and they become unproductive.'[5] The answer to the problem, he thinks, is to put the young where everyone else is and where the action is, 'inside the economic institutions where the productive activities of society take place'.

Much the same verdict has been reached by educationists who do not necessarily share the ideology of the deschoolers. From now on, some de-emphasizing of the importance which has come to be attached to the kind of organized, institutionalized learning catered for in schools, colleges and universities has to be bargained for. The search for alternative forms of organized learning, already begun, needs to be undertaken with a new sense of urgency. More necessary still, we need to revise our ideas about what counts as 'learning'. How far the application of modern technologies of communication will help in the devisal of a new institutional framework remains to be seen. The Open University may be seen as a tentative step in this direction, arguably the most significant British achievement in recent decades. If only from the point of view of cost-effectiveness, it represents a more rational use of resources, its course offerings and performance to date comparing more than favourably with those of any of the lavishly endowed conventional foundations, old or new. Despite its critics and detractors, not to mention the political and other handicaps under which it operates, the OU has at least gone some way towards releasing students from the age-old constraints of time and space. While the personal relationship between teacher and taught remains as desirable as ever, it is no longer absolutely necessary to require students – or for that matter adolescents who have mastered the basic skills – to assemble at a given place and time, or to insist that they reach given standards of attainment by a certain age. While the ideal of a 'learning society', in which education is no longer confined to the early years of life and becomes instead an ongoing, all-involving process affecting the individual's work and leisure activities throughout his career, may seem utopian and remote, any idea of schooling as a once-and-for-all 'preparation for life' is clearly due for revision. Changes in the life cycle demand a life style which admits of no clean break between 'learning' and 'living'. A logical consequence of ceasing to regard schooling as the be-all and end-all of education is a shift in the focus of attention, hitherto concentrated on the learner's life between the ages of five and sixteen, and a greater concern with the parts played by agencies other than the statutory system. As community service, education can no longer afford to put all its eggs in one basket.

Among other things, this explains why forward thinkers the world over are impressed by the prospects opening up in the field of lifelong education and why plans and policies to this end are now being formulated – more actively by our colleagues in the European community as a whole, be it said, than here in Britain. Torsten Husén, for one, is sceptical about the effectiveness of schooling as it is organized at present. In his valedictory address to his associates on relinquishing his chair of educational research at the University of Stockholm, he made it plain that an open disavowal of their professional faith was called for:

> It might seem impertinent, not to say mindless, to appear before an assembly of educators to challenge the merits of the school as an educational institution. It would be like addressing a congress of clergymen to question the competence of the Church to minister to man's religious needs. During the hundred years that have passed since public elementary education became universal in Western Europe, much of what the school does has become so institutionalized that the resulting pronounced matter-of-course character is somehow assumed to be rooted in the metaphysical.[6]

There lies the initial difficulty which has to be overcome. We are all creatures of history, living in a schooled society. The latter's rise and progress in England has been accurately charted by David Wardle. The point he makes at the outset of his survey of the formative period of the English system provides a fitting preamble for the arguments to be pursued in these pages. As he says,

> As an intellectual proposition most people are prepared to accept, if they are asked to ponder the matter, that more learning takes place outside than inside schools. Indeed, it is obvious that in the first five years of life and in the lengthy period after formal school-ing is completed, the great majority of our learning is done uncon-sciously without deliberate intent, and certainly without the intervention of teacher or building.
>
> And yet, unless our attention is specially directed to the question, we continue to see education as an activity which takes place in an institution specially set aside for the purpose, and which is given by professional teachers. In all advanced industrial societies, and in an increasing number of 'developing' countries, all children spend a substantial period in formal schooling, and as the de-schoolers point out, there is a tendency for the length of this period to be used as an index of a society's progress. Among the most advanced nations length of schooling is being replaced as an index by the proportion of pupils who proceed to higher education – and higher education, of course, is carried on in colleges and universities, institutions of formal learning in the same class as schools.
>
> A mental effort is needed to think away the identification of 'education' with 'schooling', but in historical terms the dominance of the school is very recent.[7]

All of which helps to explain what this book is about and why much of what it has to say may either exasperate or baffle the reader who dislikes being asked to 'think away' assumptions and ideas which he has long accepted.

The first task, accordingly, is to tease out the necessary distinctions between 'education' and 'schooling'. That done, the next step is to examine the ways and means by which, over the centuries, 'learning' has come to be regarded as a commodity purveyed by professional teachers in the classroom – to the extent that nowadays any signi-ficant 'learning' in the absence of instruction tends to be played down, if it is not ruled out of the reckoning altogether. Criticism of the effects and defects of formal schooling is becoming widespread nowadays, and not only among the ranks of the deschoolers. There is a good deal of loose talk about the need for 'alternatives', very little about the practical implications. Administrators, teachers and parents cannot be blamed if they remain unimpressed by theoretical arguments which seek to draw a vital distinction between formal schooling and education: they require some demonstration of what can be done and what happens when the attempt is made. At this point, therefore, it seemed timely to include an account of one small-scale project modelled on the original Parkway Program, the first 'school without walls'; small-scale and short-lived because of the constraints imposed upon it by a bureaucratic system. The idea of learning outside the school raises two major issues in any future theory and practice of education. The first of these is the one which is commonly referred to, for want of a better name, as 'lifelong learning'. The other concerns the as yet largely unexplored domain of informal learning – in the home, at the workplace, in community life – in which the normal teacher–pupil relationship does not apply. Instead of envisaging education as people-processing, a generative theory is proposed which treats the learner as a responsible agent, free to act on his own initiatives, not necessarily submissive to the controls imposed upon him by his mentors, in short, capable at all stages of development of getting an education for himself.

Husén's summary of his own position, arrived at as a result of analysing the mass of research evidence made available by International Educational Achievement and other investigations, provides as appropriate a starting point as any for a critique of education and schooling:

> During the last decade the gospel has spread that institutionalized education accounts for the major portion of economic growth. It has been asserted that education should therefore be allowed to grow more rapidly than other areas in the public sector. Society should see to it that everyone gets as much formal education as he can usefully assimilate. For a couple of decades now the majority of teenagers in Europe have gone to full-time schooling instead of working with their elders outside the school walls. I think it is time to take a critical look at institutionalized education without necessarily letting the pendulum swing to the other extreme and requiring complete 'deschooling'. I think it is of the utmost importance that we try to establish our bearings now when the

school as an institution seems to be on a collision course with society at large.

We have to be rather ruthless in pointing out which holy cows in education we have to get rid of. I do not pretend to have conducted a systematic culling operation. Suffice it to say that some of the time-honoured conceptions have been questioned . . . comparative studies of the outcomes of school instruction have led me to the belief that we have grossly overemphasized the didactic aspects of education. The tricks and formal procedures in the classroom that play such an immense role in teacher training in the last analysis clearly account for only a tiny portion of the variation in learning outcomes between classrooms.[8]

At a time when financial cutbacks, fuel shortages and other restrictions threaten to disrupt the educational services – services already suffering from internal disruption – it may not be popular to say that possibly no great harm will be done as a consequence. Perhaps a frugal regimen is what we most need. At the very least, next time we see the headlines – 'SCHOOLS CLOSED FOR LACK OF HEATING: PUPILS' EDUCATION AT RISK' – we might do worse than remind ourselves that we do not *have* to believe everything we read in the newspapers.

2 Education and schooling: what's the difference?

In the first place, why bother to look for a distinction between the two terms? Why all this fuss about the use of words which everyone recognizes to be fuzzy, and why pretend to feel concerned if they *are* commonly taken to be interchangeable? Many would say that the question, 'What is the difference between education and schooling?', if not actually improper, involves a verbal quibble and to that extent should be dismissed as a non-problem. English usage is essentially flexible in these matters, after all, not given to the terminological exactitude of other European languages. In this connection Professor Titone's international micro-lexicon (Fig. 1, p. 12) affords some interesting comparisons.

Sociologists, for their part, do not insist on any firm distinction between education and schooling. For them the organized learning which takes place in schools and similar institutions is a social *fact*. They have a point, of course. For practical purposes we must agree that entries in *Who's Who* informing us that so-and-so was 'educated at Eton and Trinity' are in some sense correct: it would be highly pedantic to object that, strictly speaking, the word ought to be 'schooled'!

Chameleon-like, the meaning of the word 'education' is as variable as its contexts in time and space. It is too late in the day to protest that it was invented in the eighteenth century by schoolmasters who wished to give their work a spurious and inflated self-importance. The truth is that ever since mass schooling was first introduced the enlargement of its influence and control over the young has fostered the impression that there is little or no significant difference between education and schooling. Formerly, the family, the Church, apprenticeship, neighbourhood and other social agencies played a major role in the *rearing*, *nurture* and *upbringing* of children. Significantly, these words are no longer fashionable in the technical jargon of education. As R. S. Peters remarks in his essay 'The justification of education', 'There is a general concept of "education" which covers almost any process of learning, rearing or growing up. Nowadays, when we speak of education in this general way, we usually mean going to school, to an institution devoted to learning.'[1]

This extension of the word 'education' to cover a wide range of functions can be seen as resulting from the gradual takeover by state-controlled bureaucracies of responsibilities which were originally discharged either by individuals on their own behalf or by informal, voluntary organizations. This aggrandizement is so obvious that it scarcely needs to be illustrated. Thus, in recent years, teacher training colleges have been renamed colleges of education, an honorific title which owes more to status-seeking than to anything else. A similar pretentiousness is the trademark of most histories of education, in which the relative insignificance of the part played by formal schooling in the cognitive and personal development of the young has been consistently suppressed. To date, in Sol Cohen's judgement, most historians, in confusing education with schooling, stand guilty of the sin of parochialism ('writing a narrow history of the schools') and the sin of evangelism ('seeking to inspire teachers with professional zeal rather than attempting to understand what really happened').[2] Ministers of education would, no doubt, be very surprised if they were advised that their titles of office were misleading and that it might be better for all concerned if they reverted to calling themselves ministers of public instruction. Most professors of education would be indignant – for the same reasons as were the sophists in Socrates's day – if it were put to them that they were violating some as yet unwritten Trade Descriptions Act, still more indignant if it were suggested that they were condoning practices which were positively miseducative.

INTERNATIONAL MICRO-LEXICON OF EDUCATIONAL TERMS

Compiled by Professor R. Titone, University of Rome

English	Italian	French	German
education formation training	*educazione*	éducation	Erziehung Bildung
education instruction	*istruzione*	instruction	Bildung Unterricht
teaching	*insegnamento*	enseignement	Lehren
educator	*educatore*	éducateur	Erzieher
teacher instructor	*insegnante*	instituteur professeur	Lehrer
teacher professor[1]	*professore*	professeur	Lehrer Professor[2]
learning	*apprendimento*	apprentissage	Lernen

education
science of
  education
educational
  philosophy
philosophy of
  education
	pedagogia	science de l'éducation	Pädagogik
			Erziehungswis-
			  senschaft

educationist
educational
  philosopher
	pedagogista	(théoricien de
		  l'éducation)
			Pädagog

pedagogy
  (USA)
didactics (GB)
teaching
  methodo-
  logy (USA)
	didattica	pédagogie	Didaktik
			Unterrichtslehre
			Methodik

pedagogue
  (GB)
(pedagog:
  USA)
	didatta	pédagogue	Didaktiker

[1] *Teacher* for primary and secondary pupils; *Professor* for university students.
[2] *Lehrer*, general term; *Professor* = *Herr Professor*: epithet reserved for university teachers.

Fig. 1　International micro-lexicon of educational terms

A good example of the professional educationists' intellectual arrogance is to be found in *The Logic of Education*. Referring to the hazy views of education held by laymen, Hirst and Peters write:

> Their understanding has not become differentiated to the extent of needing a special word for referring to the passing on of what they think is valuable. They have *a* concept of education, for they use the term to refer to what goes on in schools and universities. But they have not *our* concept. The only trouble about dealing with the objection is that people who lack our concept of education are, at the moment, rather numerous. 'We', in this context, are in the main educated people and those who are professionally concerned with education; and 'we' are not in the majority of people who use the word 'education'.[3]

This feigned humility might be more convincing were it not for the fact that what the authors are pleased to call 'our concept of education' is derived from, and relates much more closely than the layman's to 'what goes on in schools and universities'. As such, it is woefully out of sympathy with the man in the street's aspirations and experience. The 'understanding', 'knowledge' and 'learning' they champion stem from a world of discourse which has always been the exclusive preserve of scholars. This explains, incidentally, why their recommendations for curriculum renewal based on the traditional 'disciplines' must be seen as a forlorn, last-ditch attempt to resuscitate the Seven Liberal Arts – which are as remote from the felt needs of the majority of pupils today as they were from those of medieval serfs. (A reminder, this, of T. S. Eliot's saying, 'No humanist, *qua* humanist, ever had anything to offer the mob.')

But, surely, it will be said, most of us are well aware of the difference between education and schooling and cannot be accused of supposing that one is the same as the other. In fact, although many of us privately recognize the need to draw a distinction we find it difficult to do so; and in public we tend to go along with the opinion that no great harm can come of treating the two terms as synonymous. The general view would seem to be that education and schooling, like love and marriage, go together; in the words of yesteryear's popular song, 'You can't have one without the other'.

'TEESIDE TEACHERS' STRIKE: PUPILS MISS EDUCATION', a newspaper headline announces. Children attend school in order to receive an education, thinks the average parent – in the same way that shoppers go to the supermarket to buy groceries. 'Education', in short, has come to be thought of as a commodity; and 'schooling' provides its service station. Since the latter is the monopoly of the 'education system' it is hardly surprising that the notion of education without schooling should have come to seem a contradiction in terms.

Are we only playing at word games, then, in seeking to draw a distinction? Granted, both terms belong to the class which Wittgenstein described as blurred at the edges, interpenetrating and shading off into each other so imperceptibly that there seems to be no saying for certain where schooling ends and education begins. As Polanyi says, 'we must accept the risks of semantic indeterminacy, since only words of indeterminate meaning can have a bearing on reality, and that for meeting this hazard we must credit ourselves with the ability to perceive such bearing.'[4] Seeing that it is useless to look for definitions, and in view of the close family resemblance between education and schooling, what harm can there be in treating them as if they were synonymous? We cannot ignore the social fact that 'ordinary language has lost the ability to distinguish between procedure and substance, schooling and education, curricular participation and learning'.[5] But it would be folly, nevertheless, to conclude that the affinities between 'education' and 'schooling' mean that the words are identical.

For the sake of clarification, the first step is to pinpoint the essential characteristics of the two concepts. The following list enumerates some of these in the form of propositions. If any of these propositions is held to be unarguable it will be because a clear distinction is self-evident. If, on the other hand, a valid objection can be raised against any of them the objection will at least serve as a cue for further discussion.

1 *'Education' is much the fuzzier of the two concepts*
Schooling is a tangible process, embodied in institutions: it has its 'outward and visible signs', whereas *education* corresponds rather to an 'inward, invisible grace'. In other words, whether or not a person has been subjected to schooling admits of no argument: whether or not he can be said to have been educated is more doubtful.

2 *'Education' is a more socially prestigious word than 'schooling'*
In Ryle's terminology 'education' is an *achievement* word, 'schooling' a *task* word. Alternatively, 'education' is U, 'schooling' non-U.

3 *There is a part-whole relationship between schooling and education*
Schooling is only one among a number of social agencies concerned
with the process of education.

4 *There is a means-end relationship between schooling and education*
School serves a propaedeutic purpose in making education possible.
It is, as Bruner says, an *enabling* process which helps the learner to
become a responsible agent. 'Education' is what happens when he
leaves his instructor behind and takes off on his own. Carl Bereiter,
in an article entitled 'Schools without education' in the *Harvard
Educational Review*,[6] argues forcibly that we would do well to drop
the pretence that schools exist to provide pupils with an 'education':
far better, he thinks, to cut our losses and agree that all they can
rightly be expected to do is to provide basic training.

**5 *'Schooling' is largely concerned with training in specific skills
whereas 'education' is all-pervasive in its influence***
We usually say that a man has been schooled in this, that or the other
field of knowledge – mathematics, physics, law, letters – but we speak
of him as 'educated' without any such qualification. According to
R. S. Peters, *trained* suggests the development of competence in a
limited skill or mode of thought whereas *educated* suggests a linkage
with a wider system of beliefs.

Objection

A. N. Whitehead maintained, rightly, that any liberal education
worth the name must enable a man to *know* something well and to
do something well. Again, in *The Evolution of Educational Theory*,
Sir John Adams warned against the futile and effete notion of 'the
man who is educated, just that and nothing more'.

**6 *Animals can be schooled but only human beings can properly be
said to be educated***
Dolphins, even killer whales, can be taught, instructed, conditioned,
trained, 'gentled' – schooled – to perform all manner of engaging
tricks. Possibly the greatest danger in the current tendency to identify
education with schooling is that it leads ultimately to a dehumaniza-
tion of theory and practice. In the last resort, education has to do
with what M. V. C. Jeffreys has called 'the sacred and hidden identity
which no techniques can reach'.

Objection 1

'School is the one difference between men and animals. Animals don't go to school. In the Free Development of their Personality, swallows have built their nests in exactly the same way for millenniums.'[7]

Objection 2

As late as the nineteenth century English usage saw nothing wrong in speaking of the education of animals and even plants. The confining of 'educated' to 'man' is of comparatively recent origin.

7 *Schooling has its detractors but everyone, apparently, is in favour of education*

Anti-school criticism has a long history, too long to recapitulate here. One has only to think of Quintilian's castigations of the vices of Roman schools, of Luther's fulminations against them as 'slaughterhouses of the mind', of Rousseau's contempt for 'jeunes professeurs', of Pestalozzi's sad comment on the pupils of Geneva, 'Sie kennen viel und wissen nichts', of Dewey's complaint about 'the divorce of school from life' – and, in the contemporary situation, of Kozol's *Death at an Early Age*, Freire's *Pedagogy of the Oppressed* or John Holt's round assertion that 'Schools are bad places for kids'. Yet in denouncing *schooling*, all these critics urge the cause of *education* and stress its benefits.

Objection

These criticisms apply only to bad schooling, not to schooling *per se*.

8 *Under certain conditions, schooling can be shown to be miseducative – which would be impossible if schooling and education were invariably identical*

Just what these 'certain conditions' are, and how they arise, should therefore be our immediate concern. See point 15 below for further discussion. Suffice it for the moment to say that evidence suggests that, for a substantial proportion of non-academic teenagers, prolonged schooling is too much of a good thing. For many, the extra year at school (since the raising of the school leaving age) merely confirms and reinforces the anomie, frustration and low ego concepts which they have acquired en route and from which they are unlikely to recover. The overt objectives of the secondary school, measured in terms of cognitive achievement, mask its covert objectives – the hidden curriculum which condemns a majority of its pupils to the role of third-class citizens. 'The fact that much of what goes by the name of education, i.e. schooling, teaching, and learning, does not necessarily assist in the optimization of human life, and in fact is often non-, mis-, or even anti-educative, signifies the general inadequacy of the educationists' preparation for, and comprehension of their role.'[8] New ventures, like the so-called School Without Walls, must therefore be seen as necessary attempts to mount a rescue operation, releasing young adults from enforced confinement and restoring them to their rightful place as active members in society. Plutarch's saying, 'The City is the best teacher', is at the heart of many of the significant innovations and experiments in educational reform today. Over-schooling, we are now beginning to realize, has the effect of prolonging childhood and adolescence unnecessarily; it is a device for preserving the learner in a state of submissive dependence. Despite its protestations to the contrary, it does everything possible to sidetrack, if not actually deny, the will to be free, to be different, to 'do one's own thing' – which explains why so many of the young nowadays are driven to seek outlets for personal satisfaction outside the school system. Task forces, youth volunteers, community service – these are the growth points for tomorrow's education.

9 *Schooling is imposed on the learner willynilly, but education is liberal in the sense that it implies the existence of a responsible free agent*
To be *in statu pupillari* is to submit to the authority and discipline of a mentor. Voluntary learning admits of no such need. In Rousseau's terminology, school learning is *labor* (being consciously subject to external, adult authority) whereas spontaneous, playful learning is *opus*. In Illich's terminology, it is the difference between a *bureaucratic*, rule-bound learning situation and one which is *convivial*. In Piagetian terms, it is the difference between *assimilation* and *accommodation*.

Objection 1
In the case of young children, compulsion, however arbitrary, is necessary for their protection. Moreover, even as adults, most of us

are grateful for having been forced to learn and do things against our personal inclinations. Says Peters, 'Gifted teachers are precisely those who can get children going on activities which have no initial appeal to them.'[9]

10 *Educere aut educare? In general, education corresponds to the former, schooling to the latter*

Debates about the derivations from these Latin verbs are mostly claptrap. At the same time, they serve to highlight the difference between those two schools of thought which, for the sake of convenience, are commonly referred to as 'teacher-based' and 'child-centred'. Hitherto, educational theory and practice have been predominantly 'teacher-based', the assumption being that education was a process which was administered to the learner – a matter of doing things to him and for him – *not* a process in which he was the prime mover.

The Socratic method, Rousseau's negative education, Dewey's Progressivism, activity methods and integrated day curricula in primary schools, resources for learning projects *et al* – all these represent an attempt to put into practice the theory that in the first and last resort the learner must be encouraged to get an education for himself. In the past, this theory and practice failed to find universal acceptance because adults were convinced that children were incapable of doing anything of the sort and could not be trusted with the responsibility. Hence the stress on classroom instruction.

In the original edition of his masterly review of resource-based learning projects, L. C. Taylor took a somewhat gloomy view of their chances of succeeding. In the second edition, he is decidedly more optimistic. As he says, 'The pace of change is now such that "recurrent" education is likely to become the general experience. An independent, resource-based style of learning provides a more suitable preparation than does class teaching for continued studies.'[10]

To repeat, schooling serves a propaedeutic purpose in making education possible. The point is made more simply and elegantly by the children of Barbiana: 'The teacher gives to a boy everything the teacher himself believes, loves and hopes for. The boy, *growing up, will add something of his own*' [my italics].[11]

It is this 'growing up and adding something of his own' which the professional educationist tends to ignore. Preoccupied with the 'forms of knowledge' which are 'public' only in the sense that they are the private monopoly of intellectuals, his concept of education is restrictive. The 'knowledge' he peddles belongs to the realm of uncommon sense (as Bernstein categorizes it) and largely rules out the world of commonsense learning and existential knowing. Schooling normally relies heavily on external discipline; education presupposes the exercise of inner freedom and self-discipline.

11 *Schooling promotes rational thought: education is the development of personal judgement and understanding*

Objection

Even Socrates seems to have been doubtful about the possibility of making men wise. Why not settle for more tangible objectives?

12 *Schooling is necessarily institutional, education not so*

In all societies, schooling represents a systematic attempt to organize learning collectively. Education, by contrast, is the concern of the individual. Ideally, the interests of the individual and of society coincide. In so far as there is a conflict of interests it is arguable that there is a vital difference between schooling and education.

The self-educated man may be a rarity in the modern world, but to speak of him as self-schooled makes no sense at all.

13 *Schooling ends sooner or later, but education is a continuous process which ends only with death*

Properly conducted, schooling sets the pupil on the road to lifelong learning. The indications are, however, that too often it does nothing of the sort.

14 *Education is to schooling as theory is to practice*

Thus, 'schooling' is what we actually get, 'education' is what we are *supposed* to receive. What we get (with schooling) is:

a Instruction
b Custodial care
c Socialization
d Classification

What we are *supposed* to get is something more than the sum of these parts: 'the nuture of personal growth', 'the whole man', etc., etc. Let us examine these four main functions:

a As regards *instruction*, courses are often irrelevant or so organized as to ensure that many pupils are left with a permanent sense of failure and inferiority. Despite the best efforts of curriculum developers to validate the hypothesis that 'Any subject can be taught in some intellectually honest form to any child at any stage of development', the verdict must be that the search for a viable alternative to an academic type of secondary education has failed. Secondary schooling on the traditional model caters for a certain kind of intelligence, emphasizes the importance of symbolic skills and bestows its favours and rewards on those pupils – predominantly middle class – who abide by the 'principle of deferred gratification'. Inevitably, the effect of formal classroom instruction is to depreciate the pupil of average and below-average ability: a depreciation which one critic, not without cause, has styled *The Great Brain Robbery*.

b *Custodial care*, so far as young children are concerned, may be a necessary function of the modern industrial society *in loco parentis*; but is it altogether cynical to see it, later on, as a street-clearing operation designed to keep teenagers out of circulation and to preserve them in an indeterminate status, a limbo between childhood and adulthood?

c *Socialization*, in practice, means training children to accept the conventional wisdom, by confirming the values and requirements of an acquisitive, consumer society.

d *Classification*, seen by sociologists as the main function of any educational system, involves the selection and grading of pupils for their future occupational roles. It results in the kind of schooling which is geared to examination requirements and intense competition for paper qualifications. So organized, schooling becomes a bitter game where, in the nature of things, there are relatively few winners and many losers. In this stressful situation, learning is mostly *labor*, and *opus* gets short shrift. Granted, because of the complex division of labour in advanced industrial societies, some method of selection and grading is essential. The question is whether this function ought to be discharged primarily by the school. As things are, many of the decisions affecting the learner's future occupational role are taken prematurely: at early age he is labelled fit for this, that or the other category in the Registrar-General's list – and the labels may stick for the rest of his working life. Worst of all, he may come to accept the evaluation placed upon him by the school.

As for the examination fetish, there are good reasons for thinking that it has now reached the stage when it is on a par with the selling of indulgences in Luther's day. In too many cases, these paper qualifications bear little or no relation to the learner's on-the-job performance: a wholesale racket which is nicely satirized by Ivar Berg in *The Great Training Robbery*.[12]

Both as regards the parts and the sum of the parts, then, there is a blatant credibility gap between our professed theory of education and its practice in schools. Clearly, a distinction has to be drawn between what is (i.e. schooling) and what might be (education).

Objection

All this proves is that we live in an imperfect world. Socrates's comment (in *The Republic*) about the impossibility of implementing idealistic plans seems relevant here.

15 *Schooling, i.e. the compulsory institutionalizing of the young, is an invention of nineteenth-century industrial mass production: an ersatz process, compared with the liberal education always associated with, and reserved for, a leisured class*

On this reckoning, the objections raised previously to points 7 and 9 can be dismissed on the grounds that compulsion, at any rate beyond early adolescence, is one of the conditions which make for bad schooling. Easy as it is to make light of the unwillingly-to-school syndrome, we must take note, as the cultural anthropologists have done, of the fact that it is the hallmark of education systems in *all* civilized societies. Unlike their coevals in primitive societies, children are required to attend school and learn things which are of no immediate interest or obvious relevance to them. Hence, as already noted, the preoccupation with work (*labor*) at the expense of play (*opus*).

Yet the original Greek word for school meant 'leisure' (Latinized as *ludus*). So long as the learner was able and willing to submit voluntarily to the discipline of being *in statu pupillari* this sportive element could be retained, even in conditions which were spartan, not to say repressive. Ælfric's *Colloquy* and Harting's *Parfait Boke for Keping Sparhawks* provide typical examples of the conditions laid down by medieval schoolmasters for the acceptance of would-be pupils. Briefly, these were that before being taken in hand the applicants had to show (*a*) that they were keen, (*b*) that they were prepared to undergo the master's discipline, (*c*) that they had the necessary aptitudes. Only if all three conditions were satisfied was a genuine master-disciple relationship possible.

Once legalized compulsory attendance for *all* was introduced, however, schooling inevitably gravitated towards the extreme end of the bureaucratic spectrum, i.e. it ceased to be 'convivial' and for some pupils, at least, came to resemble a penitentiary. The sharp contrast between the urbanity of Victorian Oxbridge tutorship and the harshness of Mr Gradgrind's classroom points the moral. For pupils who were not particularly keen in the first place, whose willingness to submit to their teachers' discipline could only be induced by fear (usually of corporal punishment) and whose aptitudes were non-scholastic, compulsory attendance often turned out to be a brutalizing experience, akin to that of conscripts on a barracks square.

Objection

How about teach-ins, integrated day curricula, ETV (educational television), extracurricular activities, adventure courses, open schools, simulation and gaming? Are not all of these to be seen as attempts to reintroduce the needed sportive ('convivial') element in the educational process? Once again the model of schooling which is being criticized seems to be one which is in many aspects already out of date.

16 *Schooling puts a heavy premium on verbal reasoning and on testable cognitive skills (scholarship), but these cannot be considered the sole criteria of educational achievement*

During the nineteenth century literacy was the main stock-in-trade of the schools. Ever since the invention of printing, indeed, our ideas about what constitutes 'learning' and 'knowledge' have been book-based. Just how these ideas came to be legitimized – or rather institutionalized – has been elucidated by Father Ong in his study of Ramus[13] and by Marshall McLuhan in *The Gutenberg Galaxy*. We forget that two of the most influential educators in the Western world, Socrates and Jesus Christ, left no written record of their teaching.

The extent to which our educational theory and practice, even our philosophies of education, are themselves institutionalized explains the curious blind spot which prevents most people, none more than professional educationists, from recognizing the many kinds of informal, non-verbal learning which receive no credit in schooling.

Was Michelangelo an educated man? R. S. Peters thinks not, apparently! Says he, 'We do not call a person "educated" who has simply mastered a skill even though the skill be very highly prized such as pottery.'[14] Or sculpture, it is fair to ask? What sort of cognitive perspective is it, one wonders, what can pass judgements like this?

The case of Michelangelo, a typical pre-Gutenberg artist, is worth pondering if only to make the point that cultural values are relative, not absolute. It is true that he wrote sonnets and that, under protest, he painted the ceiling and wall of the Sistine Chapel, but for him sculpture was the supreme art, painting a next-best form of creative expression and literature a poor third. 'Whereof one cannot speak, thereof one must create an image', was the sum of his philosophy. What he had to 'say' could not be adequately communicated in words: it had to be hewn, at times in a white heat of fury, from the mute block. So the sonnets, moving as they are, lack the *terribilita* of his Last Judgement; and that awesome fresco, in turn, is not so sublime as his Moses: while none of them can match the unspeakable pathos of the Rondanini *Pietà*.

Educational psychologists, of course, are not alone in attributing man's intellectual superiority to the use of language. There is no denying, either, that systematic thought is largely dependent on speech, and that the disseminative power of thought has been vastly increased by the invention of printing. A good deal less attention has been given to the fact that man's *spiritual* development has more often than not manifested itself in non-verbal forms. All languages express either feelings, appeals, or statements of fact, and while it can never be proved, it is tempting to suppose that primordial language was mainly emotional. Language is rooted in tacit, existential experience, just as the 'meaning' of Michelangelo's statues was originally hidden in the senseless marble: invariably, the attempt to make the ineffable explicit is a 'raid on the inarticulate'. Not surprisingly, non-verbal communication appeals to the imaginative genius (one thinks of Keats's 'O for a life of sensations rather than of thoughts'), just as it does to ordinary people whenever they reach the point when, as they say, words fail them.

Schooling, however, is pre-eminently a matter of verbal learning and our educational psychology one which equates intelligence with verbal reasoning. We need a more human evaluation. The extent to which our modes of thought have been moulded by 400 years of reading and writing can scarcely be exaggerated. Only recently have a few perceptive thinkers become aware of it and dared to crack some of the time-honoured, case-hardened suppositions which determine our current theory and practice of education. The new theory and practice, as yet dimly envisaged, will conceive of education not as one process confined more or less to schooling but rather as a family of processes.

17 *Schooling is necessarily formal and deliberate, but education can be both informal and non-deliberate*
It is often said that education is what is left when everything learned at school has been forgotten. The inference seems to be that education, like digestion, is largely a matter of unconscious assimilation. Schooling implies the need for conscious effort on the part of the pupil, compliance with regulations, obedience to the dictates of adults, 'paying attention'. Schooling, in short, means undergoing corrective treatment. Education, on the other hand, is what one makes of one's schooling. Presumably this is what Nunn had in mind when he said that 'Character is what each of us makes out of his temperament'. For better or for worse, one *receives* a schooling. One acquires an education. Education is the Pygmalion at work in each of us: as St Augustine put it, 'The Master is within'.

18 *Education is perfectly possible in the absence of schooling*
Thomas Huxley thought so, as did Margaret Mead's aunt. Oddly enough, even R. S. Peters agrees: 'In the end, education is something that only the individual can achieve for himself. . . . He can do it in solitary confinement.'[15]

3 Education and schooling: a spectrum of opinion

In theory there is no place for superstition in the social sciences: in practice the sibylline utterance still has power to sway the deliberations of educationist and layman alike. Amid the present tumult, certainly, ancestral voices prophesying war are not easily stilled. Should they be heeded? Can they be trusted?

Schools are in crisis, and so are the people who attend them. The former is a crisis in a political situation; the latter is a crisis of political attitudes. This second crisis, the crisis of personal growth, can be dealt with only if understood as distinct from, though related to, the crisis of the school.

Schools have lost their unquestioned claim to educational legitimacy. Most of their critics still demand a painful and radical reform of the school, but a quickly expanding minority will not stand for anything short of the prohibition of compulsory attendance and the disqualification of academic certificates. Controversy between partisans of renewal and partisans of disestablishment will soon come to a head.[1]

Statements of this sort are so full of passionate intensity, so oracular in their assurance, that they carry conviction, if not the ring of truth.

The difficulty is to decide whether they are arrant nonsense, or even downright lies, or whether they contain a kernel of wisdom which is hard to swallow only because it is so unconventional. 'Schools are in crisis.' Where, it may be asked? How does the 'crisis' manifest itself, seeing that in many countries the majority of parents, teachers and pupils seem to be tolerably satisfied with their schools? And are there really any grounds for thinking that there is a 'quickly expanding minority' of abolitionists? As for any threat to the educational legitimacy of the institutions in which they work, most teachers, academics and administrators will be inclined to dismiss it as mere fee-fi-fo-fum, too patently absurd to be taken seriously. Very few, one imagines, will find their equanimity troubled by what Neil Postman calls 'My Ivan Illich problem'.

Since Illich swept up from the South Country, I have been obliged to admit to unsuspected attachments to certain social structures, which attachments a genuine revolutionary like Illich has obviously abandoned. As a matter of fact, several times in recent months I have returned soberly and respectfully to a passage in the Declaration of Independence that I had previously been inclined to dismiss as merely a conservative cliché:

Prudence, indeed, will dictate that governments long established should not be changed for light or transient causes and accordingly all experience hath shewn, that mankind are more disposed to suffer while evils are sufferable, than to right themselves by abolishing the forms to which they are accustomed.[2]

As a radical critic of the *status quo* in American schools and colleges, Postman is no slouch, but when it comes to envisaging a world sans schools, sans pupils, sans teachers, sans summer vacations, sans diplomas, he confesses that his mind boggles. Common sense decrees that it is just not going to happen. Hence his Ivan Illich problem: is his refusal to go the whole way and agree to the total dismantling of the education system simply due to intellectual cowardice or, worse, to sheer obtuseness – or is he right in persevering on the long march through existing institutions? To ask, 'After deschooling what?', not only begs the question, he concludes – it puts the cart before the horse: it should be, '*Before* deschooling what?'

Tomorrow, there are going to be about 45 million kids showing up for school. Schooling as an institution may or may not be dead, which is a question that makes for swell lectures at Cuernavaca. But the kids certainly aren't dead. They are *there*. And what happens to them tomorrow matters – and next term, and the term after that. And it just won't do to write them off. Not by me. Because, as I see it, some part of their lives is my problem. And if Ivan Illich isn't interested, then I figure that's *his* problem.[3]

Between the devil's advocacy of the extremists and the ca' canniness of stick-in-the-mud traditionalists, where does one make one's stand? For born rebels, especially the young, the former may have a strong appeal, but how can we be sure that in yielding to it and casting themselves in the role of freedom fighters they are not irresponsible iconoclasts? The secret of the oracle lies in its ruthless disregard of what others think is reasonable: out of the blue, it declares that everyone is out of step except itself – which explains its extraordinary power to create dilemmas in the minds of would-be activists. Could it be that the oracle is right and that the scruples of the great majority whose forward thinking is characterized by its moderation simply mask their squeamishness – that when it comes to the crunch they are paper tigers? Is it the weakness of intellectuals to want to cling together for the sake of mutual support? Even Postman, as forthright a thinker as any, rationalizes his pulling back from the brink by reminding us that John Holt, Jonathan Kozol and all the others who have contributed to the recent literature of educational dissent did the same.

For those in positions of responsibility, on the other hand – mostly middle-aged and middle class – no such dilemma exists. For them, unquestionably, the vote will be for preservation orders, arguably because (whether they intend it so or otherwise) any policy which ensures that the education system is maintained more or less intact protects their vested interests. In academic circles a position slightly left of centre seems to be the most daring that can be bargained for: anything bolder is liable to be called heretical or merely incomprehensible. In schools, colleges and departments of education such questions as 'What is the difference between education and schooling?' rarely arise, and when they do they tend to be treated as of no great concern anyway. A typical reaction when the question is posed is to counter with the puzzled query, 'Why do you ask?' – though this is not so typical, alas, as the frank admission that the respondent has never really thought about it before. Is this because teachers and educationists have their noses so close to the grindstones of routine – getting on with the job as they call it – that they are unable to stand away from their work and take a detached view of it. Or (nasty thought) is the question merely 'academic' after all? What for example, would an analytical philosopher have to say about it, or a specialist in educational research, a sociologist, a vice-chancellor, a town planner, or for that matter even Ivan Illich himself?

With these uncertainties in mind, I drew up the following list of what seemed to me to be the key questions, arranged more or less in order of priority. Before going on, the reader may find it useful to ponder each of these ten points for discussion. Sending out questionnaires is a forlorn exercise at the best of times, and in a case like this, where each of the points raises issues which demand book-length treatment in order to do them justice, the respondents might have been excused for thinking the questionnaire a piece of calculated impertinence and consigning it without more ado to the wastepaper basket. It speaks well for their courtesy that they did nothing of the kind. Not surprisingly, few of them had the time or the patience to complete the entire list. Even so, their off-the-cuff comments, terse as they are – in some instances monosyllabic! – are revealing. If they do nothing more, they show that each of the individuals concerned has his own 'Ivan Illich problem' and resolves it by striking a balance, which to him seems honest, between the claims of radicalism and conservatism. The answers also reveal a wide measure of agreement on the all-important question of the difference between education and schooling. They are presented here without further comment with the author's grateful acknowledgements for permission to reproduce them.

THE QUESTIONNAIRE

1 Education and schooling: what's the difference?
2 What's wrong with schooling anyway? – and how is this question answered in different cultural contexts?
3 How seriously do we take the idea of deschooling – has its rhetoric outrun its rationale?
4 Given modern technologies of communication, what practical alternatives to organized schooling can be envisaged?
5 Do the existing alternatives – e.g. open schools, free schools, mini schools, schools without walls – merely represent a lunatic fringe

or are they symptomatic of a breakaway movement which will eventually see the ascendancy of a counter-culture?

6 Is the school as a bureaucratic institution a proper study for industrial archaeology? (i.e. does it reflect nineteenth-century conditions?)

7 Should the non-stop expansion of the educational services be regarded as a form of cultural pollution?

8 Is it in the nature of things that the process of education should suffer from a permanent cultural lag?

9 Since the education system is part of the wider socio-economic system is there any prospect of the reform of schools succeeding?

10 If the answer is yes, is there a viable strategy for overcoming the forces of inertia and the vested interests which combine to ensure the maintenance of the educational establishment?

SOME REPLIES

1 *From Ivan Illich, Centro Intercultural de Documentacion, Cuernavaca*

Educatio prolis is what cats and mothers do with their young, quite distinct from 'instruction' or '*docentia*'. In the eighteenth century the word was appropriated by schoolmasters to give more importance to the task they were employed to do. Today it designates the invisible commodity which results from the industrial production process called schooling. I fear the societies' commitment to the mass production of this commodity will survive the breakdown of societies' reliance on school systems to produce it. Alternative devices for the production and compulsory consumption of measurable (operationally verifiable) programming which goes under the name of 'education' are indeed more feasible and less tolerable. Systems alternative to school systems are now on the verge of replacing traditional curricula in many areas. They are potentially more effective than traditional schools in conditioning people for life in an economy dominated by industrial production. They are therefore more attractive for management of our societies, more seductive for the population subject to their operant conditioning and more insidiously destructive of fundamental humanist values. It is necessary to expose the fallacy involved in the ideal of standardized and compulsory education in order to guarantee that the deschooling of education leads to a deschooling of society.

2 *From C. A. Doxiadis, Director, Centre for Ekistics, Athens*[4]
1 The ancient PAIDEIA.
2 I do not believe 'schooling' is wrong.
3 I do not think of deschooling but of better schooling.
4 No one that can replace schooling.
5 I think it is the result of an explosion (see *Daedalus*, fall edition).
6 I do not know.
7 —
8 I think yes.
9 Certainly yes, when we conceive the total explosion and how to deal with it.
10 We *must* conceive the whole, and then we can certainly deal with the parts.

3 *From Professor Dr Wolfgang Mitter, Director, Deutsches Institut für International Padagögische Forschung*
1 Education can be defined as a process including all the kinds of formal, deliberate and explicit socialization, whereas schooling only refers to the organized and institutionalized sector of education, focused (as far as civilized societies are concerned) on the instruction of knowledge and the development of cognitive abilities.
2 Schooling can be interpreted as a constituent revelation of man's alienation in a world in which his relation to nature is determined by technology and science to a growing extent. Alienation is the necessary result of human history, the question 'what's wrong' can only be answered with regard to the possibilities of keeping the alienation process under control.
3 If deschooling is suggested as a means of totally abolishing schools, this should be understood as a rhetorical question. Its rationale, however, points to the necessity of counterbalancing the dehumanizing trends of school development.
4 Modern technologies of communication can certainly open a wider sphere of unorganized learning. Whether they succeed depends on the stage of self-recognition and self-assertion of the individuals concerned. As these qualities can only grow in a long process, permanent help given by educators and teachers is necessary. It is inconceivable that this help can be safeguarded without a certain amount of organized schooling, especially for children and adolescents.

5 Open schools (in the widest sense of the term) are alternatives to the existing school systems in so far as they indicate the idea of a breakaway movement and confront the existing school systems with their own problems. From this point of view open schools should be encouraged and promoted as far as possible. Considering the fact that one cannot expect to have a sufficient number of extraordinary educators, qualified and with initiative, to run open schools, the existing alternatives only point to a counter-culture in the shape of concrete Utopia.

6 In its present organizational form school seems to resemble a bureaucratic institution suitable for study by industrial archaeologists. This does not mean, however, that school systems as national institutions could do without regulations and directives.

7 Educational services are necessary; they can be interpreted as a necessary means to provide people with information and advice, considering the fact that traditional formations of education (families, neighbourhoods) have broken down as a consequence of horizontal and vertical mobility in modern societies. There is the danger, however, that these services tend to limit the spheres of individuality and privacy beyond societal needs.

8 So far all the endeavours to adapt education to the cultural standard of the corresponding age have not been realized satisfactorily. This task certainly remains open.

9 Prospects of school reforms depend very much on the tendencies of the socio-economic system schools form a part of. Educators should not be discouraged from regarding schools as a counterbalance to the meritocratic and technocratic effects of social systems focused solely on economic growth. They should be fully aware of the permanent challenge and the necessity for putting forward innovative strategies in the dichotomy of fundamental goals and pragmatic objectives.

10 Within the framework outlined in point 9, viable strategies should be developed and encouraged.

4 *From Professor Alberto Granesi, Director, Facultá di Magistero, University of Cagliari, Sardinia*[5]

Prima facie it is clear that 'education' may be taken as meaning: (*a*) an activity, (*b*) a result. It is debatable whether meaning (*b*) necessarily implies a positive value. R. S. Peters argues that one cannot logically affirm that a person has been educated unless he has been changed for the better. This argument is not very rigorous in that it does not distinguish between the ethical quality of (*b*) i.e. the result, and its congruence with (*a*) i.e. the objective of the activity. To accept Peters's argument, one must presuppose that education in sense (*a*) necessarily involves an effort to change for the better. In other words, it remains to be proved that the activity of educating necessarily means a deliberate effort to change the learner for the better.

One may educate a person with 'highly satisfactory' results in intolerance, violence, race hatred, etc., and it may be conceded that such results are the best possible for anyone who educates in this way. I would like to point out the illogicality of an educative activity that is knowingly and intentionally aimed at changing the learner for the worse. No educator can remain indifferent to the thought that what he does in the name of 'educating' may really be miseducative.

Considered as a result, 'education' is not logically reducible to any of its multiple components. It belongs to a logical category different from all the single processes which determine it. Teaching, inciting, suggestion, exhortation, punishment, example, counselling and guidance activities are not necessarily 'education' in the sense that they may not necessarily contribute to an educative result and in the sense that they are distinct from 'education' – as task and achievement invariably are distinct. (Competing is distinct from winning although it is necessary to compete in order to win.) Obviously this is not to say that 'education' is a separate, 'spectral' process encompassing all the others which have as their outcome the improvement of the person. It would be wrong to conclude that because 'education' cannot be identified with this or that particular process it is itself a nonprocess. What cannot be established with certainty is the connection between the manner and method of the educational process and its outcome (as is shown in the pseudo-Platonic dialogue 'On virtue'). The philosophical myth of self-education partly expresses the uncertainty of the connection between the educative activity and the educational result. Efforts to establish a scientific pedagogy must be seen as an attempt to render this connection less dubious and precarious.

Accordingly, there is no logical contradiction in maintaining that to send a child to school is not the only, or even the best, way to educate him. The concept of 'education', in any case, broadly coincides with that of the organization of learning even if the organized forms of knowledge (the ones which constitute the curricula of educational institutions) are not necessarily the ones that produce the best results. To analyse education in terms of the organization of learning is a more useful way of defining the connection between 'education' and 'schooling' because 'schooling' is the typical form of organization. But 'schooling' is not the only possible form: the goals of education do not necessarily have to be attained through this means. Neither education nor learning necessarily imply the need for teaching. Logically there can be (and historically there has been) education without schooling. Conversely, schooling is conceivable only in relation to an educational objective which may or may not be achieved: there are no *a priori* guarantees that 'schooling' means the same as 'education'. This is not to say that 'education' is an alternative process. 'Schooling' is one of the possible forms of the organization of learning, whereas 'education' is rather a family of activities directed to the attainment of (*a*) a result that is judged to be morally sound, (*b*) that result and (*c*) the 'ideals' or criteria by which the result is judged. The problem of deciding whether 'schooling' constitutes a valid form of the organization of learning cannot be resolved solely in terms of logic but only by empirical proof (historic, political, ethical etc.). What the school actually does achieve must always be studied in a given social and economic context.

In short, it can be said that 'schooling' constitutes a moment or a level of education not logically separable from other moments and levels or from the complex of task-achievement which characterizes the formative process of modern democratic society and, indeed, of any community of rational beings.

5 *From Professor J. P. Tuck, Head of the School of Education, University of Newcastle-upon-Tyne*

Your questions stir in me the simple idea that complete reschooling in a community organized as ours is would produce confusion, since we depend on institutions to order our affairs and introduce coherence in our way of life.

But this does not mean that the inevitable tendency of institutions to ossify should be encouraged, and I think the healthiest approach to the future of schools is that they should develop approaches and practices which make them more flexible and adaptable and so become able to provide the kind of education which 'deschoolers' would like to see, yet also the experience of living in a community devoted to purposes which are desirably detached from some of the purposes of the community as a whole.

6 *From Professor Frank Musgrove, Sarah Fielden Professor of Education, University of Manchester*

1 These are really antithetical. Literally, I suppose, to be schooled in anything is to be disciplined, ordered, contained.

2 Deschooling: schools for everyone are recent (100 years), and on any historical perspective eccentric. They are really a remarkable confidence trick and one wonders how it came off as well as it did.

4 The significant invention was the circulating library, as Lovett and the Chartists knew. 'Modern technologies' make decentralized 'information retrieval' perhaps a bit more efficient.

5 I don't think they are a lunatic fringe: the counter-culture *is* the new education.

6 I'm not sure that archaeology can throw much light on bureaucracy – except, perhaps, by uncovering organizational layers or deposits in organizations which have changed, e.g. an elementary school becomes a secondary modern, becomes a comprehensive.

7 Yes. I would agree, I think, with Richard Livingstone that education is a matter of exclusion, selection and good taste.

8 Education as schooling: yes.

9 Not really. I imagine we shall need testing, diagnostic and grading agencies for certain purposes. We might call these agencies schools. (We *do* call these agencies schools.) Extramural and extracurricular activities provide the clue to what is genuinely adaptive and truly 'relevant'.

7 *From Professor G. H. Bantock, School of Education, University of Leicester*

1 Education, ideally, should be liberal. Schooling undoubtedly tends to be instrumental, but liberal elements need not necessarily be excluded. Undoubtedly, however, the job looms much larger in most minds than culture.

2 I think the answer to this is implicit in my answer to question 1. I

might add, perhaps, that schooling emphasizes testing and examinations which, while not necessarily anti-educational, can be so. Yet testing is an important part of the educational process because it enables the student to measure himself against a standard.

3 I am not quite sure what is meant by taking deschooling seriously. If you mean do I consider it a serious alternative to the present system, my answer is no, I would like the reforms within the system. If you mean do I think the deschooling movement is likely to spread and become serious in that sense, my answer is I don't really know; I think it possible, but unlikely.

4 I doubt if modern technologies of communication offer any practical alternative to organized schooling, because I doubt the persistence of children unless supervised directly by teachers. The Open University is possible because it attracts people of comparatively mature age, who have already acquired a good deal of self-discipline, and this would not be the case where children are concerned.

5 My answer here really is implicit, I think, in No. 3. I don't like what I have heard about the counter-culture, which seems to me to involve an element of romantic pathology.

6 I don't think I altogether understand No. 6.

7 Not necessarily.

8 I would tend to think so, because by its nature education tends to be preservative in transmitting the known culture rather than innovative. This is the case even in creative or problem-solving exercises. Children can't be genuinely original because they just don't know enough, and in order to solve problems it is necessary to have a good insight into the traditional structure of the area within which the problem-solving is to take place. You can't solve problems in a vacuum.

9 Reforms are always taking place, though not all reforms are necessarily good things. Even within the socio-economic system there is always a good deal of play permissible in what can possibly go on in classrooms. In England at least no one positively dictates to a teacher exactly what he shall teach.

10 Genuine reforms in education, in my view, do not exist on the macroscopic scale, or only marginally so. They only occur in any important sense in the interplay of minds in a classroom or in any other teaching situation. This, of course, is our mistake over thinking that organization is so important, and the present

disenchantment with comprehensive education which is pretty well widespread throughout Europe and America illustrates my point. Any genuine reform, therefore, only comes as a result of the indirect influence we exert in teacher training and elsewhere over the quality of mind of our students who are going to teach in the schools. This is not exciting, heady stuff, but then I have always maintained that teaching is not an heroic exercise, but a matter of a very large number of small decisions taken in particular situations in classrooms.

8 *From Professor W. A. Campbell Stewart, Vice-Chancellor, University of Keele*

Education and schooling – your various questions would take many pages to attempt to answer. Here are a few headlines. In a Western society, when all the talk has subsided, some kind of schooling is necessary. In some settings continuous training might take the form of the passing on of traditional learning in the small community life of family or tribe, but this is not a feasible approach to a nation of children predominantly in urban situations where the prerequisite skills of literacy and numeracy are of obvious advantage, indeed of necessity. With that said, I believe the potential for education of people with initiative, interests and various abilities can be much more flexible than it has been hitherto. Put in another way, there has to be a continuing compulsory element and the range of what is voluntary and individual can now be better understood and encouraged. Your symposium[6] could well address itself to the modes of education now becoming available; the institutions or means of providing those modes; the relationships between existing educational administration and provision, with the possibilities of compulsion and option which could be offered. The lunatic fringe might be examined as a creative minority or as a dogmatic anarchy together with the relationships of fringes of any kind and the so-called 'establishment'. Indeed a useful study could be made of the notion of 'educational establishments' as a cliché which sometimes enables people to take off into private fantasy and delusion. The implications of 'establishment' as a necessary framework are often distorted (by critics and by 'establishment' practice) into a self-deluding ideology, while the implications of 'anti-establishment' tend towards a romantic or utopian anarchism. Education to my mind requires a disciplined approach to experience and knowledge as well as a dynamic of interest and originality. These things in turn require a stable framework in a society interested in a continuing and developing culture. Herein lies my opposition to the common emphasis in statements supporting deschooling.

9 *From Professor Ben Morris, Advanced Studies, School of Education, University of Bristol*

You ask me what is the difference between education and schooling. There are clearly different sorts of answers to this question. One is to treat it in terms of institutions, and the school is clearly only one of the agencies which societies entrust with the upbringing of the young; the others being the family or family substitutes and the community, including various other sorts of institutions like religious bodies. At a more fundamental level, however, and in the sense in which Mark Twain meant his own remark to be understood, I would I think simply copy Doxiadis, whose answer strikes me as very good.

Education is the discovery of what it means to be human – including the destructive as well as the creative potentialities. Schooling is necessarily concerned with only partial aspects of such discovery.

10 *From John Eggleston, Professor of Education, University of Keele*

Concerning the first question which you regard as the most important, I think all I need to say is that I entirely agree that there is a difference, but then sociologists have been saying this for years – you can get it all in Durkheim's *Education and Society* in which he points out very clearly the comparative recentness and relative insignificance of schooling, or at least, formal schooling as part of the total process of education or socialization. I suspect that it is the relative ease with which schools and their curricula may be influenced or even controlled that has led us to overestimate the importance of schooling as against education at a time when the informal agencies of education are increasing in significance and are likely to do so on an even greater scale in the immediate future. I would imagine that the development of television, for example, and I don't just mean 'schools' television, has already effectively dissolved much of the artificial barrier between education and schooling. The Open University seems an interesting example here.

R. H. Turner recently delivered a lecture in which he presented an interesting thesis whereby he defined schooling as a set of institutions that were originally concerned to provide 'second-hand' experience for a population satiated with rich primary experience of life in home, community and factory, but who lacked the means of getting at secondary experience – the knowledge of events and phenomena not directly available to them. His argument was that since schools were set up to serve this purpose the social situation has changed, so that children are now rich in secondary experience through the mass media but are often devoid of first-hand experience, possibly living on a housing estate where there are almost no models of adult roles available to them other than the milkman and the postman (and these both likely to disappear within the next decade). He then presents a picture, which to me seems plausible, of schools rapidly changing, creating and exposing their pupils to 'first-hand' experience. If one takes this view of the new curricula in many primary schools, and a few secondary schools, it seems that the school system is already deschooling itself in many of the ways envisaged by the 'deschoolers'.

4 The knowledge market

When asked how he came to formulate his general theory of relativity, Einstein is said to have replied, 'I did it by refusing to accept an axiom.' For an educationist to dare to question the popular credo of his profession is, arguably, more difficult than it is for a physicist, if only because axioms affecting the lives of human beings are not so easily disproved as they are in the natural sciences. Examples of folklore so time-honoured as to be taken as axiomatic are not hard to find, but for the moment two will suffice.

One of the most widely accepted assumptions in education has been that exposure to teaching is highly related to student learning – and in a linear fashion. That is, we have assumed that a 50 per cent increase in full-time schooling would result in a 50 per cent increase in the knowledge retained by students. We have also taken for granted that formal schooling accounts for the major share, if not all, of the knowledge and skills that young people acquire. Therefore, in order to improve standards, it is necessary to increase the number of years of schooling, or the number of hours a subject is taught per week, or both.[1]

Although the various research findings are not conclusive, there is enough evidence to prove that assumptions of this kind need to be seriously challenged. As Husén observes,

> The interest that several international and national technical assistance agencies have begun to show in nonformal or out-of-school education is an important symptom. Programs in which the common denominator is a better integration of education and working life have already been launched in the developing countries, and more will possibly follow. It is possible that as these experimental programs progress, the developed countries will find that they have as much to learn from the underdeveloped world, as they have to learn from us.[2]

A second axiom which is rarely questioned is the one which assures us that schooling is a preparation for adult life, a means to an end – the end being some competence in the world of work. Although he is critical of the 'new alienation' which the deschoolers complain of, Douglas Holly recognizes that there is a sense in which, for many pupils, if not for all, compulsory school attendance *is* profoundly alienating. As he says:

> Our society has conditioned people to believe that work is an alien imposition: work is by definition opposed to liberty and leisure. Not only secondary modern pupils believe this – the authors of the Newsom Report believe it as well. Two things necessarily follow: (*a*) work is something imposed, requiring external discipline or internalized 'self-discipline' to ensure its completion; (*b*) enjoyment is not to be expected in conditions of work and is only to be purchased as the result of work. From this springs the whole Judeo-Puritan ethic and the whole instrumental attitude to education – education as a means-to-an-end rather than an end-in-itself.[3]

– and he adds:

> to fulfil the requirements of a co-operative human determination of society in the future, the content of formal education will have to be not merely reformed but revolutionized. Such revolutionary change can't be effected by tinkering with this or that curriculum. Probably the very term 'curriculum' is a hindrance to revolutionary change. Unless it is used in a very general sense it tends to suggest a course of learning to be followed as an end in itself, something

contrary to the idea of education as realization and learning as a process.[4]

If there is anything in the charge that knowledge has come to be treated as a commodity, packaged and purveyed by a closed shop – i.e. the school system – then it behoves us to ask just how this has come about. The first task is to demonstrate why the theory and practice of education we have inherited are no longer adequate, and the extent to which they rest on folklorist fallacies. In previous ages, of course, such a demonstration would have been relatively easy. The world over, pedagogues and pedants have always been mentioned in the same breath, dull dogs who could safely be left to carry on with the business of child-minding, just as babysitters are today, because society at large had more important things to do. If they took themselves seriously, that was their affair: no one else did. It is only since they stopped calling themselves pedagogues that educationists have been able to command the enhanced public respectability they now enjoy, a change of status which occurred as recently as the turn of the century. By the same token, it is only since they stopped calling themselves alchemists that chemists have become 'respectable', with this important difference that in their case the change of status was earned by discarding a pseudo-theory in favour of a genuinely scientific one. As a consequence, the processing of materials has long since ceased to be a mystery, but the so-called 'education of the masses' – people-processing – has yet to be demystified. On the face of it, to assert that educationists still cling to theories as antiquated and misbegotten as those of the medieval alchemists may seem widely irresponsible; and to assert, further, that they have been responsible for perpetrating the greatest confidence trick of all time may sound merely ridiculous. Fortunately, both assertions can be backed by solid historical evidence.

To begin with, suppose we list some of the popular fallacies which have come to be shared by the educationist and the layman alike:

1 'Education is the influence exercised by adult generations on those who are not yet ready for social life.'
2 Education is responsible for the transmission of culture.
3 It is necessary to attend school in order to obtain an education.
4 For practical purposes, *education* and *schooling* are interchangeable terms.

5 Standards of educational achievement are closely related to the length of regular school attendance.

6 Sound learning depends to a great extent upon efficient teaching.

7 Schooling fosters 'continued capacity for growth' and the development of self-discipline.

8 For practical purposes intelligence can be identified with verbal reasoning.

9 Learning must have a cognitive core.

10 Secondary schools provide general and special education for all pupils.

11 Only a minority of disaffected, maladjusted teenagers are dissatisfied with the provision made for them in secondary schools.

12 Life earnings are closely related to the number of years spent in formal schooling.

13 The expansion of the educational services at all levels is a sign of increasing equality of opportunity.

It would be easy to add to the list, but these unlucky thirteen may be taken as representative of the hallowed, hollow myths of which our secular faith in education is composed. Most people would probably say that each of these statements was perfectly sensible. The first (Durkheim's definition) may have been reasonable in 1900, but is totally unacceptable now that the implications of the 'continuous process' of lifelong learning can no longer be ignored. In the same way, all the other statements can be shown to be either patently untrue or in need of serious qualification. They only *seem* sensible because historical determinants prevent us from discriminating between myth and reality. Hence the need to elucidate the ways and means by which our educational theory and practice have been institutionalized.

CLOSED SHOP AND RESTRICTIVE PRACTICES IN THE
ACADEMIC COMMUNITY

'Accurate scholarship can unearth the whole offence', says Auden, though in this instance it seems that we need to go beyond Luther in seeking for its *fons et origo*. Seeing that it is at the heart of the matter we might begin with Cicero's declaration, *Appelari caeteros homines, esse solo eos qui essent politi propriis humanitatis artibus*[5] (We are all called men but only those of us are truly human who have been civilized by the studies proper to culture), but Quintilian provides as good a starting point as any, if only because he ranks first among the 'great educators' who successfully combined practice and theory. The *Institutio Oratoria* was at once a master craftsman's exposition of the methodology for the professional training of a public speaker *and* a prescription for the production of the good man. To be sure, Quintilian's formula, *vir bonus dicendi peritus*, puts the cart before the horse, for throughout his treatise the main emphasis is constantly placed on the special aim, i.e. professional training, the assumption being that the general aim will somehow be achieved incidentally through the civilizing influence of liberal studies.

Once instituted, 'The education of the orator' became *the* model for pedagogues in the Western world. It was a model which endeared itself to the medieval schoolmen, for whom the spoken word was still the main medium of communication, even more so to the Renaissance humanists, and with slight modifications it remains operational to this day.

The exclusive, inbred nature of this ancient tradition has been analysed by Father Ong in one of the most erudite *tours de force* of contemporary scholarship, *Ramus: Method and the Decay of Dialogue*. Apart from students of medieval philosophy, few educationists would have heard of this work, let alone thought of consulting it, had they not seen it mentioned and quoted at length in *The Gutenberg Galaxy*. Many of McLuhan's insights into the subtle and startling shifts of modes of thought and perception which took place during the transfer from an oral to a print-dominated culture derive from this source. Ong's chapter entitled 'The pedagogical juggernaut' is particularly revealing.

Ong's researches scarcely bear out Illich's contention that modern educational practice (schooling) is based on a pseudo-scientific theory propounded by that arch-alchemist Comenius. They suggest that the belief in people-processing – 'If a man is to be produced it is necessary that he be formed by education' – is much older, as is the associated belief that the process of education is essentially a classroom activity. Ong's thesis, however, far from invalidating Illich's, reinforces it. As he says:

> The 'schools' with which the term 'scholasticism' is obviously related are commonly taken today to mean cliques or sects of philosophers, as when we speak of disputes between the various schools. . . . But in medieval times, when *universitas* had gained

currency as the word for corporations, what we today would style various philosophical schools were spoken of commonly as 'ways' (*viae*). . . .

Although *schola* in the sense of a philosophical sect may occasionally be encountered, the prevalence of this term in medieval and Renaissance Latin derives largely from its use to designate a classroom. This goes back to Cicero, who borrows the word *schola* from Greek and employs it to mean, among other things, the place where lectures are given. The various *scholae* of Ramus and others are to be understood thus to mean lectures which are heard in *scholae* or classrooms.[6]

Because the *universitas*, as an incorporated guild of scholars, operated as a closed shop it was influential in delimiting the concepts of 'knowledge', 'learning' and 'teaching'. 'Knowledge' came to mean the kind of information which was only obtainable from the doctor's or the magister's *lectio*. 'Learning' was the measurable verbal content of the *lectio*. No significant 'learning' was held to be possible (or at any rate admissible) in the absence of teaching. Above all, the academic community legalized the notion of education as a package deal, a business transaction which conferred a privileged status on its members while withholding any sort of recognition from outsiders. For the *universitas*, 'knowledge', 'learning' and 'teaching' were, first and foremost, marketable commodities. In order to carry on its business, and to protect its interests, it created its own examination requirements.

As Ong explains:

The ancient pre-university did not have the concept of an examination in the medieval or modern sense – a sample of knowledge through which, by a kind of extrapolation, the whole 'content' of a person's mind can be calculated. There is no word for this in the classical tongues because there is no concept or practice for it to designate – *examen* means a swarm of bees, or, at best, such consideration or weighing of matters as might enter into judicial questions. The examination for certification in a teachers' guild as apprentice (bachelor) or master, or for the related 'licence' to teach from the Papal Chancellor, with the peculiar notions of intellectual competence which such examinations and the inaugural ceremony of *inceptio* implied, were the products of the teachers' guilds or university situation itself. As purveyed under the supervision of a corporation, knowledge naturally tended to be viewed less as wisdom transmissible only in the context of personal relationships than as a commodity. It could be measured – indeed, it had to be – which meant that it could be manipulated in terms of quantitative analogies.[7]

(Here beginneth the doctrine which holds that 'Whatever is exists in some amount', a doctrine on which modern educational psychology, educational assessment and techniques of research are based.)

Accordingly, attending school was one and the same as training to be a teacher. In a society which was information-poor, teaching defined itself as the man-who-knows-telling-those-who-don't. 'Instead of being a search for the truth, "dialectic" or "logic" became the subject a teacher taught to other young teachers in order to teach them how to teach, in their turn, still other apprentice teachers and so on *ad infinitum*.'[8]

Ad infinitum is right. This is how the educational establishment came into being. On this reckoning, what counts as 'knowledge' is what is taught and 'learning' tends to be restricted to the classroom. The existence of other sources of knowledge and other forms of learning, while not actually denied, receives no 'official' recognition. A clear demarcation between the 'uncommonsense knowledge of the school and the *commonsense* knowledge, everyday community knowledge, of the pupil, his family and his peer group'[9] (as Bernstein puts it) is established once and for all – a demarcation whose boundary strength derives from the organization of the *universitas*.

On this reckoning, 'education' without 'schooling' is inadmissible, a contradiction in terms. The outcome, as we have seen, is a cognitive psychology which equates intelligence with verbal reasoning, and a philosophy of education which insists that sound learning in the absence of effective teaching is virtually impossible. If we are looking for a point in time where pedagogues first began to enjoy the social esteem which previous ages had denied them, here it is. The medieval *universitas* enabled them, by cornering the market, to exercise an influence out of all proportion to their numbers or their importance.

The pedagogical bent of the universities resulted in the constant agitation of a group of inter-related terms; not only teaching (*doctrina*), learning (*disciplina*), method (*methodus*), but also art (*ars*) and science (*scientia*), and more or less implied as the complement of any and all of these, nature (*natura*). The notion of teaching largely controls the others in this complex – even nature, so that, for Ramus, 'natural' dialectic, or, as we will call it, the 'nature' (*natura*) of dialectic, will be what a little boy knows about dialectic from having used it in discourse unwittingly before he takes up the subject at school.

The other terms, of course, exercised some influence on the notion of teaching, too. This traditions more or less took for granted that teaching is carried on abstractly, since knowledge was generally equated with abstract or scientific knowledge. What is not conveyed abstractly or explicitly is not taught. *Doctrina* is *scientia*.[10]

Hence,

> having possessed itself thus of dialectic, the instrument of philosophy, teaching inevitably reaches out to include all philosophy. Philosophy becomes what you *learn* when you are *taught* in school. That philosophy may be the love of wisdom is not denied, but the assertion becomes quite nugatory when faced with the unassailable fact that philosophy is in reality defined by the pedagogical situation.[11]

From its seemingly modest beginning in the twelfth- to thirteenth-century *universitas,* the closed shop of the academic community has progressively extended its influence and strengthened its control over the education system. The pedagogical juggernaut keeps on rolling, snowball-fashion, carrying all before it. Today, it is not merely philosophy for a minority of students, but *all* forms of knowledge for *all* people that are 'defined by the pedagogical situation'. How else to explain the fact that education has come to be regarded as all one with schooling?

That this 'education' remains firmly rooted in institutions for the training of teachers goes without saying. As an academic study, it has grown up in Britain since 1890 in university departments and colleges devoted more or less exclusively to this purpose. What passes for theory of education', then, is pre-eminently a theory of instruction. Its 'logic' continues to be the logic of domination – only today it lacks the authority of its heyday. Its 'learning', despite protestations to the contrary, remains closely identified with traditional scholarship. Its 'knowledge' gives pride of place to abstract, symbolic skills with the result that the kind of tacit, personal knowledge of life as it is lived is rigorously excluded – another way of saying that what cannot be sieved through the mesh of examinations is simply ignored or openly disparaged. In a society which is information-rich, its 'teaching' assumes a self-importance it no longer possesses. Its 'philosophy' is as scholastic as the one which gave birth to it.

Look here upon this child and on that. The first is a middle class boy of professional parents, IQ 120, an A-stream grammar school pupil, a regular concert-goer, fond of Bach – the kind of boy who is clearly destined to pass his O and A levels in music with flying colours. The second is a secondary modern school D-streamer, IQ 95, whose chances of gaining any sort of academic award are rated by his teachers as nil. Child A is knowledgeable about Beethoven's quartets (which count) and reads, writes and converses fluently. Child B is a mine of information about the Top Twenty (which don't count) but is semi-illiterate, as well as inarticulate.

To be sure, the contrast is simplistic. Nevertheless, it illustrates the polarization between academic and non-academic types of learner which characterizes all modern education systems. Many are called but few are chosen. During the past thirty years a vast amount of sociological evidence concerning the many who are variously described as deprived, disadvantaged or underprivileged has been amassed, and clinical analysis of the factors involved continues to be one of the chief preoccupations of contemporary research. These factors may be thought of as *external* to the classroom situation and *internal*, i.e. inhering in the organization of the school itself. In so far as they are *external*, the evidence points to a conclusion with which most of us are only too familiar :

> Middle class family socialization of the child is a hidden subsidy, in the sense that it provides both a physical and psychological environment which immensely facilitates, in diverse ways, school learning. The middle-class child is oriented to learning almost anything. Because of this hidden subsidy, there has been little incentive to change curriculum and pedagogy; for the middle-class child is geared to learn; he may not like, or indeed approve of, what he learns, but he learns. Where the school system is not subsidized by the home, the pupils often fails.[12]

Recent studies, notably Lacey's *Hightown Grammar*, have drawn attention to the fact that the polarization formerly ascribed to environmental influences loosely grouped together under the heading of 'social class' can be explained in terms of the school organization itself. Again, experience in the field of curriculum development, where the high hopes originally entertained by the planners have not been fully realized, has led to the conviction that a policy of new wine in old bottles is fated to fail. Between 1945 and 1955 curriculum renewal was conceived of as a relatively simple problem, a matter of updating textbooks and revising the content of courses. After 1955 a more sophisticated strategy was adopted and a series of major projects was launched – SMSG, PSSC, Chem Study *et al.* in the USA, Nuffield Science and all that in England – characterized by an insistence on the prior need for defining objectives, for careful attention to the analysis of the structure and sequence of the field of knowledge or skill which the learner was expected to master, above all by the conviction that the educational achievement and capabilities of the mass of average and below-average children could be enhanced if sufficient care was taken in devising an appropriate methodology. This conviction was typified by Bruner's now famous hypothesis, according to which 'any subject can be taught effectively in some intellectually honest form to any child at any stage of development'. While it would be foolish to say that this optimism has been falsified in the event – in fact, a great deal has been accomplished, especially in the new mathematics, in physics, chemistry and biology – the only possible verdict on these high-powered, not to mention costly, efforts in curriculum development must be that they amount to a few skin grafts, not a major organic transplant. Far from schoolchildren being given a new lease of life, the proportion of apathetic, anomic teenagers appears to be increasing. Truancy, indiscipline and violence are a cause of growing concern in secondary schools in the USA, Britain and elsewhere. The reason is plain. It may be true that it is possible to teach any subject to any child if sufficient resources can be concentrated to achieve this improbable feat. By the same token, we know that it is possible to teach a dolphin to perform all manner of extraordinary tricks, but the ability to do so in an aquarium leaves all the other dolphins in the sea unaffected. In short, these impressive curriculum projects may have worked wonders with 'subsidized' pupils under able teachers, but they remain essentially élitist in the sense that they have little to offer the mass of ordinary children.

It is no accident, therefore, that in his introduction to *The Relevance of Education* Bruner himself admits to a certain disillusionment: at the end of the day, he confesses, we are left wondering whether the school itself is not part of the problem rather than a solution to the problem of curriculum renewal. Significantly, this is the position reached by Husén in Sweden. Just as stage 1 (1945–55) was too facile in thinking of the curriculum in terms of subject matter alone, so stage 2 (1955–70) now begins to look rather naïve in its reliance on improved methodology. Stage 3, which we are now entering, widens the focus so as to see the curriculum as the *total learning situation* – a situation which necessarily includes the school as an institution.

But the school as an institution is only a microcosm of the education system as a whole. So far, the theory of education systems is in its infancy, yet the analyses of social scientists and social critics as different in background and approach as Earl Hopper, Pierre Bourdieu, Raymond Aron, Aldo Visalberghi, and Basil Bernstein agree in certain respects, showing, as they do, how the selective and managerial procedures first adopted by the medieval *universitas* have had far-reaching effects upon mass schooling in modern industrial societies.

Implicit in Hopper's typology of education systems is the assumption that in industrial societies formal schooling is the main mechanism of selecting, recruiting and allocating children to their future occupational roles.[13] The education system, in other words, answers to and serves the complex division of labour. As McLuhan says (for once, the pun is unintentional!), 'It is, indeed, the homogenizing hopper into which we toss our integral tots for processing.'[14]

As societies industrialize they develop specialized and differentiated systems of education. Such systems have three primarily manifest functions: the selection of children with different types and levels of ability; the provision of the appropriate type of *instruction* for the various categories of children created by the selection process; and the eventual *allocation* of trained personnel either directly to occupational roles or to agencies which specialize in occupational recruitment. Because the last two functions are closely linked to the first, the structure of educational systems, especially those within industrial societies, can be understood primarily in terms of the structure of their selection process.[15]

The criteria for selection differ widely from one education system to another – Hopper distinguishes four ideal types of ideology which he calls 'aristocratic', 'paternalistic', 'meritocratic' and 'communistic' but in general the outcome is a pattern of classification which is much the same.

In Bourdieu's view, cultural reproduction and social reproduction go hand in hand, and the education system must be seen as a device for ensuring that the dominant classes retain their hegemony. *Plus ça change plus c'est la même chose.*

In fact the statistics of theatre, concert, and, above all, museum attendance (since, in the last case, the effect of economic obstacles is more or less nil) are sufficient reminder that the inheritance of cultural wealth which has been accumulated and bequeathed by previous generations only really belongs (although it is *theoretically* offered to everyone) to those endowed with the means of appropriating it to themselves.[16]

As he says,

Analysis of the specifically academic mechanisms according to which apportionment is effected between different institutions makes it possible to understand one of the most subtle forms of the trick [*ruse*] of social reason according to which the academic system works objectively towards *the reproduction of the structure of relations between the sections of the dominant classes* when it appears to make full use of its own principles of hierarchical ordering. Knowing, first, that academic success is directly dependent on cultural capital and on the inclination to invest in the academic market (which is itself, as is known, dependent on the objective chances of academic success) and, consequently, that the different sections are recognized and approved by the school system according to the size of their cultural capital and are also, therefore, all the more disposed to invest in work and academic prowess, and knowing, second, that the support accorded by a category to academic sanctions and hierarchies depends not only on the rank the school system grants to it in its hierarchies but also on the extent to which its interests are linked to the school system, or, in other words, on the extent to which its commercial value and its social position depend (in the past as in the future) on academic approval, it is possible to understand why the educational system never succeeds quite so completely in imposing recognition of its value and of the value of its classifications as when its sanctions are brought to bear upon classes or sections of a class which are unable to set against it any rival principle of hierarchical ordering. . . . In short, the effectiveness of the mechanisms by means of which the educational system ensures its own reproduction encloses within itself its own limitation: although the educational system may make use of its relative autonomy to propose and impose its own hierarchies and the university career which serves as its topmost point, it obtains complete adherence only when it preaches to the converted or to lay brethren, to teachers' sons or children from the working or middle classes who owe everything to it and expect everything of it. Far from diverting for its own profit children from the dominant sections of the dominant classes . . . it puts off children from the other sections and classes from claiming the value of their academic investments and from drawing the economic and symbolic profit which the sons of the dominant section of the ruling classes know how to obtain, if necessary, better situated as they are to understand the relative value of academic verdicts.[17]

If the translation of this passage is a trifle turgid, the meaning is plain enough: to him that hath shall be given. The selective mechanism which Bourdieu rightly styles a *ruse* is precisely the one invented by the *universitas*. Its essentially fraudulent nature was perceived by the youngsters from Barbiana whose *Letter to a Teacher* is one of the ablest, wisest and most moving books in the recent literature of education, and while the fraudulence may be more grossly apparent in Italy than in other European countries, it is as well to recognize that it is inherent in the pretence which *all* education systems make to provide for equal opportunity.

At the end of the five elementary years, eleven children have already disappeared from the school. . . .
'Schools are open to all. All citizens have a right to eight years of school. All citizens are equal.'
But what about those eleven. Two of them are equal to nothing at all. To sign their name they make a cross. One of them has one-eighth equality. He can sign his name. The others have two-, three-, four- or five-eighths equality. They read after a fashion but cannot understand a newspaper.[18]

The irony of it is, of course, that although these juvenile protesters are unschooled their little masterpiece is proof enough that they are well and truly educated. Before jumping to the conclusion that the royal road to social justice necessarily leads to a further enlargement of the statutory education system – more nursery schools, more university places, more in-service and retraining courses, more services of every kind – it is vital to understand that irony.

Aron's critique of the dialectics of modern industrial societies, aptly summarized in the title of his book, *Progress and Disillusion*, is at once non-committal and gloomy. There is, he decides, a fundamental contradiction between the egalitarian aspirations of these societies and their hierarchical organization. The distinction drawn between the gifted few who receive special treatment as first-class citizens (whether as gentlemen or technocrats), and the many who receive only the basic training needed to make them efficient workmen and producers, is built into the structure of industrial society itself. 'Is it feasible to think of educating everyone so that each man can realize his full potential, if not in work, at least in leisure?', he asks, 'Or is it not more likely to foresee a society in which these millions and millions of human beings will be able to enjoy certain comforts, but will be condemned to the creative existence of termites?'[19]

Useless for the existentialists to proclaim the no-thingness of man: by its very nature an industrial-technological society is depersonalized and treats individuals as things. Whether we diagnose this state of affairs as *alienation*, as *anomie* (i.e. absence of internalized norms), or as *other-directedness*, is really immaterial. Whichever diagnosis is preferred, one ultimately arrives at the same conclusion, which is that the sense of loss, of anonymity and helplessness, experienced by the individual in a mass society springs directly from the structural characteristics of industrial civilization. Short of the Great Refusal advocated by thinkers like Marcuse and Illich there is no exit from the squirrel's cage of economic growth and endless production. As things are, there is no prospect of a 'revolt of the masses: as a political platform, the Great Refusal is a non-starter', thinks Aron.

Only a few people are prepared to say *no* and are proud of not yielding. As long as the machine of production continues to turn and to bring more goods to almost everyone from year to year, the masses will accept their fate passively. But this acceptance represents alienation nonetheless and for two interrelated reasons.

Civilization still treats men like objects, it permits the commercial or political manipulation of consumers or pseudocitizens, it maintains a climate of competition between individuals and nations even though the productive capacity would be sufficient to secure a simpler and less frantic life for everyone.[20]

Visalberghi's reading of the situation is no less despondent. The writing is on the wall, he thinks, and unless our anomic society can take avoiding action in time, it is headed for a future which looks like being suicidal. In the existing situation he notes the following tendencies: (1) the explosive rates of growth in the educational services in both developed and underdeveloped countries; (2) the accelerating growth of knowledge; (3) the growing difficulty of finding manpower for menial and less gratifying types of work; (4) the use of the school system as the main agency of selection for and allocation to different types of work; (5) the adoption of policies of neo-colonialism (e.g. 'guest workers' in Germany, immigrant labour in Britain); (6) the increasing difficulty of meeting the non-stop escalation of the costs of maintaining the educational services; (7) the emergence of deschooling theories; (8) the growing dissatisfaction, frustration and unrest among pupils in the upper secondary schools and among students in higher education; (9) increasing support both from international, national and voluntary organizations for 'permanent education' as an alternative to the further expansion of continuous schooling on the present lines.

Taken together, these tendencies point to a future in which education will be open to all, and in which at the same time it will be necessary for more people than ever before to possess high-level intellectual skills. On the other hand, the number of interesting, self-gratifying occupations which require relatively low-level intellectual skills will decrease sharply, as will the inclination to engage in 'dirty' jobs. Hence the dilemma. As it is, students qualify in ever-increasing numbers – a case of over-production and over-schooling which gives rise to widespread fears about the unemployment of graduates.

Faced with these problems, the authorities responsible for educational policymaking must choose between three possible alternatives. In the first place, they may decide to resist expansionist tendencies, selecting only the ablest pupils for advanced secondary and higher education, i.e. preserving a two-track system. In the second, they can profess to accept mass education at every level while secretly devaluing it, thus leaving the responsibility of selection to the socio-economic mechanisms which have operated in the past. Under such a plan, outwardly more 'democratic' and 'liberal' than the first, schools would be conceived chiefly as 'parking areas' and leaving certificates would be token awards, without any legal or market value.

The first of these alternatives is likely to appeal to autocratic, reactionary regimes, say fascist Spain or the Colonels in Greece. The second has an uncanny resemblance (or has it?) to current developments in the United Kingdom and the USA. Either way, thinks Visalberghi, the outcome is bound to be a pseudo-meritocracy.

The third alternative, as yet nowhere in sight, is so visionary as to seem merely utopian. It envisages a 'new classless society' in which all citizens would engage at some period in their lives in humble, menial occupations as a matter of duty. This would not necessarily involve compulsory direction of labour, only a voluntary rotation of work.

> Nobody will be confined to such activities except for short initial periods. Everybody will be trained for higher jobs and will be able to spend his 'educational credit' for changing and/or upgrading his skills. Careers should be quite independent from school qualifications possessed before being employed, and only partially linked to specialization obtained through formal education: on the job training would be at least equally important. Therefore many people would prefer to cultivate themselves more personally than in any institutionalized way. All these are requests rather commonly made by authors supporting permanent education (and also by 'deschoolers'); but in the system of vertical job rotation they seem much easier to be fulfilled.[21]

When it comes to the question of whether such a model is politically viable, Visalberghi is frankly sceptical, not without good reason. If it were to become operational it would presumably involve, if not a zero rate of economic growth, at least a slowing down of the continuous rise in the Gross National Product – and before that could happen there would have to be an all-round, dramatic change of values in consumer societies. It may come to this, of course, but nothing short of the imminent threat of ecological disaster will make it possible. Everything points to the conclusion that in Western Europe at any rate the second alternative will be chosen. 'In my end is my beginning.' This is where the pedagogical juggernaut has led us.

Just where we go from here must be a matter for speculation. In this connection, Bernstein's paper 'On the classification and framing of educational knowledge' has some interesting pointers to offer.[22] He begins by distinguishing between two types of curricula – *collection* and *integrated*. In the former, the contents (subjects, disciplines, courses) are clearly bounded and insulated from each other, whereas in an integrated curriculum the boundaries are either non-existent or blurred and the contents stand in open relation to each other. On the basis of this distinction, Bernstein outlines a more general set of concepts: *classification* and *frame*. *Classification* refers to the degree or strength of boundary maintenance between the various components of the curriculum. *Frame* refers to the degree of control teacher and pupil possess over the selection, organization and pacing of the knowledge transmitted and received in the pedagogical relationship. The resulting typology of educational knowledge codes remains largely hypothetical, but it does help to explain the 'divorce of school from life', first institutionalized in the medieval *universitas* and derided by a succession of critics from Montaigne and Rousseau down to John Dewey and the present-day deschoolers.

Derided, yes, but never dislodged. Once established within the walls of the *schola*, the classification of 'educational knowledge' became rigid, as did the frames marking off formal academic learning and informal existential learning.

This formulation invites us to ask how strong are the frames of educational knowledge in relation to experimental community based non-school knowledge? I suggest that the frames of the collection code, very early in the child's school life, socialize him into knowledge frames which discourage connections with everyday realities, or that there is a highly selective screening of the connection. Through such socialization, the pupil soon learns what of the outside may be brought into the pedagogical frame. Such framing also makes of educational knowledge something not ordinary or mundane, but something esoteric which gives a special significance to those who possess it. I suggest that when this frame is relaxed to include everyday realities, it is often, and sometimes validly, not simply for the transmission of educational knowledge, but for purposes of social control of forms of deviancy. The weakening of this frame occurs usually with the less 'able' children whom we have given up educating.[23]

The answer to Bernstein's question, 'How strong are the frames of educational knowledge in relation to experimental community based non-school knowledge?' is clear enough.[24] No less clear is the fact that in a permissive society these frames are visibly weakening, witness the advent of schools without walls, of team teaching, of the vogue for interdisciplinary courses in universities, of the merging of community education with community service, of the proliferation of voluntary non-statutory organizations and agencies – youth volunteers, nursery play groups, task forces, etc. – whose functions admit of no clearcut distinction between 'education' and 'welfare'. Witness too that the teacher's professional role, formerly defined as that of an instructor, has become so diffuse that it is hard to say just how or where it differs from that of other social workers. Witness, again, the growing conviction that the immurement of teacher trainees in monotechnic institutions like colleges of education is no longer advisable. With respect, judging by his comments in the last two sentences quoted above, it seems that Bernstein's own frames of reference constrain his thinking about what counts as 'educational'. It is true that anyone trying to organize a 'school without walls', involving the block release of pupils from full-time school attendance, will meet stern resistance from the authorities in England (sterner still in Scotland) and that the most he can bargain for is the release of 'dead-end kids' who have been written off as deviant. This is by no means the case, however, in the less tradition-bound conditions of the USA where community- and home-based schools have been organized successfully with pupils drawn from the whole spectrum of ability from drop-out to college preparatory. The popularity of the Parkway Program, admission to which is by public lottery, is no flash in the pan : if the regulations governing school attendance were to be relaxed, with credit given for non-school learning and activies, who can doubt that the response of many teenagers (whose motto is 'Get where the action is') would be immediate and enthusiastic? Who can doubt, too, that socialization of this kind would be a better preparation for lifelong learning than the one which insists on keeping them cabin'd, cribb'd, confin'd – a captive audience within a pedagogical frame?

DOING VIOLENCE TO THE PERSON: THE LOGIC OF DOMINATION

Sophisticated as we like to think we are, we are rightly scornful of medieval plumbing, yet curiously unmindful of the stranglehold exerted by archaic modes of thought on our educational theory and practice; curiously ignorant, too, of the course of events which enabled the vested interest of a guild of pedagogues to decide what counts as learning, knowledge and education. Lest it be thought that the excursion into the sociology of modern education systems side-tracks the original argument (that the empire-building which gave rise to state systems of education was accomplished on the basis of a colossal confidence trick) it seems timely to examine another piece of historical evidence.

So far, all that has been proved is that the theory of education which originated in the *universitas* was, in fact, no more than a theory of instruction. As such, it could hardly be accused of being pseudo-scientific, seeing that it was intended to produce scholars and did precisely that. It was only when this model was adopted for the compulsory schooling of the masses that it became specious and pretentious. This, for three reasons: (1) because its concept of education was restricted to the learner's school life; (2) because the theory undertook prime responsibility for the 'making of men'; (3) because its professed aim of initiating the child into adult society masked its covert aim, which was to prepare him for the world of work.

As regards (1) it is as well to recall what Durkheim had to say on the subject in his essay on 'Education: its nature and role':

> Education is the influence exercised by adult generations on those that are not yet ready for social life. Its object is to arouse and develop in the child a certain number of physical, intellectual and moral states *which are demanded of him by both the political society as a whole and the special milieu for which he is specifically destined* [my italics]. . . . In a word, education is the methodical socialization of the young generation.[25]

This definition, he tells us, was arrived at by abstracting the characteristics of different education systems in the past. Three objections to it immediately come to mind. First, the definition appears to rule out any possibility of lifelong learning: 'education' is for the child, not for his parents. Second, it rules out the influence of peer groups: the learner is 'not yet ready for social life' and the responsibility for educating rests with adults alone. Third, the definition derives from a concept of society which is essentially ambivalent. (In one context, 'society' is treated as a *fact*, external to the individual and constraining him: in another, 'society exists exclusively in the mind of the individual'.)

Durkheim's attempt to explain away this Cartesian dualism is not very convincing:

> In each of us, it may be said, there exist two beings which, while inseparable except by abstraction, remain distinct. One is made up of all the mental states that apply only to ourselves and to the events of our personal lives: it is what might be called the individual being. The other is a system of ideas, sentiments and tendencies which express in us, not our personality, but the group or different groups of which we are part; these are religious beliefs, moral beliefs and practices, rational or professional traditions, collective opinions of every kind. Their totality forms the social being. *To constitute this being in each of us is the end of education* [my italics].[26]

Curiouser and curiouser. According to this, education has nothing whatever to do with the nurture of personal growth. Can it be that Durkheim's preoccupation with the 'collective conscience' was due to his desire to establish sociology as an independent science at all costs, even at the cost of talking psychological nonsense? On his own admission, the separation of the social and individual being was only made possible by means of intellectual abstraction. If, in fact, the individual internalizes this collective conscience, in what sense can he be said to be not ready for social life?

Durkheim recognizes that the child is no passive *tabula rasa*, but this does not prevent him from coming down firmly on the side of nurture rather than nature:

> Education does not make a man out of nothing, as Locke and Helvétius believed; it is applied to predispositions that it finds already made. From another point of view, one can concede, in a general way, that these congenital tendencies are very strong, *and very difficult to destroy, for they depend upon organic conditions on which the educator has little influence. Consequently to the*

degree that they have a definite object, that they incline the mind and character toward narrowly determined ways of acting and thinking, the whole future of the individual finds itself fixed in advance, and there does not remain much for education to do [my italics].[27]

Any suggestion that at all stages of development the human organism might be capable of ordering its own life – 'doing its own thing' – was not in keeping with Durkheim's temperament, not with his methodology. Not for him a philosophy of *natura naturans*: he shied away from it, affecting to dismiss these innate predispositions on the grounds that they were 'very general and vague'. Not so general, nor so vague, it may be thought, as the 'collective conscience'! Throughout, he is openly contemptuous of child-centred theorists like Montaigne and Rousseau. His concept of education is unashamedly authoritarian, typical of a nineteenth-century French bureaucrat. It assumes the same helplessness in the learner as in the subject of hypnotic suggestion. Like the hypnotist, the teacher and parent must speak to the child in a commanding tone.

He must say: *I wish*; he must indicate that refusal to obey is not even conceivable, that the act must be accomplished, that the thing must be seen as he shows it, that it cannot be otherwise. If he weakens, one sees the subject hesitate, resist, sometimes even refuse to obey. If he so much as enters into discussion, that is the end of his power. . . .

Now, these two conditions are present in the relationship that the educator has with the child subjected to his influence: (1) The child is naturally in a state of passivity, quite comparable to that in which the hypnotic subject is found artificially placed. His mind yet contains only a small number of conceptions able to fight against those which are suggested to him; his will is still rudimentary. Therefore he is very suggestible. For the same reason, he is very suggestible to the force of example and much inclined to imitation. (2) The ascendancy that the teacher naturally has over his pupil, because of the superiority of his experience and of his culture, will naturally give to his influence the efficacious force that he needs.[28]

There could hardly be a more explicit, or a more wrong-headed, declaration of faith in the logic of domination than this. 'Break their wills betimes', is the sum of its advice. Far from the child being the father of the man, he is to be treated like an unlicked cub, bludgeoned, if necessary, into the shape of the social animal, the end product of the educational process. The child's nature is to be transformed by force. (Durkheim does not mince matters: the word 'force' is repeated again and again, as if to underline his unrelenting conviction that the teacher-pupil relationship must always be one of dominance and submission, a battle in which there can be no give and take.) 'The object of education is to superimpose, on the individual and asocial being that we are at birth, an *entirely new being*. It must bring us to *overcome our initial nature*; it is on this condition that the child will become a man.'[29] This is the doctrine of education as initiation, a secular version of the doctrine of original sin which has been restated – it can hardly be resuscitated – more or less word for word by R. S. Peters in our own day. According to this nineteenth-century industrial ethic, the 'natural man' needed to be transformed into the 'social man', to undergo a second birth, to be programmed for the role in life for which he was specifically destined. It is the ideal of the inner-directed man, the man who has been provided with a built-in code of values and conduct which is intended to last him until he dies – and which he is unlikely to change because he has been rendered incapable of doing so. Its imperatives admit of no denial, only acceptance.

Duty remains. The sense of duty is, indeed, for the child and even for the adult, the stimulus *par excellence* for effort. Self-respect presupposes it. For, to be properly affected by reward and punishment, one must already have a sense of his dignity and, consequently, of his duty.[30]

Back to innate predisposition, then! Here, Durkheim seems to concede the essentially dynamic nature of the child which he refuses to recognize elsewhere. It is this dynamism which is at the heart of modern developmental psychology (of all the life sciences for that matter), of Chomsky's theory of generative grammar, of Gombrich's theory of aesthetic perception (in *Art and Illusion*), of Popper's evolutionary approach to epistemology (in *Objective Knowledge*). As Stuart Hampshire notes in his review of the latter book, the basic common factor in what, for want of a better term, may be called organismic thinking is the understanding

that the perceiving mind always has a set of expectations, a primitive hypothesis, as it searches for features that will either fit or falsify its expectations: that the hypothesis-forming and testing attitude to the world is built into the organism and that in this respect scientific knowledge is a natural extension of common-sense knowledge. We are programmed always to look at the environment with specific questions relevant to our needs in mind.[31]

It is a view nicely summarized (or satirized?) in Harvard's First Law of Animal Behaviour which states that: *If an organism is subjected to regular, pre-determined schedules of reinforcement and maintained in a rigorously controlled environment the outcome is that the organism behaves as it bloody well pleases.*

Durkheim's educational theory literally does violence to such a view. Today, it is clearer than it was at the turn of the century that his model is not only inadequate but positively mischievous in its effects. In fairness it should be added that he would be the first to acknowledge this were he alive today. Futurology was not his métier but he was well aware of the transience of the best-laid schemes for educational theory and practice.

When, under pressure of increased competition, the division of labour increases, when the specialization of each worker is at the same time more marked and more advanced, the universe of discourse of common education will necessarily be limited, and, therefore, the characteristics of the human type will also become limited. Formerly, literary culture had been considered as an essential element of all human culture; and now we are approaching a time when it will itself no longer, perhaps, be more than a specialty. In the same way, if there exists a recognized hierarchy among our faculties, if there are some to which we attribute a sort of pre-eminence and which we should, for this reason, develop more than others it is not because this dignity is intrinsic to them; it is not because nature itself, from all eternity, has assigned this eminent rank to them; but it is because they have a higher value for the society. Also, as the scale of these values necessarily changes with the society, this hierarchy has never remained the same for two moments in history. Yesterday it was courage that was in the foreground, with all the faculties that military virtue implies; today it is thought and reflection; tomorrow it will perhaps be elegance of taste, sensitivity to artistic matters. Thus, in the present as in the past, our pedagogical ideal is in every detail the work of society.[32]

To his credit, also, Durkheim was careful to distinguish between 'education' and 'pedagogy'. What he failed to realize was that his thought was backward-looking, vitiated by what Whitehead called 'the vicious assumption that each generation will substantially live amid the conditions governing the lives of its fathers and will transmit those conditions to mould with equal force the lives of its children.' The doctrine of education as initiation may have preserved a certain plausibility in Victorian times – Elizabeth Barrett suffered under its tyrannies and so did Sissy Jupe – yet it was already non-sensical in Durkheim's lifetime. Seventy years later we find the author of *Future Shock* still inveighing against it.

It remains to consider some of the deleterious effects of this hang-over from the past.

1 Because education was conceived of exclusively as the upbringing of the young the logic of domination became its ruling principle. In theory and practice, education was understood to be a process in which the strong (adults) masterminded the development of the weak (children). To be *in statu pupillari* meant undergoing special treatment at the hands of one's elders and betters just as the patient in the operating theatre is submitted to the surgeon's knife: the analogy may be unnecessarily gruesome but underlines the point we are making, viz. that education was thought of primarily in terms of what was done to the learner and only secondarily, if at all, in terms of what he was able to do for himself.

Methodologically, this theory found its typical expression in the applications of Herbartian psychology – the famous five steps for the preparation of lessons which helped to lay down the narrow gauge railroad for the pedagogical juggernaut in the age of steam. Far from being discredited, it retains its place intact in the conventional wisdom. Revamped, it finds its champions in educational technologists like B. F. Skinner and educational philosophers like R. S. Peters: above all, even in a permissive society it has the broad approval of public opinion which, if it no longer agrees that children should be seen and not heard, is unshaken in its conviction that 'adults know best'.

2 Since education was for the young, the only ones who could spare the time for it, it quickly came to be identified with full-time school attendance. Educational theory, accordingly, had to bite off in practice more than it could chew. It might, and did, talk airily of 'the

continuous process', 'nurture of personal growth', 'general and special education', 'the whole man', all this and heaven too, but invariably these statements of aim were a blend of piety and cant, for the simple reason that none of them was realizable within the learner's school life. The appalling inefficiency of the school system is largely due to its attempt to do too many things at the same time. Even those of its objectives which are relatively clearcut – instruction in the 3 Rs, for one – are not being fully achieved. Some 20 per cent of boys and girls entering secondary schools have a reading age at least two years behind their chronological age. Half of them at present receive little or no remedial treatment and can be expected to fall further behind by the time they reach school leaving age. Peter Clyne's survey for the Russell Committee indicates that there are at least 2 million adults in England and Wales whose basic education is seriously deficient – an estimate which is almost certainly conservative.[33]

Because time was so limited, the curriculum inevitably became overcrowded, a collection of bits and pieces of uncommonsense knowledge. For the same reason, the school's classificatory function, selecting and grading pupils for their future roles, assumed greater and greater importance. Because decisions had to be taken prematurely, as still happens at 11 plus (not to mention 16 plus and 18 plus), an element of enforced stress entered into the learning situation. Intense competition became the rule. Nor was this the worst of it for, as Lindeman points out,

> Education conceived as a preparation for life locks learning in a vicious circle. Youth educated in terms of adult ideas and taught to think of learning as a process which ends when life begins will make no better use of intelligence than the elders who prescribe the system. . . . Education within the vicious circle becomes not a joyous enterprise but something to be endured because it leads to a satisfying end.[34]

3 Among other things, this explains why schooling has always emphasized *labor* at the expense of *opus*; and why pedagogical theory appeals to the 'principle of deferred gratification'. Although the doctrine of education as initiation professed to offer the learner a preparation for 'life', this was never more than a cover for its real intention, which was to prepare him for the world of work. Whether it was bare literacy for elementary school pupils who were going to

become factory hands, or classics for Oxbridge undergraduates destined, as Dean Gaisford freely admitted, 'to positions of considerable emolument', the underlying assumption was that earning a living was of paramount concern. This assumption, stemming from belief in the primal curse which expelled Adam from Eden and doomed Everyman to live forever by the sweat of his brow, was central to the Protestant ethic. Neither the political economy of Marx nor the sociological theory of Durkheim questioned it for a moment. The human life cycle was thought of as composed of three stages: childhood, adulthood and old age. This division, which held good for all except the idle rich until the second half of the twentieth century (when it still holds good for most!) is neatly summarized by Jean Le Veugle:

> On considerait que la jeunesse, l'âge adulte et la vieillesse étaient respectivement l'âge de la formation, celui du rendement et celui du repos.
>
> Au cours du premier âge, dans la famille, à l'école et en apprentissage les jeunes se preparaient à prendre quelques années plus tard leur place dans la société. Celle-ci serait sensiblement la même que dans leur enfance, avec seulement quelques années de plus. Au cours du deuxième âge, il s'agissait de travailler, à l'atelier, dans les champs ou au bureau, et de mettre au profit, pour soi, pour so famille et pour la société, ce qu'on avait appris au cours du premier âge. Quant au troisième âge, réservé, à une minorité de gens – car la moyenne d'âge limité de la vie était beaucoup moins élevé qu'aujourd'hui – c'était l'âge de repos, de la sagesse due à une longue experience de la même vie sociale, des conseils donnés aux plus jeunes.[35]

(It was considered that youth, adulthood and old age were respectively the age of education, work and retirement. During the course of the first age the young prepared themselves for their future role in society, in the family, at school and in apprenticeship. The latter, broadly speaking, was an extension of their childhood. During the course of the second age, it was a matter of working in factory, office or on the land, and of making use of what one had learned during one's youth in order to produce a profit for oneself, one's family and society. As for the third age, reserved as it was for a minority – for the average expectation of life was very much lower than it is today – it was the age of rest, of the wisdom due to long experience of an unchanged social life, of advice given to the young.)

Of the three ages of man, adulthood was by far the longest and the one in which the ineluctable necessity of labour bulked largest. Leisure, such as there was, meant rest and relief from physical and mental exhaustion, or was otherwise construed as idleness and carried its own guilt complex. Thus transformed by industrialism, the Christian virtues embodied in the Protestant ethic were carried over into the school system which inculcated, among other values, a sense of duty, obedience to superiors, utter reliability, willingness to work for small returns (if necessary, for no returns at all), and above all, a fatalistic acceptance of lowly status. For the schoolmaster, as for the factory owner and the priest, 'Blessed are the meek' had a strong appeal when it came to policymaking.

Hence the stress on *labor* and the sheer joylessness of traditional schooling. Hence too, the constant heavy reminders from parents and teachers alike that 'Life is a serious business', that you must 'make the most of your chances or you'll regret it later', etc. Hence again, the poohpoohing of methods of teaching which resorted to play, or any innovation which answered however faintly to the description of 'progressive'.

All of which is perfectly understandable, of course. To the extent that most of us remain inner-directed, a theory and practice which seeks to fit out the learner for life with a built-in code of morality and with the basic vocational skills which will help him to 'get on in the world' cannot fail to seem plausible. But in a society in which work no longer plays anything like the all-important role it did in the nineteenth century the adequacy of such theory and practice must sooner or later be called in question. Technological and demographic changes have brought about an entirely new situation which demands not so much a revision as a drastic reformulation of our ideas about the nature of the educational process. It is not simply that the average working week is becoming progressively shorter, holidays with pay more frequent, foreign travel easier, standards of living higher, life expectation longer; nor that, in future, it will be necessary to enrol for in-service and recycling training in order to keep abreast of developments in one's chosen occupation. The implications of the fact that, for the first time in history, the toiling masses are in sight of a society in which leisure will be the central element have yet to dawn on us. All at once, Rousseau's paradox, 'The great object is not to save time but to waste it', ceases to be nonsensical.

As defined by Dumazedier, 'Leisure is activity – apart from obligations of work, family and society – to which the individual turns at will for relaxation, diversion and broadening his knowledge and his spontaneous social participation, the free exercise of his creative capacity.'[36]

Activity apart from obligations to which the individual turns at will for the free exercise of his creative capacity may well be taken as the formula for the kind of education which has to be envisaged henceforth. As a formula, it is poles apart from the one recommended by Durkheim. 'To educate' becomes an active verb, with the learner, not the teacher, in charge. Not what is done to him by others but what he does for himself becomes the guiding principle. *Labor* turns into *opus*. The wheel of events which began in the Greek *schola* and Roman *ludus* is coming full circle and in theory, at least, a society in which work is play and play is life need no longer be considered a Shavian whimsy. Integrated day curricula in primary school, simulation and gaming exercises for business executives, voluntary task forces and the host of activities and agencies loosely lumped together under the name of community service – each in its way evidences the trend towards an educational practice which is non-pedagogical. Will it ever return us to a state of affairs in which it will be possible to recapture the intellectual serenity displayed in Plato's *Symposium* where everyone is at ease and no one, least of all Socrates, is concerned to outsmart his fellows? Too early to say. But, hopefully, current trends point in this direction.

4 Nature denatured. One of R. F. Mackenzie's best stories (in *State School*) deserves to be taken as a parable. Maybe it needs to be taken with a pinch of salt, but it has the ring of truth. It concerns a young Highlander, Mike McAllister, who broke the world's record for truancy. Mike's total school life, it appears, consisted of one half day's attendance. The circumstances which allowed him to get away with it are easily explained: living in a remote glen in Wester Ross, he was seriously ill at the age of five and so delicate a child thereafter that he was not sent to school until he was seven, by which time he had developed his own life style and considered himself well on the way to being grown up. He was placed in the baby class and took

such a poor view of the indignity that he never returned. Sheer isolation and a rugged terrain kept this Scottish Émile out of the clutches of the school attendance officers. His childhood and adolescent days were spent in crofting, shepherding or roaming the far hills in search of foxes and deer.

Now Mike has three brothers, all of whom left home to attend the nearest secondary school and eventually the university. These three are now doing well in their respective professions. Each year during the summer vacation the family is reunited. On these occasions, blood being thicker than water, there is never any trace of bad blood between Mike, the stay-at-home, and his three well-educated brothers: no inferiority complex on his part, no condescension or embarrassment on theirs.

The moral of the story is pointed by the local gamekeeper. In his opinion, Mike is the pick of the bunch: sure, the others are doing well in Aberdeen, Glasgow, or wherever their calling has taken them, but so far as he is concerned they are no better than 'sookit oranges'.

Pedagogue's pride, alas, prevents parables of this sort from being taken seriously. Amusing, perhaps, but meaningful only because Mike's case is taken as the exception which proves the rule, the rule being that education without schooling is next to impossible. That schooling can be a denaturing influence rarely or never occurs to us, and when it does we dismiss any such idea as preposterous. In this connection, then, we might do worse than listen to the views of the Provost of King's College, Cambridge, someone we are bound to take seriously, if only because of his academic distinction. As Dr Leach points out, most of the learning involved in the process of growing up is informal and only a small part of it is acquired as a consequence of going to school. Our speech, the way we walk, the way we sit down, the kind of clothes we wear, our tastes, manners, values – in short, our whole way of life – all this is part and parcel of the process of education, but very little of it can be ascribed to formal schooling. He goes on:

If we take the very broad sociological view that, in human society as a whole, education signifies the total process of socialization – that is to say everything that is transmitted by learning from one generation to another – then we can break down this very broad category into several components:

(1) *Habits*, which are learned informally at home or school or place of work
(2) *Skills*, learnt formally at school or by some other systematic form of training
(3) *Knowledge*, mainly acquired by conversation and by reading. We acquire 'knowledge' mainly because it is interesting. It has little utilitarian value.

When we break down our categories in this way we can see immediately that these different facets of the total educational process are mutually in competition. Any form of learning takes up time and if you exaggerate the time spent on formal school education then you will inevitably cut back on the more informal but perhaps equally valuable process of informal socialization. To take a case in point: anyone who has ever had anything to do with university undergraduates must be aware of the problems posed by young men and women who are academically very advanced but socially and emotionally very backward. It isn't that they have had too little education; they have been educated with the wrong kind of mix. Many of my own past pupils would certainly have been much better adjusted to adult life if they had had much *less* academic pressure imposed upon them at school and spent more time just learning to know their fellow men.[37]

Dr Leach here raises the crucial issue: is formal schooling such a good thing that in order to attain it we are prepared to prejudice informal non-school education? Already, the signs are that formal schooling means, in effect, over-schooling. Not only has the time spent on it increased, both in terms of the length of compulsory attendance and of the proportion of the learner's daily life, but so has the importance attached to it. The sin of pedagogue's pride has always been to affirm that the process of education is all one with schooling, whereas the truth is that education is a *family* of processes, of which schooling happens to be one.

Perhaps now the connection between Dr Leach's maladjusted undergraduates and the Highland gamekeeper's appraisal of Mike's learned brethren as 'sucked oranges' is becoming a shade clearer. It remains to be seen what the connection is between both groups, as products of the education system, and Skinner's pigeons.

Skinner's pigeons? Perish the thought! A moment's reflection, nevertheless, should remind us of the close similarity between the carefully controlled conditions imposed on schoolchildren in their classrooms and those which make it possible for silly birds to go through the motions of a passable game of table tennis. In both cases the subjects are housed in a box. In both cases, their behaviour is shaped for them by outsiders. In both cases they are hived off from the rest of their kind, reared in an artificial, aseptic environment which does its best to prevent intrusions from the world outside. (This, incidentally, in the name of socialization!)

For the most part, birds or boys, the subjects are amenable to this kind of treatment. They have little choice in the matter. Middle class children, we know, are oriented to learn almost any old rubbish in school, just as Norway pigeons which have been bred and born in the laboratory will respond like zombies to a process of operant conditioning. Why, then, should certain working class children be less tractable – and why is it that Skinner's experiments would run into difficulties, or break down altogether, if they were repeated with wild rock doves and wily wood pigeons? The very success of schooling in inducing habits of acceptance and docility is the measure of its denaturing influence. 'Gentling the masses' – 'promoting the type' as it came to be called in the early twentieth-century American jargon – operates on much the same lines, and with much the same effects, as battery farming. J. S. Mill's fears that state education would turn out to be a contrivance for moulding everyone to a common pattern have been realized to an extent which few of us care to recognize. Only rank outsiders, the Mike McAllisters of this world, remain unaffected. Only the eccentricity of an A. S. Neill was immune to the pressures of conformity – which is why his reputation is certain to be honoured among the great educators long after all our ministers and professors of education have been forgotten. 'Democracy, the votes of the masses castrated in their cradles', the GOM pronounced in his swansong.[38]

The jungle fowl, alas, is now a *rara avis* but battery hens are to be counted in their millions.

5 A theory of education originally designed for the production of scholars became specious once it was enlarged and undertook prime responsibility for the making of men. As adumbrated by Comenius and followed up by thinkers like Locke, Helvétius, Owen, Herbart and others, it fostered early industrial society's belief that the

education of a 'multitude of laborious poor' was essentially akin to any other manufacturing process. The same techniques of prediction and control could, it was believed – and the belief persists – be applied no less successfully to the shaping of human behaviour. As a consequence, all that side of the learner's life which had formerly been left to informal experience – *natura naturans* – was either belittled or suppressed altogether, superseded by techniques of management which sought to bring about a kind of secular conversion. Iron ore or infants, the raw material had to be converted into the finished article, preferably in a saleable form and bearing a mass production trademark.

Admittedly, the methods used were never quite so inhuman or so Procrustean as this. But whether it was Mr Gradgrind deliberately reducing little Sissy Jupe to a state of abject impotence or Arnold of Rugby dominating his sixth formers by sheer force of personality, the aggressive intent was never more than partly concealed. The theory held that doing things to children (benignly if possible, nastily if there was no other way, and always in their long-term interest, needless to say) was vitally necessary and vastly more important than anything children could do for themselves. Useless for Rousseau to protest that 'Our pedantic mania for instruction is always leading us to teach children the things they would learn better of their own accord'. Useless, because the pedagogue's claim to be indispensable was embedded in a theory of education which had its genesis in the medieval *universitas*. Any validity it may have had in a society which was information-poor has now been lost, and for ever.

6 There remains, finally, the objection that a theory of instruction masquerading as a theory of education is hopelessly outdated for the simple and obvious reason that the problems arising in post-school learning are virtually excluded from its terms of reference. By its own definition, education is for the young. Hitherto, it has had a great deal to say about 'Immaturity – its uses, nature and management' (the title of Bruner's essay), little or nothing about what happens thereafter. Yet if there is any truth in the saying that life begins at forty there is a sense in which it can be said that education begins when schooling is left behind. The test comes when, for the first time, the pilot waves goodbye to his instructor on the tarmac and takes off on his own. With the best will in the world, a theory of

education which focuses its attention on the short segment of the human life cycle occupied by the learner's school life is bound to be blinkered. The game is up unless it raises its sights. In short, what counts as 'education', 'learning' and 'knowledge' nowadays is not for pedagogues to decide.

5 Learning in the community: organizing a school without walls

A frequent and deserved criticism of theorists like Illich, Curle and other contributors to the recent literature of educational dissent is that they are persuasive enough in arguing the case against formal schooling but singularly unhelpful, and extremely vague, when it comes to explaining what can be done to provide practical alternatives. It may be, of course, that they have served a sufficient purpose in arousing in their readers a sense of discontent which would otherwise have remained dormant and that it is unrealistic to ask more of any reformist writer. Still, example counts for more in the estimation of most teachers than a bookful of precepts. It needed a Pestalozzi, after all, to prove that *Émile* was not simply the romantic effusion of an idle dreamer – and a half-crazed, rather disreputable dreamer at that.

Whether we attribute it to the deschoolers (Illich, Reimer, Goodman, Holt, Kozol, *et al.*) or to eminent figures in the field of academic educational studies (Husén, Bruner, Curle, R. M. Hutchins *et al.*) the fact is that there is today a wide and growing measure of agreement about the need for alternatives. Carl Bereiter, Professor of Educational Psychology at the University of Toronto, has put the case as succinctly and convincingly as anyone. Broadly, the argument is that the learner's social attitudes and value system bear little or no relation either to the *length* or *type* of courses followed in school. Informed opinion agrees with him in concluding that the effects of schooling have been greatly exaggerated. 'Schools do not, and cannot, successfully educate – that is, influence how children turn out in any important way. The most they can do successfully is to provide child care and training.'[1] The behavioural changes which have given rise to unrest on the campus and in the classroom – and which occasionally manifest themselves as demonstrations of 'student power' and 'pupil power' – have been brought about by social forces outside the schools. The realization that these extramural forces are vastly more potent than any that can be brought to bear on pupils in the classroom serves to undermine the theory on which schools are supposed to operate. In North America, at any rate, 'The word seems to have passed down from college to high school and now to the more with-it elementary school populations that a great deal of school work is pointless, that grades do not really tell you how good you are, and that school rituals are a subject for derision.'[2]

So far as the primary school is concerned, thinks Bereiter, the only honest solution is to cut our losses and concentrate on the two objectives which the school *can* achieve – training in the basic skills and the provision of custodial care. This, he insists, is what the public is paying for and to pretend that anything more, or better, is being offered is nothing less than fraudulent. As things are, parents cannot sue the authorities if, as often happens, their children are illiterate and innumerate by the time they reach the age of eleven or twelve. A primary school staffed by specialist instructors (a kind of 3 Rs brigade) and child care aides (an 'activity and experience' brigade) would represent a more rational division of labour than the one we have. Among other things, this would mean the disappearance of the all-purpose teacher.

While this advice may be hard to take, what follows is sterner still. 'It is not at all certain that the high school will survive as an institution. The pressures toward its disintegration are much stronger and the reasons for its survival much weaker. For adolescents, institutionalized child care is unnecessary and training needs are so diverse that it makes little sense to cram all sorts of training within the same four walls.'[3] In other words, once adequate norms of attainment in literacy and numeracy are virtually guaranteed for all, say by the age of thirteen, the way is open for the teenager to pursue his own learning strategies independently as and where he chooses. In a society that is information-rich, formal schooling beyond the primary stage is fast becoming an anachronism.

Before 1970 anyone expressing views so trenchant as these would have been given short shrift. Even today, when they are being openly voiced in high places, they are strenuously denied by professional educationists and administrators who have a vested interest in the maintenance of the existing system and who not unnaturally feel threatened by any suggestion which looks like querying their authority. For all that, the indications are that the bureaucratic controls over the lives of the young, not least those requiring full-time school attendance, are slowly loosening. For the sociologist, if not the educationist, the ecology of the underground anti-school movement provides an intriguing study. Analysis of the distribution of free schools in the USA, for example, shows that more than half of them are located in four states (California, New York, Illinois and Massachusetts), with the main concentrations in cities like San Francisco, New York, Chicago and Boston. Without necessarily arguing that American trends set the pattern for the future on this side of the Atlantic, the portents are surely clear enough. It is no accident that the highest incidence of truancy and juvenile delinquency *everywhere* is to be found in the congested areas of big cities. The mistake is to gloss over the problem by saying that it is not typical of the country as a whole: a mistake because it overlooks the fact that every significant move forward in the history of education has been made in the context of urbanization. In tomorrow's megalopolis the kinds of problem which are at present confined to the ghetto districts will almost certainly assume greater and nastier dimensions – and the kinds of solution now being proposed in the name of 'alternatives to schooling' can be expected to win more general approval. As it is, since the raising of the school leaving age to sixteen, many teachers, faced with the task of coping with unwilling, not to say rebellious, adolescents, are inclined to wonder whether the game is worth the candle. The young nowadays no longer evince that 'spirit of docility' which the Protestant ethic, as interpreted by the pioneers of mass education in the nineteenth century, could safely demand of them: they are not prepared to keep quiet and put up with the treatment meted out to them by regulations which, rightly or wrongly, they see as curtailing their personal freedom. Social, political and economic pressures may combine to keep them in a detention camp longer and longer, but the lines of force drawn by the secular trend towards early physical (and emotional) maturity, not to mention the daily experience of life outside the classroom, are pulling in precisely the opposite direction. In the unseen tug of war that is taking place in contemporary culture between formal schooling and the networks of informal learning made possible by the media, *something* has to give. That something is the institution which we have hitherto known as the school. No amount of systems maintenance can preserve it indefinitely in its present form.

THE IDEA OF A SCHOOL WITHOUT WALLS

So much by way of argument. How to clinch it by acting upon it? In *The Free School* I outlined one of the earliest attempts to translate radical theory into radical practice, the Parkway Program in Philadelphia, well publicized as the first 'school without walls' – and followed it up with an imaginary account of what might happen if a similar breakaway venture were to be launched in a Scottish setting. Here, then, was the germ of an idea which may have made for stimulating reading, but which would have come to nothing had not the author been put to shame at a Students' Representative Council meeting in which a questioner asked, 'Why the hell don't you do something about it instead of talking so much?'

Why not, indeed? Accordingly, I made the first tentative step of consulting the Yellow Pages of the Glasgow area telephone directory and drawing up a provisional list of community resources – factories, chain stores, hospitals, zoos, museums, car distributors, Automobile Association, offices, hotels, airports, etc. The next step was to send a tentatively worded letter to each of these organizations asking whether they would be prepared to accept fourteen to fifteen year old schoolchildren and, if so, in what numbers, for how long and under what conditions. The initial response to this casting of bread on the waters was overwhelming: roughly two-thirds of the organizations answered in the affirmative. Let it be said that this was the first lesson which was learned before the project got off the ground: the enormous goodwill displayed by people in responsible positions who could offer their services. That there was a rich catchment area of resources for learning awaiting exploitation was never for a moment in doubt. Sad to relate, the lessons which had to be learned before any tapping of it could begin were nothing like so encouraging.

Even so, the knowledge that there was no lack of backers for a project of this kind prompted a small group of lecturers in the university departments of education and psychology and the local college of education to get together and form a joint planning committee. It was agreed that if a project of this kind was to have any hope of gaining acceptance from an education authority and the school(s) concerned it would need to be carefully organized and monitored as a piece of serious educational research. A sound experimental design was essential. Nor was it enough that the project should be given an air of academic respectability: if its proponents were to enlist the co-operation of administrators, teachers, pupils, parents and personnel in the 'host' organizations they owed it to themselves in the first instance to clarify their rationale.

RATIONALE

The reasons for wishing to mount the project were based on four main assumptions, the first of which could hardly be stated openly without causing offence.

1 Since there was obviously no prospect of securing block release from school attendance for pupils engaged on certificate courses, it was assumed that the experimental group would have to be drawn from the lower streams of the fourteen to sixteen year olds. Unlike the Philadelphia situation where a public lottery allows teenagers covering the entire spectrum of ability from 'college preparatory' to the hardened drop-out to opt for admission to the Parkway Program, the Scottish view was that, with a few exceptions, the proper place for teenagers was in the classroom. The exceptions, needless to say, were the slow and backward learners, the would-be early leavers who were either marking time or showing signs of restiveness. These, it was felt, were the pupils who stood to gain little or nothing in the way of scholastic attainment by staying on for the 'extra year'. What they were *really* learning was that they were hopeless failures, that, as they frequently admitted, 'We're no' clever, Sir. We're the dummies.' For them, the effect of being compelled to remain at school was to confirm and reinforce the low ego concepts and the fatalistic acceptance of their own inadequacy which they had acquired during their school career. If this assumption was in any sense correct then there was some justification for mounting a rescue operation and for believing

that in releasing these pupils from the bondage of the classroom the results could hardly be worse than under the *status quo*. In any case, on purely tactical grounds, the chances were that the necessary permission to go ahead with the project would only be granted for a minority of dead-enders, though not, be it said, for the notorious troublemakers.

2 A second assumption was that community resources – businesses, industry, social and governmental agencies, etc. – were capable of offering guidance for secondary school pupils and of doing so more usefully and extensively than was normally possible in occasional, brief out-of-school visits. That many of them were eager to volunteer their services and to establish closer contacts with the schools was already clear.

3 A third, and more challengeable, assumption was that even below-average ability fourteen to fifteen year olds could take greater responsibility for shaping their own courses and for behaving responsibly in learning situations where they were not constantly supervised by a teacher. Given the opportunity to 'go it alone', they might succeed where pussyfooting didacticism had hitherto failed.

4 Finally, there was the assumption – to be honest, little more than the hope – that if pupils were allowed to see how school-based learning was put to use in the world of work and public service its relevance might become more apparent than it usually seemed to be. Failing this, at least the experience of being released from full-time attendance for a period of several weeks might help to improve their attitudes to school and to life in general. If, at the end of the exercise, any measurable gains in cognitive skills (i.e. scholastic attainment) proved to be minimal or non-existent, no matter; much more important, it seemed, was the question of the *personal* development of the pupils. If the pre-tests and post-tests used in monitoring the experiment were to have any hope of yielding significant results it was vital that the block release scheme should last for at least one whole term.

PRELIMINARY PLANNING

In due course, the outline of an experimental design and proposals for the organization and administration of the project were drafted and circulated among directors of education in the Clydeside conurbation. Only one professed any initial interest: the others declined, presumably because they were heavily preoccupied with their own RSLA schemes and satisfied that these needed to be tried out first.

In the event, the one possible 'taker' saved the project from being stillborn. Personally he liked the scheme but said that he was not prepared to make any move unless it had the approval of the regional HMI. The latter, in turn, was reluctant to commit himself until the whole matter was thrashed out in discussions with the heads and staffs of any schools who might be willing to participate.

To resolve these uncertainties, the director called a meeting of the interested parties, chaired by himself, with the HMI, two representatives from the university department of education, one from the college of education, and the heads and members of staff from several comprehensive schools in the county. Invited to explain in greater detail why the project seemed worthy of serious consideration and just how it would operate, the university representatives opened the proceedings. As a combined operation, responsibilities would have to be shared. For their part, they were prepared to undertake the general overseeing of the experiment and its assessment and (trump card!) provide the services of an experienced reseach assistant who would work in liaison with teachers and community personnel and act as an organizing secretary and general factotum.

Far from being received with open arms, this gift horse was greeted with a good deal of head shaking and suspicion. Not an insurable risk was the immediate reaction, an opinion which spread round the table as speaker after speaker voiced his doubts and objections. What if there was a street accident? Wasn't it essential that the children should be accompanied at all times and in all places by a teacher? With staff shortages already acute and secondment out of the question, how could adequate supervision be arranged? If pupils had to attend for morning roll call and report back by 4 o'clock would there not be a good deal of time-wasting? Besides, schools were already engaged on similar projects of their own, so what was so special about this one anyway? Wasn't there a danger that some of the host organizations had volunteered their services from very dubious motives? What about objections from the trade unions if it turned out that pupils were actually placed in a part-time job situation? If they were to be gadding about all over the place who was going to pay for their travel expenses? How could anyone keep track of them? How were they to be selected?

In a timely intervention, the chairman felt it diplomatic to adjourn the meeting, pointing out that its purpose was purely exploratory and that there was no question of reaching a decision on the spot. Possibly teachers would prefer to talk it over among themselves and eventually come up with counter-proposals of their own.

Incidentally, here was the second lesson. While it was not quite necessary to move heaven and earth to get the go-ahead for a small-scale, modest experiment of this kind, it was evident that the lines of demarcation – status barriers if you prefer it – between central and local administrative authorities, between them and the academic community in the university and the colleges, and between head-masters and assistant teachers, were strong enough to make co-operation difficult. It was a pecking order characterized more by mutual distrust than by mutual understanding. Protocol demanded that each had his special role to play, his position to maintain, and that it was unsafe, and certainly unwise, to stir beyond it. In a word, there was precious little play in the system. Before and after the meeting, some of the younger assistant teachers expressed consider-able enthusiasm, but on seeing which way the wind was blowing during the round-table discussion they had deemed it expedient to say little in the presence of their superiors. The powerful hold exercised over decisionmaking by a hierarchy of bureaucratic controls and constraints was itself a problem in need of closer investigation.

As invariably happens in this kind of situation, the outcome was a cautious compromise. Two schools agreed to release small groups of lower stream pupils for a four-week period: anything longer, they insisted, could not be entertained. As far as assessment and evalua-tion went, this was a serious, indeed a fatal blow since it ruled out any possibility of the pre- and post-tests yielding significant differ-ences or any 'hard' evidence of the worthwhileness of the project. But on the principle that half a loaf is better than no bread, this limiting condition was accepted.

Accordingly a small steering committee consisting of a deputy director of education, two assistant teachers from school A and the project leader (provided by the university on a one-year basis) was set up to look after the day-to-day organization and management of the pilot study. As might have been expected, the work involved was very considerable and fell mainly upon the project leader. Among other things, it involved contacting as many as sixty-three different 'host' organizations, interviewing pupils in order to ascertain their interests and preferences (if any), sending explanatory letters to parents, drawing up weekly schedules and placements to suit individual pupils so far as was possible, keeping close liaison with teachers in school A and in school B (which had agreed to follow up once the pilot run had ended) and with the deputy director. All this, and a great deal more before D-Day arrived! It was a task which called for boundless energy, infinite patience, and above all a flair for getting on well with people in all walks of life. Fortunately, the project leader, Mrs Barbara Gardner, who had previously been engaged in a similar venture in the Home Base School at Watertown (Massachusetts) proved to be the ideal person for the job, so much so that this, or any other account of what happened, must be deeply indebted to her efforts. Although officially attached to the university department of education, in which she had duties to perform as a temporary lecturer, she was from start to finish very much at the centre of things, as the accompanying diagram (Fig. 2) showing the interlocking relationships between the various bodies involved in the project indicates. Onerous as it was, it was a position which was in many respects ideal for a participant observation study.

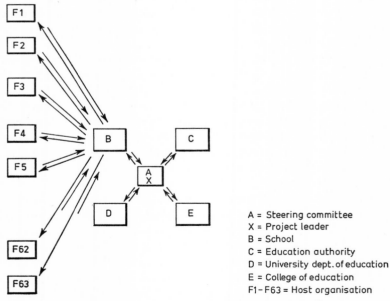

A = Steering committee
X = Project leader
B = School
C = Education authority
D = University dept. of education
E = College of education
F1–F63 = Host organisation

Fig. 2   Inter-institutional network for 'school without walls' project

THE PROJECT IN ACTION

Before sending them out to find their own way around and fend for themselves in the Clydeside conurbation, it was necessary for the pupils to be properly briefed. The school A contingent (n = 23) tended to be rather diffident and withdrawn to begin with, but after the first few days most of them responded remarkably well to being placed on trust and left to use their own initiative. Each morning they reported to the school between 8.30 and 8.45 to collect their packed lunches, bus and train fares (reimbursed by the education authority out of school funds) and arrange for contacting their supervisors by telephone during the course of the day. Each was asked to keep a diary. For the most part, pupils were sent out in pairs and spent at least two whole days in the 'host' organization in which they were expected to fit in and try to be helpful, to make the best of it even if the out-of-school experience turned out to be a good deal less exciting than they had bargained for. They were told that any misbehaviour would be immediately reported to the school. Where fairly long-distance travel was unavoidable they were exempted from the morning reporting but were required to call one or other of the staff members so that their movements could be checked.

That the briefing was well done seems to be borne out by the fact that absenteeism was virtually non-existent and that scarcely any problems, and no real emergencies, arose. In one case, due to a misunderstanding, a girl arrived at the workplace and found that the firm was not expecting her: she called the school, returned and was immediately rescheduled in another resource centre. In another a minor tiff between two boys and a foreman who objected to what he regarded as horseplay was quickly composed. All in all, relations between children, teachers and workers could hardly have been better.

What happened out there in the 'host' organizations was uncannily like the imaginary description of the activities of a 'school without walls' in *The Free School*, so much so that there is little point in repeating it here. Fig. 3 records a typical week's schedule. Washing an elephant, helping mentally handicapped children, being given the freedom of a television studio, serving customers in a department store, preparing food in a hotel kitchen, making a film, tube-winding, serving alongside a receptionist in an airport – these were some of the

Learning in the community project   Name   School A boy

National Savings Bank	Hubert Burns, plasterer and slater	Mill Service Station	Hubert Burns, plasterer and slater
Jan 22	23	24	25	26

Hubert Burns, plasterer and slater	Thomas Capstick, electrician			a.m. Renfrew and Bute Constabulary p.m. Glasgow University Television Service
29	30	31	Feb 1	2

Normandy Hotel		Mill Service Station	
5	6	7	8	9

Automobile Association	British Caledonian Glasgow Airport		
12	13	14	15	16

Fig. 3   Learning in the community project

varied and extraordinary learning situations in which pupils found themselves. Not that they were always stimulating, novel or rewarding. As the feedback from the pilot study in school A soon showed, the tendency was for boredom and frustration to set in where there was not enough for pupils to do: being shown around the place and left in the role of passive observers was not enough. (Unfortunately, time did not allow of any correction of this fault before the follow-up in school B but in retrospect most of the 'host' organization personnel agreed that in any future operation of this kind it was essential for pupils to be placed on something like the same footing as other young employees.)

What did these teenage guinea pigs make of it all? What, if anything, did they learn? Did their attitudes towards school and, more important, to life and work, change? Extracts from their diaries are as reliable a source of evidence as any:

'I suppose the most valuable [thing] was looking and behaving yourself. We tried our best to behave ourselves and look decent. . . . The handicapped children's hospital made me uncomfortable. I just couldn't handle them and was scared stiff in case one of them had one of their turns.'

'It was better today as we actually got working. We learned to work the machine ends by a tape and earphones. It was just as if we were going to start work and we just got what the other tube-winders got when they started. We never really felt left out.'

'Did the same as the day before. I don't want to go through the routine because it was just exactly as the day before. Except the more you do a thing the better and faster you get. You learn by your mistakes. And don't do it again. I have made a lot of mistakes but don't usually make them twice.'

'Today I was peeling onion, slicing cucumbers, diced mushy carrots for the soup. Then I was sent to the storeroom and packed tins and orders on the shelves. After that I helped the chef turn steaks and take the sausage out of links and rolled in on the pastry [*sic*]. Then I put a whipped egg over the pastry to brown the sausage rolls. Then after that I helped to arrange cakes for a wedding, then I sliced more onion. I found it quite interesting but hard to get used to.'

In the post-project interview each of the participants was asked to say what he or she liked or disliked about learning in the community and whether different aspects of out-of-school experience seemed important or not. The responses are summarized in Table 1. Not

I will read you a number of things that may have happened to you during the project. Would you tell me whether you liked or disliked each one, whether it was important or not for you, or whether it didn't happen. (post-project, n=40)

TABLE I

	Like	Dislike	Important	Not important	Does not apply/ Don't know
1 Doing things you can't do in school	37	1	24	9	1
2 Having to travel on your own	17	12	17	10	9
3 Finding out about a variety of jobs	37	1	33		2
4 Meeting different kinds of people	37	2	23	9	3
5 Being able to do things you want to do	34	1	26	5	3
6 Finding out about some jobs in detail	32	4	29	5	2
7 Getting off regular lessons	28	7	6	22	4
8 Finding out more about yourself	25	2	28	3	8
9 Having to do things on your own	28	5	22	6	6

Is there anything we've left out?	
Nothing left out:	29
No response:	4
Don't know:	1
Catch up on lessons:	1
More travel:	1
Liked meeting people:	1
Being treated as adult:	1
Go to more places:	1
Teachers go on initial visit:	1

surprisingly, pupils thought that the main purpose of the experiment was to introduce them to a wide range of job situations and that apart from pre-vocational training any benefits to be derived from it were incidental. Significantly, however, there was a heavy vote for 'doing things you can't do in school', for 'meeting different kinds of people' and 'being able to do things you want to do'. The somewhat mixed feelings about 'having to travel on your own' were probably accounted for by the weather – January, February and March are not the pleasantest months for getting around in Lowland Scotland!

EVALUATION

It was recognized, of course, that any attempt to 'measure' attitude shifts was invalidated once the decision to limit the experiment to four weeks had been taken. In school B, where a matched sample of children remained in school while the experimental group was released, no meaningful comparison between 'experimental' and 'control' was possible for the same reason. In the pre- and post-tests all the children were rated on the Wilcoxon Alienation Scale and a semantic differential scale dealing with attitudes to family affairs, friends, leaving home, earning a living, school, etc. In the circumstances, the psychologist was left with a thankless task in administering such tests, knowing in advance that no statistically significant results could be obtained. Rather more revealing were the pupils' answers to a series of questionnaires completed after they had settled in again (or had they?) to normal classroom routines. This, for instance:

Are there advantages in staying on at school after fifteen for people who are not taking exams?

(percentages)

	Some advantages	No advantages	Don't know
School A Experimental	30.4	52.1	17.3
School B Experimental	29.4	70.5	0
School B Control	11.1	83.3	5.5

Advantages of staying on: (total for three groups)
   More education: 7
   No jobs available: 3
   Get better job: 2
   Get a second chance: 1
   Maybe sit O levels: 1
   Too young to leave: 1

By far the most fruitful source of evidence, however, was to be found through participant observation, notably by the project leader and also by teacher supervisors. All agreed that noticeable changes in attitudes *were* detectable, too slight to amount to anything like a transformation of personality, but becoming more pronounced towards the end of the four-week period. Parents corroborated this impression, many of them saying that their children talked a good deal more openly about what they were doing than they had ever done before, that they were less nervous, livelier and more self-confident. Resource personnel were of the same opinion, adding that what they had seen of these children had strengthened their desire to establish closer contacts with the schools.

Most pupils started out by being unsure of themselves, tentative, reserved, tongue-tied in the presence of adults, apparently without any definite interests and with little or no idea about the kind of occupation they wanted to follow on leaving school. They asked very few questions either in or out of school. They were reluctant to talk about their experiences or to confide in others, even their parents, about their hopes and fears. As the weeks went by, however, they gradually became more forthcoming: they organized themselves in business-like fashion each morning, began to co-operate more with each other and to volunteer suggestions, criticisms (and complaints!) to the staff without being asked. Wherever they happened to be sited, many of them were able to size up their placement more perceptively than anyone had dared to expect and most, after the first few days of standing around and watching from the sidelines, discovered that they were not content to remain passive spectators. Their initiative increased in some degree, though not by leaps and bounds – except in the case of an undersized, shy fourteen year old boy who felt several inches taller after helping to wash an elephant! Again, two boys who felt that they were wasting their time took it upon themselves to go and talk to the manager who was so impressed by their frankness that he forthwith assigned the pair of them to regular duties. All showed signs of being freer and more open in their contacts with staff members both in and out of school. Initially there had been some concern that pupils might take advantage of the newly found freedom and treat the whole affair as a month's holiday. Any such fears proved to be unfounded.

True, any findings from so limited and short-lived a project are bound to be inconclusive. Nevertheless, for those engaged in it, there was no resisting the conclusion that if any cognitive gains were negligible the gains in personal maturity were certainly not. As an attempt to bridge the frontier between formal schooling and genuine education, the project, in however small a way, was an unqualified success. While it has to be acknowledged that learning in the community is only feasible for a minority and to that extent ought never to be put forward as if it were a universal alternative, the fact remains that this project was offered far more resources than it could possibly use in the very short time allocated. In this connection, Mrs Gardner's final comment is worth quoting:

> The question of how these resources can best be used is one that needs the attention of businessmen, teachers and pupils. Though there has been relatively little contact in the past, it is fairly obvious that many common problems are faced by schools and community institutions. Both groups tend to bemoan the lack of contact between them, but in fact the problem seems to be more one of access than of intentions and goodwill. It takes time to build up a pattern of communication that will last through personnel changes. The experience of this project, however, would indicate that many people are feeling the need for such co-operation for a variety of reasons at this time, and that a serious attempt at broader co-operation would be met with mutual enthusiasm. Schools and businesses of course have different functions, and both have limitations of time and personnel as well. Nevertheless, the areas of overlap are sufficiently large to warrant further effort.

As the student said, 'Why the hell don't you do something about it?' The trouble is that when one tries there is never any assurance that the effort will bring about anything more than minor, evanescent changes. Too often it seems that the surface ripples of innovation die away, leaving the troubled waters beneath as troubled as before. Introducing a measure of play into a rigid system is a slow, hard business, full of setbacks, snags and disappointments. But at least the onus is on us all to keep trying.

6 The vision of Edgar Faure

It seems that losing a war can be good for the soul of a nation. For France, certainly, the bitter humiliation of the years of occupation found its catharsis in the quenchless spirit of the Resistance; and it is from this source, more than any other, that the mainspring of social, economic and educational reform – transformation, rather – has come since 1945. To belong to the Resistance meant leading a double life, outwardly compliant, secretly committed with fellow conspirators to a cause which seemed hopeless. Membership called for qualities of heroism very different from those displayed on the battlefield. The odds against surviving, let alone winning, were tremendous – and a fate worse than death awaited those who were discovered. It was an experience shared by many prisoners of war, but one which the British people as a whole were spared (though not entirely during their trial by fire during the Blitz).

Compared with Britain, where 'reconstructionism' was in vogue long before the end of hostilities, French *planification* in the immediate post-war period was altogether more radical and ambitious. Comprehensive as it was, the 1944 Education Act (England and Wales) was neither so far-reaching nor so determined as was the Langevin plan; and the fact that the latter was never formally adopted or legislated for *en bloc* by the French parliament does not alter the case. In the event, educational reforms in the two countries have followed the lines laid down in 1944–5, the English ones a cautious blend of stop-go, conservative-socialist policymaking, the French ones, after a hesitant start, gathering greater momentum under the guidance and control of the Commissariat Général au Plan. It is true that the idea of education as a continuous process was written into the 1944 Act, but the revolutionary nature of its implications and the ways and means of implementing it have not aroused the vigorous public debate which has helped to make France the leading proponent of *l'éducation permanente* in the European Community.

More so than England, France was in no mood to forgive and forget the sins of omission of its pre-war education system: its excessive intellectualism, its traditional classical curriculum, its neglect of scientific technology, its narrow élitism and hordes of *déclassés*. If not first in order of priority, education was a major political issue which had to be taken seriously. After liberation, the leaders of the Resistance pledged themselves to the cause of a new social contract. For a time, though to a lesser extent, the same held good of the English situation. As its chief architect, the Butler Act had a front rank politician who was genuinely interested in education. Following his retirement from active political life, however, successive governments have failed to produce anyone of the same calibre: so far as ministers of education are concerned, the British record to date has varied from good, bad to mostly indifferent. Education may be a branch of politics but in these islands it remains a pretty slender one. To be sure, public spending on the educational services has progressively increased, but those in charge of these services have been more concerned with the administrative aspects – keeping the system in tolerably smooth running order – than with fundamental thinking or with long-term planning. As a nation, we lack the inspired educational leadership of a truly great statesman.

That France was destined to become a dominant, if not *the* dominant, Western European power in the last quarter of the twentieth century seemed highly improbable, to say the least of it, in 1944. That year saw the emergence of a middle-aged lawyer, Edgar Faure, as a prominent member of the French Committee for National Liberation, then attached to the government in exile in Algiers. A year later he appeared at the Nuremberg court as one of the French representatives on the international tribunal for the trial of Nazi war criminals. Elected as the Radical Socialist deputy for the Jura division (1946–58), he served under a succession of short-lived, unstable governments as Secretary of State for Finance, Minister of Justice (1951), Minister of Finance, Economic Affairs and Planning (1952), President of the Council of Ministers (1955), Minister of Agriculture, and Minister of Education (1968–9). As if the cares of high office were not sufficient to keep him busy, he continued his professional and academic career, earning a formidable reputation as prosecutor or defence counsel in a number of *causes célèbres*; and engaged in teaching and research as Professor of Law in the Universities of Dijon and Besançon. Always a good constituency man, he campaigned tirelessly in the cause of regional development, organizing the Committee for Economic Expansion in the Franche-Comté and Belfort and similar projects in eastern France. No doubt because of his known Leftist sympathies, Faure was the President of the Republic's nominee as leader of missions to China in 1963 (an account of which is given in his book *Le Serpent et la Tortue*), to the USSR in 1964 – where he was received with acclaim by the Soviet authorities – and to Egypt and Tunisia in 1965. He is currently (1973) President of the French National Assembly. His life style as an author is suggested by the titles of his numerous publications: *L'Éducation nationale et la participation* (1968), *Philosophie d'une reforme* (1969), *L'Ame du combat* (1970), and *Ce que je crois* (1971). Incredibly, in his spare time he has written several detective stories under the pseudonym of Edgar Sanday!

In view of Faure's long, varied and distinguished career it may seem naïve to regard his appointment as chairman of an international commission on the future of education as the culmination and crowning achievement of his lifework. For wealth of experience, for sheer drive, above all for the ability to take a global view of the problems and prospects, UNESCO could not have made a wiser choice. Whether or not because the spirit of the Resistance remains strong within him, this extraordinary politician somehow contrives to maintain his place in high office, a pillar of the establishment, while at the same time keeping contact with the various underground protest movements which provide the cutting edge and élan of intellectual and political life in France: a balancing feat which would be suicidal for anyone of the same eminence in public life in Britain. It is as if Mrs Thatcher were privately in league with the organizers of Scotland Road Free School and regularly sought advice from LSE activists and the more turbulent elements in the new universities. Hard to imagine a Royal Commission in this country going out of its way to interview rebels as notorious as Ivan Illich or Paul Goodman: harder still to credit that if they did they would be so open-minded as to take notice of the evidence of such witnesses and actually be influenced by them in making their final recommendations.

Yet this is precisely what happened in the preparation of the commission's report *Apprendre à être (Learning to Be)*, the UNESCO document masterminded by Edgar Faure and bearing the forceful imprint of his personality. Not even the massive Robbins Report was so exhaustive in its inquiries; it is impressive if only in its survey from China to Peru of ongoing projects and experiments in the educational world, only in this case what emerges is no insular plan but the grand design for a new theory and practice which is universal in its applications – the 'master concept' of lifelong education.

Granted, the theory is not exactly novel; and its enunciation is open to the criticism that it is, at best, utopian, at worst so vague as to be capable of meaning anything or nothing. What *is* novel is the immense sweep of its proposals and the high seriousness of its statement of principles. In places one is reminded of the *Great Didactic*, that other *chef d'œuvre* of grand design which three centuries ago must have seemed as preposterously tall an order to the average reader as this one does today.

Learning to be? To many, the title may seem to have a curiously vacuous ring. Learning to be *what*, they ask? The answer (reminiscent of Dewey's 'continuous reconstruction of experience'): 'Man is an unfinished being and can only fulfil himself through constant learning.' Gone for ever is the notion of education as a process restricted to the years of infancy, childhood and youth: gone, too, the monopoly of learning by so-called educational institutions. In their place we are asked to envisage a learning environment in which the resources of society at large will be available for all, a life of learning which begins at the moment of birth and continues, as Illich says, 'up to, and in the moment, of my death'.

Though it refrains from using the word 'crisis', the report begins with an analysis of the stresses and strains in contemporary society, in particular the widespread dissatisfaction with its political and educational institutions. Formal democracy, which allows citizens to elect their leaders periodically, can no longer meet the growing demand for active participation: at most, it provides the individual with a minimum of juridical protection from the arbitrary exercise of power. Again, any genuine social democracy must be considered out of the question so long as classes are divided by marked inequalities of educational opportunity. Hence, education must be regarded as a domain in which political decision-making is of primary, not secondary importance.

As things are, it argues, fears that technological developments are out of control, and that the values of a consumer society are determined for it by mindless demands for economic growth, must be taken seriously. On the other hand, there can be no turning back the clock: 'Science and technology must be fundamental elements in any educational enterprise – so as to help the individual to control not only natural and productive forces but social forces too, and in so doing to acquire mastery over himself, his choices and action; and finally, for them to help man to develop a scientific frame of mind in order to promote the sciences without being enslaved by them.'[1]

The report goes on to note those features in the present situation which, in common with other observers, it regards as unprecedented. To begin with, for the first time in history there is the worldwide tendency for educational development to *precede* economic development. Secondly, because of the accelerating pace of cultural change, education is faced with the task of preparing the young for a social life which is certain to be unlike any experienced hitherto. Thirdly, there is a growing distrust, not to say downright rejection, of many of the products, forms and values of institutionalized education.

The malfunction of much educational practice makes renovation of education *necessary*. Changes in socio-economic structure and the scientific and technological revolution make it *imperative*. Scientific research and technological progress related to education, combined with growing awareness among the people of the world make it possible.[2]

As proof of this assertion, which may be taken as a fair specimen of Faure's fervid rhetoric, the report instances the recent advances made in such fields as biology, neuropsychology, genetic epistemology, linguistics, information theory, semiology and cybernetics, each of which it sees as having a part to play in the eventual formulation of what can only be called a general systems theory of lifelong education.

If all that has to be learned must continually be re-invented and renewed then teaching becomes learning and, more and more, education. If learning involves all of one's life, in the sense of both time-span and diversity, and all of society, including its social and economic as well as its educational resources, then we must go even further than the overhaul of 'educational systems' until we reach the stage of the learning society.[3]

The contemptuous inclusion of 'educational systems' within quotation marks makes it plain that this is an open invitation to dissent. To be critical of the established order is a *sine qua non* for forward thinking which can never evade 'the primordial necessity of placing educational problems in an over-all context and seeking answers to this all-important question – does the educational apparatus, as now conceived, really satisfy the needs and aspiration of man and societies in our time?'[4] This means, it insists, that we are morally obliged to inquire into the powers now vested in the education system, its myths and the validity of its aims. Only if we do so will it become apparent that the system cannot possibly continue to evolve along the lines, and according to the rates, laid down for it hitherto. Demands on the educational services are increasing all the time and there are no signs of the pressure of demand being relaxed. At the same time, resources are limited, unequally distributed, often grossly wasteful, with the result that some national systems are already finding it difficult to make ends meet. Sooner or later, probably sooner than the authorities expect, the supply and demand equation cannot fail to bring about an 'energy crisis' unless alternative resources are found and exploited.

Until quite recently, to ask 'Is there any point in public education?' was almost unthinkable, except for drop-outs. Today, some of the most respected figures in academic circles in the USA are joining in inquiries starting from that very question. One of these, instituted by the Center for Policy Study at the University of Chicago, has as its chairman Dr Robert M. Hutchins, who is reported as saying: 'The political community should be required to justify the prolonged detention of its citizens in an educational system. We need to answer the question whether public education is any longer useful. If so, on what terms? If not, what is the alternative?'[5] Without prejudging the issue, it may be added that the Rand report, prepared for the US President's Commission on School Finance, gives some dusty answers to these questions.[6]

Schooling represents a labour-intensive industry, in which teachers' salaries are by far the costliest item in the bill, yet the research evidence as summarized by the various International Educational Achievements projects has led Husén to the conclusion that amount of instruction makes nothing like so significant a difference as is commonly supposed. The falsity of the myth which would have us believe that learning is largely dependent upon teaching needs to be exposed. That schooling is an inefficient method for the mass organization of learning is, of course, a fact which those in charge of the education system have long been aware of – John Gardner, former head of the US Department of Health, Education and Welfare is reported as saying that, 'All a high school graduate has learned in twelve years of schooling he could easily have learned in two – and, with a little effort, in one' – yet the fact tends to be carefully suppressed. Worst of all, this concentration of manpower and finance on schooling creates the mischievous impression that resources are scarce.

Of all the shams which a gullible public has been induced to accept, none is more deceitful than the pretence of providing equality of educational opportunity. Conceptually, the report argues, we have fallen into the error of confusing equal access to schooling with equal opportunity and broad access to education with democracy in education. 'Equal access is *not* equal opportunity. This must comprise equal chance of success.'[7]

There speaks the radical socialist! According to this view, which finds support in the analyses of Bourdieu and other sociologists, *all* education systems, even the most affluent and liberal, stand indicted for their failure to solve the problem of equality of opportunity. Moreover, so long as they are organized on existing lines there can be no prospect of their succeeding. What, then, is the solution?

On the face of it, the demand for 'equal chance of success' looks to be hopelessly unrealistic. However, 'once education becomes continual ideas as to what constitutes success and failure will change. The early "failure" will no longer be relegated for life to the ghetto.'[8] Only by reducing the all-or-nothing importance currently attached to the learner's school life and by giving him time, opportunities and facilities to compensate for slow starts and late development will any semblance of equality of opportunity be made possible. Only then will the school's classificatory function – the premature egg-stamping of individuals as first-, second- and third-class 'products' – cease to be regarded as final.

It follows that what we are accustomed to calling 'further', 'adult', or 'recurrent' education will become the general rule. Education will be seen as the normal culmination of schooling which will no longer be thought of as a once-and-for-all process. Before this can happen, however, there will need to be a drastic revision of the prevailing concept of 'learning' and its evaluation. School-bound learning and out-of-school learning (categorized by Bernstein as uncommonsense and commonsense, and by Bruner as 'spontaneous' and 'cultivated' or 'artificial') must be linked more firmly together. The report quotes with approval Plutarch's dictum, 'The city is the best teacher', and urges the necessity for mobilizing resources available in institutions which at present tend to be excluded from the so-called education system. Thus, Principle 3 in the report states that 'Education should be dispensed and acquired through a multiplicity of means', and Principle 9 that 'Lifelong education means that business, industrial and agricultural firms will have extensive educational functions'. Principle 4, again, affirms that 'An over-all, open education system helps learners to move within it both horizontally and vertically and widens the range of choice available to them'.

Urgent as the need is for internal reform of the 'education system', therefore, the search for viable alternatives – new institutions, fresh resources – is no less vitally necessary; otherwise inequality of provision is bound to persist. Growing demand will result in ever fiercer competition for what *seems* to be a shortage of resources. This, in turn, will have the effect of aggravating class distinctions and a general sense of alienation in a society best characterized as a pseudo-meritocracy.

In a key passage, *Learning to Be* focuses attention on the existential problems which futurologists and educational planners too often prefer to ignore:

> Science – focused on defining objectives, modernizing methods, on cybernetic organization and efficiency – and government authorities – anxious to prescribe rationally organized educational systems for their citizens – are confronted by the demands for the right to initiative, to individual inventiveness, to creativity, to be different. The aversion which people feel towards the rationalization of educational procedures must lead us to expound new concepts and these tend to go against the laws of scientific development.

People react to the process of mechanized integration by proclaiming rights to individual originality.[9]

Having previously nailed its colours to the mast of scientific technology, the report may seem at this point to come perilously close to contradicting itself. Basic to the entire argument, however, is the conviction that science and technology, between them, can provide the means of achieving the good life for individual and society alike *if* they are brought under control for humane ends. Learning to be, then, means learning to be aware, active, informed, responsible. This *is* the *'continuous process'* – and it cannot begin too early. Of all the general principles enunciated, none points the way to future theory and practice more surely than Principle 14: 'The new educational ethos makes the individual the master and creator of his own cultural progress. Self-learning, especially assisted self-learning, has irreplaceable value in any educational system.'[10]

There is no denying that in some respects *Learning to Be* could be said to be a thoroughly woolly document, untidily presented and unconvincing in its arguments. Already out of print, it has aroused little interest in the English-speaking world and a great deal of unfavourable comment from educationists at home and abroad. A mountain of verbiage unredeemed by even a ridiculous mouse of a policy with any hope of a viable future, then? A vision which invites only derision?

Typically, the report ends with the flamboyant imperative: 'the indispensable remoulding of all its elements – theory and practice, structure and methods, management and organization – must be completely rethought from one and the same point of view'[11] – a tall order by any reckoning, the more so since it is by no means clear what this one and the same point of view is to be. Despite its shortcomings, nevertheless, the report gives at least three clues which are certain to prove invaluable in the eventual formulation of that point of view: (1) in seeing the learner as 'master and creator of his own cultural progress' at all stages and levels of development, *not* as one who is largely dependent upon, and submissive to, the dictates of his mentors; (2) in cutting down to size the part played by formal schooling; (3) in switching the focus of attention from the established education system to the wealth of resources for learning that await exploitation in the community.

The first of these clues provides the starting point for what might be called a generative theory of education, a theory totally different in all its aspects and dimensions from the one we have put our trust in hitherto – the one which interprets itself in practice as people-processing (i.e. with the emphasis on a dominant–submissive relationship between teacher and taught). The second clue is virtually the same as the one offered by the deschoolers and by leading educationists like Husén, Curle, Bruner and others who do not necessarily agree with the ideology of deschooling but who are increasingly sceptical about the effectiveness of formal schooling under the existing system. The third points the way to the concept of education as lifelong learning.

7 Lifelong learning in an age of technology

The realization that education is never simply a matter of formal schooling and that it spreads over into community life as a whole is, of course, in no way novel. When Grundtvig started the Danish folk high schools, when Henry Morris followed suit with his Cambridgeshire village colleges, or when Danilo Dolci founded his centre at Partinico to encourage self-help among a depressed and fatalistic Sicilian peasantry, they were, in however small a way, initiating a reform movement – and a movement of ideas – which was destined to gather momentum. Each in his local context was inspired by the ideal of an educative society, and concerned to give practical expression to that ideal. Basic to their philosophy was the conviction that schooling served merely as a propaedeutic, albeit a necessary one, for a process which was co-extensive and coterminous with the interests of individual and society alike. Also implicit in it was the conviction that the learner, even in the early days of infancy, needed to be entrusted with an active role. Thus, Dolci's *maieutico*, outlined in his verbatim accounts of informal discussion groups in which children and adults talk freely and unaffectedly in an attempt to resolve problems of common interest, typifies the new non-didactic approach.[1] Elevated to the level of political theory, this approach tends to find its outlet in ineffectual talk of 'participatory democracy' as well as in advocacy of a new deal in education of the rather unpractical kind represented by *Learning to Be*.

The trouble is that projects for the restructuring of society which have proved highly successful on a small scale soon run into difficulties at the macro-level. Given the wise leadership of a Grundtvig, a Morris or a Dolci, it may be possible to create enclaves of personal freedom, but as Robert Owen learned by bitter experience – and as Professor Armytage has shown in *Heavens Below* – invariably they turn out to be short-lived; and if, as working models of a near-perfect society, they are not without influence in an imperfect world (as witnessed, for example, in the Israeli kibbutz) their failure to bring about major changes in the organization of the nation state or its way of life has to be acknowledged.

In the immediate post-war years, when 'reconstruction' was a word for educational theorists to conjure with, Sir Fred Clarke argued the case for an educative society as forcibly and eloquently as anyone before or since. As far back as 1931 he had written:

> In the world that is coming, education, as distinct from schooling, will be a duly supervised function of the social life as a whole, in all its parts. When each institution – industry and Church and family and voluntary society – has its proper place, we shall see better than we do now the true purpose of the school. . . .
>
> It is a sign of immaturity and a defect of thinking when attempts are made to adapt the school to every form of educational need. The more mature and developed society that is coming will recognize more fully than we do now how thoroughly *socialistic* the project of public education is. Steadily but surely all forms of social activity will be adjusted to the needs of educational service. Housing, public health, social insurance, radio service, town-planning, industrial regulation – all these will be viewed more and more in their educational aspect. We shall ask when we take measures in regard to them: 'What value can this have for the end of citizen-making?' *And we shall be quite ready to take a pupil out of school if society can find better provision for his real education.*[2]

Nearly half a century later, who dare say that this optimistic forecast has been fulfilled? Although the intervening years have seen notable advances in welfare-statism, not to mention some striking developments on the part of voluntary agencies – nursery playgroups, industrial training schemes, youth volunteers, community centres, teachers' centres, adult education networks, citizens' bureaux and the rest – it is useless to pretend that they are so well provided for or so well co-ordinated that 'each institution has its proper share'. If anything, we have relapsed more and more into the habit of thinking that the school must adapt itself 'to every form of educational need', allowing it to assume responsibilities which it is incapable of discharging. As a result, arguments which could be put forward with quiet confidence and without seeming to be in any way doctrinaire two generations ago now have to be restated. Mercifully, if belatedly, authoritative opinion is at last coming round to the view so admirably summarized by Sir Fred.

Today, when a Frenchman speaks of 'l'éducation permanente', an Italian of 'educazione permanente', or an Englishman of 'lifelong learning', there is no guarantee that all three are talking about the same thing: the political, cultural, economic and other differences between these three nations (and others inside and outside the European Community) inevitably give rise to different interpretations, different shades of meaning. What we *can* be sure about is that all are agreed, in principle, that the pioneering efforts of men of vision now need to be followed up by a concerted drive towards the formulation of national and, indeed, international plans. In principle, yes. Unfortunately, this is one of those areas of discourse where it is hard to see the wood for the trees. Proposals which meet with approval and objectives which look sound enough when stated on paper tend to lose their force when it comes to acting upon them. With so many claims being pressed and so much unfinished business to attend to, agreement in principle quickly turns into disagreement about fixing priorities. Where is one to begin, with aims so diverse and far-reaching?

If only for the sake of clearing the ground, which means ridding ourselves once and for all of the identification of 'education' with 'schooling', it seems advisable to take a closer look at what is involved in the notion of an educative society.

I THE EDUCATIVE SOCIETY

Always on the understanding that it can have no *direct* bearing on the problems of organization encountered nowadays in advanced in-

dustrial societies, the Athenian city-state may be taken as the prototype of an educative society, arguably the best known to historians of
the Western world. It was a society in which political, religious and
economic institutions were so completely in harmony that to grow
up as a participant member of it was a sufficient education in itself.
Theatre, temple, agora, baths, shopping centre and civic buildings
were all public, open to all and within easy walking distance. It was
a closely knit community in which person-to-person relationship
came naturally: on his way from his home to address the assembly,
Pericles might meet and talk with as many as 150 of his fellow citizens. Everyone joined in the Pan-Athenaic processions and half the
population attended the performance of a new tragedy or comedy.
This all-in-together ethos is epitomized by the inscription carved on
the tomb of Aeschylus which simply read – or so the legend goes –
'He was at Marathon.' If not altogether egalitarian, it was a society
in which, for freeborn citizens at least, status counted for little. In an
emergency, it was understood that each and all would rally to the call
of arms and do his duty, regardless of his station in life. As Pericles
said in his funeral oration, 'We do not say that a man who refuses to
engage in politics does so because he prefers to mind his own business: we say rather that he *has* no business.' Best of all, the layout of
the city-state was on a scale that was easily comprehended, spacious
yet capable of being taken in at a glance: all its parts, like the people
who lived in it, hung together in a mutual interdependence.

As a consequence, the role of the school was a very minor one –
significantly the Greek word for school meant 'leisure'. In effect,
there were *no* schools – no all-purpose schools, that is – only instructors, the *kitharistes, paidotribes* and *grammatistes* who trained boys
in the basic skills of music, athletics and literacy. The *paidogogos* was
in no sense a professional teacher, merely an attendant responsible for
seeing that the boy came to no harm while he was away from home.
Paideia, for the freeborn Athenian youth, meant vastly more than
going to school, and Pericles was not alone in extolling its virtues as a
formative upbringing. As late as Plato's day, many parents thought
it unnecessary to send their children to school, and those who did
were content with a tenuous curriculum consisting of little more
than 'Music for the soul, gymnastics for the body'. In terms of
cognitive knowledge, the *ephebos* who became a fully fledged
citizen at the age of twenty knew far less than a modern ten
year old in a primary school. Despite this, the Athenian city-state

represents one of the high peaks of European civilization, a culture which later societies have sought to emulate but have never excelled.

Our present-day concepts of 'education' are very different from the *paideia* of the ancient world, and for reasons which it is unnecessary to recapitulate here. Beyond saying that it is comparatively recent, the conflation of formal schooling to cover a wide range of functions – instruction in the basic skills, classification, socialization, vocational training, moral and religious welfare, character formation and the nurture of personal growth – has led to a situation in which the provision of services is to a great extent controlled by state monopoly. Among other things, it has fostered the illusion that the only way to obtain an education is by enrolling in a special institution, that no significant learning takes place in the absence of professional teaching, that learning, above all, implies the mastery of verbal and symbolic skills. That casual, informal learning is also possible is, of course, not denied – but this kind of learning earns no 'credit' because it has no official backing. That learning is affective as well as cognitive is similarly not denied – but the prevailing view is that the learning process must be primarily intellectual in order to be genuinely 'educational'. In this way, 'intelligence' itself has tended to become equated with verbal reasoning.

This institutionalizing of childhood and adolescence through compulsory school attendance was a late nineteenth-century invention, designed to suit the conditions and requirements of the first industrial societies and to solve the problems of mass illiteracy. The school operated as a partially closed system, virtually cut off from the life and affairs of the world outside its walls. As school life became longer and longer with successive raisings of the legal age for leaving, 'the divorce of school from life' gradually became more acute, but at the same time social, economic and political pressures combined to keep the young *in statu pupillari*, in a state of limbo.

In a genuinely educative society this separation of the life of learning from the life of action would not occur. It does not occur in primitive societies for the simple reason that in 'natural', 'spontaneous' or 'commonsense' learning the knowledge gained is always inherent, implicit in the activity engaged in – hunting, house-building or whatever form it takes. It did not occur in the city-states of the ancient world nor, presumably, in those of the Italian Renaissance, because the dichotomy between 'natural' and 'artificial' learning was nothing like so pronounced as it was to become later with the advent of mass schooling.

Now while it may be true that the educationist, like the psychologist and the anthropologist, must see his study as 'a science of the artificial', as Bruner styles it (i.e. as much concerned with the man-made aspects of human environment as with its biological and developmental aspects), it is worth asking whether the acquired characteristics of an advanced industrial civilization are in some way out of step with those of the more primitive process of evolution itself. This, surely, is what D. H. Lawrence was driving at; and one suspects that Bruner himself has something of the sort in mind when he writes:

We know from a recent study of Cole and Scribner how disruptive it is in a primitive society to introduce a form of schooling that separates knowledge from the action and the value of knowledge from the person who transmits it.

Cultivated knowledge, by contrast, is knowledge about. It is teachable away from the action – indeed, is teachable even in so detached a human institution as a school. In its most elaborated form, it is free from specification as to how the knowledge might be used. It is deeply dependent upon language and codification of a kind that is itself divorced from action – notably written language which *must* be free of the context of action in order for it to be understood. Pedagogy has been the art or the science of arranging cultivated knowledge so that it may more easily be grasped and more easily used in thought. As such, it is a policy science *par excellence*, perhaps the major policy science through which the psychology of development expresses itself. To separate pedagogy, either from the disciplines of knowledge that must be translated by it, or from the study of human development, is to cripple pedagogy and impoverish us all. It would be as unwise as separating medicine from biology.

But I also believe that our understanding of how development proceeds argues for a radical reformulation of pedagogy that would include consideration of the many powerful but indirect influences that affect the growth of mind. A culture is not only a repository of knowledge and skills and values. It is also a support system for giving hope and a sense of capability to its members. The demoralization that ensues when a culture fails in this supportive role quickly telegraphs itself to the young, particularly to the offsprings of the victims, whether the society is a developing one undergoing chaotic detribalization or a developed one with chronic unemployment. It seems to be particularly the case that the more highly elaborated forms of knowledge suffer in the transmission when the young feel that their situation is such that they will never need such knowledge.[3]

Seeing that every advance in intellectual prowess can be attributed to the civilizing influence of forms of knowledge which are so encoded as to be deliberately marked off, if not altogether divorced, from the life of action, any suggestion that these forms are divisive in their effects – favouring some and alienating others by their very nature – is bound to seem anti-intellectual. But for them, there could have been no great literature, no advanced mathematics, no freedom for abstract thought. Their dependence on second-signal symbolic codes itself implies a look-before-you-leap learning strategy and this, in turn, carries the implication that some principle of deferred gratification has to be accepted in order to benefit from them.

Nevertheless, the fact remains that the outcome of this awarding of pre-eminence to 'artificial', 'cultivated' or 'uncommonsense' knowledge is a culture which is supportive mainly for those who are academically inclined and which leaves the rest disadvantaged. Despite all the efforts that have been made in curriculum development, the feeling persists that non-certificate courses, at any rate in the later stages of secondary schooling, are pointless. This leads to the kind of situation which, reportedly, exists in a number of London comprehensives where teachers are actually discouraging their pupils from learning.[4] The inference can only be that a drastic revision of our ideas about what constitutes 'knowledge' is called for and that something needs to be done to remove the clearcut distinction between the experience of formal learning and informal experience.

Who are the disadvantaged, after all? In general, they are those who fare poorly or indifferently on the provision made for them in school, and they are *not* a minority. Normally classified as non-academic, they belong on the whole to what is loosely referred to as the working class, to a subculture which does not take kindly to a so-called 'elaborated code' of verbal language (not really a code at all, rather a liking for long-windedness, as Labov points out), and which looks for its satisfactions in the immediacy of daily experience rather than in the long-term benefits of abstract thought and the 'things of the mind'.

Throughout the ages, educational thought has upheld the supremacy of 'artificial' knowledge. Rightly so. Only recently has the suspicion dawned that in doing so it has seriously underrated the part played by 'natural' knowledge; and that the imposition of the disciplines of scholarship on patterns of growth for which they were never intended can be stultifying and too often ends by being a self-defeating exercise. Thanks to this, we are left with learning theories which are not wholly humane in their sympathies, with educational philosophies which are more concerned with propositions than with persons, and an educational practice which is essentially inequitable in that it exalts a limited range of cognitive skills for those who show the necessary aptitude for them at the expense of those who do not. While the effect of mass schooling has undoubtedly helped to raise levels of aspiration and expectation, the 'Two Nations' and the 'Two Cultures' remain divided – and in a sense more profound and more intractable than either Disraeli or C. P. Snow could have anticipated. Fairly obviously, then, any move which seeks the establishment of an educative society cannot hope to be successful if it is made along the lines laid down in the past. An entirely new approach is needed, even though this means leaving the track on which the 'education system' now runs and exploring the territories where each of us must make his own way.

2 LIFELONG LEARNING

It is as well to recognize that we, in Britain, are still searching for an appropriate term to designate the emergent concept of education as a continuous process. In France, the term *l'éducation permanente*, first coined by Bertrand Schwartz some ten years ago, originated in the wartime Resistance and was inspired by the belief, first in the efficacy of innovation and secondly in human brotherhood. Stripped of its ideological mystique, it is of course, neither peculiarly French nor particularly revolutionary. 'It amounts', says Jessup,

> to an assertion that education is, and should be seen to be, a lifelong process; that it is not a phenomenon associated exclusively with formal and traditional institutions of education such as schools and universities; that the education of an individual needs to be planned

with regard to what has gone before and what may be expected to follow (vertical integration); that it must be planned also with regard to all the roles that, at a given point in his life, the individual sustains and all the educational influences to which he is subjected (horizontal integration).[5]

Recent developments in France suggest that the motivation is mainly economic and political rather than cultural, i.e. that in practice the drive towards 'permanent education' corresponds more closely to the notion of recurrent vocational training.

For his part, the Englishman tends to look back at the extraordinary proliferation of adult courses which has followed the pioneer work of men like Albert Mansbridge, R. H. Tawney, Sir Richard Livingstone and Henry Morris in the early years of this century, culminating today in that most potent of growth points, the Open University. To his way of thinking, 'permanent education' has faintly authoritarian overtones, apt to conjure up horrific visions of compulsory courses for geriatrics! On the whole, he prefers to call it 'lifelong learning', although such a designation is so vague as to be in danger of identifying itself with a simplistic philosophy of we-live-and-learn. 'Continuing education' is too awkward. 'Recurrent education' means something quite different, less comprehensive than the global concept whose outlines are now discernible. So the Englishman, as usual, compromises and settles for calling it 'Lifelong education'. What's in a name, he asks? It is arguable that the British genius is essentially empirical and that while educationists in other countries have been addressing themselves to the theoretical aspects, the British have been busy getting down to practicalities. It cannot escape notice that whereas every British university has its department of extramural adult education, with close links between the academic community and the region, nothing comparable, at any rate on the same scale, is to be found in Italy. When all the present talk of planification has subsided, posterity may well decide that the most significant breakthrough in the late twentieth century's search for a new institutional framework suited to an age of technology was the Open University.

Nevertheless, the urgent need is for an overarching theory to encompass all the varied agencies and activities, pre-school as well as post-school, voluntary as well as statutory, informal as well as formal, which together make up the expanding universe of lifelong education. Apart from McLuhan, relatively few forward thinkers in the English-speaking world have widened their intellectual focus sufficiently to see the continuous process of education as a whole, in the way that men like Bertrand Schwartz, Jean Le Veugle, Edgar Faure and Philippe Lengrand have done in France, Aldo Visalberghi and Danilo Dolci in Italy, Torsten Husén in Sweden or Bogdan Suchodolski in Poland. The fact is that the rank and file of professional educationists are ill-prepared to meet the situation with which they are suddenly confronted today. This is because educational studies have grown up in institutions devoted more or less exclusively to the training of teachers, with the result that any expertise they possess remains concentrated on the years between five and sixteen of the learner's life. What came before and after, not being of any immediate concern to educationists, was referred to separately as 'pre-school', 'further', 'adult' or 'higher' education. In short, the process of education defined itself for them as it did for Durkheim, as the influence exercised by adult generations on the *young*. For the same reason developmental psychology came to be interpreted as the study of the *child*. Thus the educational theory we are left with is, strictly speaking, no more than a theory of *instruction*.

In this connection, a historical analogy may be helpful. In the early nineteenth century, when world history was thought of as dating from the biblical Flood, a matter of a few thousand years at most, biologists' theories of evolution were necessarily inhibited, partial, if not actually erroneous. It was only when the geologists and palaeontologists provided them with countless millions of years to play with, so to speak, that a genuinely scientific theory became entertainable. By the same token, an educational theory which is mainly concerned with developments during the learner's short school life is as blinkered as that of the pre-Darwinians – as incomplete as the proverbial railway line from Oxford to London which stopped short at Didcot.

Education conceived as a preparation for life locks learning within a vicious circle. Youth educated in terms of adult ideas and taught to think of learning as a process which ends when real life begins will make no better use of intelligence than the elders who prescribe the system. . . . Education within the vicious circle becomes not a joyous enterprise but something to be endured because it leads to a satisfying end.

If Lindeman is right, and the vast majority of young people nowadays would agree that he is, we are moving into a society in which *leisure*, not *work*, will become the central element in daily life and affairs. Without indulging in wild flights of futurology we can be tolerably sure that it will be a society which will be characterized as information-rich and action-poor. That is to say, from now on it is not going to be possible, or desirable, for the learner to master all the knowledge and skills he needs by the time he reaches the age of sixteen, eighteen or twenty-two. Much of what he learns will in any case be quickly outdated by events. Learning how to *use* information and how to adapt to changing circumstances and requirements is going to have greater survival value than memorizing a given corpus of knowledge. In a world of mass communications, acquiring information is going to be the least of his problems. Much of the information at his disposal, moreover, will be *non-verbal* – a reminder, this, that understanding media must now be seen as a top priority in the formulation of an adequate theory of education. Learning, in other words, will lose both its academic and its once-and-for-all character. In a throwaway culture, Rousseau's paradox, 'The great object is not to save time but to waste it', ceases to be nonsensical.

Against this, it seems probable that opportunities for worthwhile self-expression and the exercise of the active life of work and service may be harder to find in the automated environment of Megalopolis 2000 than they are today. What is happening in the big conurbations – the boredom and apathy in the classroom, the unrest and occasional outbursts of violence of frustrated young people on housing estates where there are all too few outlets for their creative energies, the stress and strain of industrial relations affecting management and workers alike, the neuroses of housewives with time on their hands – is symptomatic of a deep-rooted social malaise. At the school level it manifests itself in unruliness in the classroom, in truancy, in a growing disinclination to see much or any relevance in the curriculum. At the secondary stage in particular the school society is polarized into separate factions, academic and non-academic, middle class and working class, pro-school and anti-school – polarization which reflects, and also helps to perpetuate, the divisions within society at large.

If this reading of the situation is broadly correct, some serious problems immediately state themselves. First, how are we to repair the ruins created by a school life which not only leaves many non-academic pupils with a positive distaste for learning but also conditions them to a fatalistic acceptance of their own inferiority? Second, how to bridge the gap between formal schooling and the informalities of lifelong learning? Third, how is the existential vacuum created by a disappearing work-based ethic to be filled? Fourth, how is it going to be possible to ensure that the cultural capital of an affluent, leisured society will be shared by all, not simply by a master class who manipulate and exploit it in their own interests? Let us briefly examine each of these problems in turn.

How can schooling be anti-educational?

It is an illusion to suppose that any policy of lifelong education can be effectively implemented without radically changing the existing school system. True, there is plenty of unfinished business awaiting completion both at the pre-school and post-school stages – the need for more nursery schools and kindergartens, the need for more university places, for more in-service training, for more youth centres and adult courses, etc. – but no useful purpose is served in thinking of these desiderata merely as addenda. Once schooling is seen in the context of the life cycle as a whole it can no longer be treated as a self-contained entity, nor should there be any sharp break between the various stages in the continuous process of learning.

At present there is a marked disjunction between the school as a formal bureaucratic institution and the various institutions catering for adult education. At first sight, it may seem irresponsible to suggest that schooling can be anti-educational, but the evidence suggests that for a sizeable proportion of adolescents this is the case. If the overriding objective in all teaching is to leave the learner as interested and well motivated at the end of a course as he was at the beginning, then we have to acknowledge that this is one objective which has certainly not been achieved. Even if they do not drop out before then, many pupils on reaching leaving age are only too glad to turn their backs on the school, never to return. They are the victims of the 'hidden curriculum'. This 'hidden curriculum', far from being a fiction of the deschoolers, is a well-established sociological phenomenon. In addition to the declared (overt) objectives there are always tacit (covert) objectives – side effects of which teachers and pupils alike may be wholly unaware. In effect, what many non-academic pupils learn is that they hate this or that subject, that they are not clever, that no matter how hard they try they are fated to be losers. Worse still, their low ego concepts and self-depreciation often reach the point when they decide that their failure is entirely due to their own inadequacies. If this is education, they decide, they want no further part of it. For them, at least, the only possible verdict must be that schooling is anti-educational.

Just how large is the proportion of alienated anomic teenagers in secondary schools is uncertain, but even if it were only a small minority it would be wrong to regard it as a lunatic fringe of long-haired layabouts. Clearly something needs to be done to arrest the gradual takeover by the school of functions which might more properly be discharged by other social agencies. Now that learning can be spread over a lifetime it is only reasonable to ask for a redefinition and a more precise delimitation of the school's objectives. As it is, the teacher's role has become so diffuse that he is expected to be instructor, father figure, priest, judge, policeman and playmate rolled into one. If the concept of lifelong education does nothing more, it points to the conclusion that the purpose of formal schooling is to provide *basic training*.

The institutional spectrum

The boy who leaves school thoroughly disenchanted and with no prospect of gaining any sort of professional qualifications is really not so different from the young man who graduates from a university. Secretly, both share the conviction that somehow, now that their 'education' is at an end, they are free agents at last, ready to enter the world of work, ready to enjoy 'life'. To be sure, the graduate is likely to be well aware of the need for periodic retraining whereas the nearest the early leaver will ever come to participating in organized cultural activities is by joining a football supporters' club or a disco. One will be a patron and consumer of high culture, the other of low culture. Socially, they will have little or nothing in common.

The disjunction between the school as an educational institution and the various organizations providing for vocational, cultural and recreative activities for adults explains why so many pupils feel that they have come to a dead end once compulsory attendance is behind them. So long as our ideas about what constitutes an 'educational institution' are restricted to the school model it is hard to see how the disjunction can be removed. In this connection, Illich's classification of institutions into two main types – 'bureaucratic' and 'convivial' – is worth bearing in mind. Taking the post-school (tertiary) stage of education as whole it is possible to arrange the various formal and informal institutions in a spectrum. At one extreme are the old foundations of higher learning, headed by the universities, followed by the newer ones – polytechnics, further education colleges, industrial training boards, *et al.*: at the other a host of organizations ranging from Rotary, young farmers' clubs, Women's Institutes, orchestral and dramatic societies, choirs, theatre groups, nursery playgroups, natural history societies, etc., down to the peer-matching which takes place round coffee tables and at dinner parties. Where, if anywhere, do we draw the line between educational, vocational,

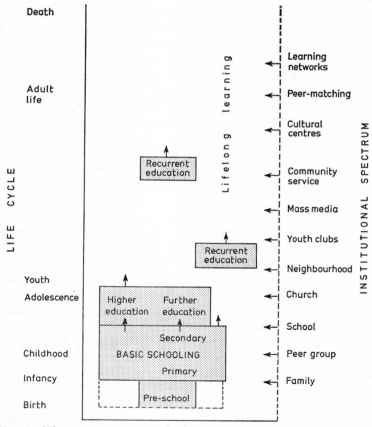

Fig. 4   The statutory system of education (shaded) as a subsystem of the educative society

cultural and recreational activities? (Before jumping in with an answer, the reader may like to remind himself that Plato's *Symposium* was a dinner party!) A mature student reading for a degree in his spare time, a young electrician studying for his National Certificate, or a housewife following a correspondence course in German, all these are 'getting an education', we say, but when it comes to the man who takes up birdwatching for the sheer delight of it or the young mother who telephones a friend to find out what to do about the baby's nappy rash, most of us tend to demur.

Demur we may, but the fact remains that the significant moves being made nowadays in the proliferating field of lifelong learning are *not* those which preoccupy the authorities – the ever-rising numbers of students enrolled for university courses, for example – but those which have their thriving grassroots in contemporary social life. In order to understand what is happening, educationists need an altogether more wholesome philosophy, more generous in its sympathies, than the arid conceptual analysis (scholasticism in modern dress) on which most of them have been reared in recent decades. Such a philosophy will undoubtedly owe more to the life sciences and to phenomenological thought than to logical empiricism or behaviourism. It would provide a sorely needed counter-attack on educational technologists like B. F. Skinner who would cheerfully dispense with human dignity and freedom as essential ingredients of the good life. Reductionism, it is now seen, inevitably leads to nihilism because it purports to explain human beings in mechanistic terms of *nothing-but-ness* and in doing so gives *carte blanche* to social engineering and the kind of educational practice which treats the learner as if he were the helpless victim of environmental forces. The new philosophy and the new educational theory and practice are, by contrast, organismic, i.e. they see the learner as a responsible agent, capable of finding his own way, making his own decisions and framing his own life style.

In similar vein is Bruner's essay on 'Immaturity',[6] as informed, sane and shrewd a diagnosis of the problems of growing up in the modern world as any yet offered. 'Let me urge', he says,

> that the process of education (whether in established schools or by other means) be conceived not just as a preparation for life but as a form of enablement selectively available throughout the life cycle. I conceive of this process as starting before the child enters school,

but it is mostly the transition from the preparatory period into one's working life that concerns me here, whether one is a school-leaver or a graduate of a college, a polytechnic or a university. There should be means available for 'returning', or 'continuing', or 'converting', or 'refreshing', or whatever. But, just as important, there must be some means of planning before departing, even if only at the level of plausible hypothesis, concerning later uses of education in one's life.

In this connection, the Council of Europe's scheme[7] for lifelong education seems apposite:

1 Basic education (schooling)
>   forming the common trunk of
2 Vocational education
>   which would evolve into
3 Recurrent education (further training, refresher courses, retraining)
>   which would develop from
4 Shaping of life to a cultural pattern.

Schemes, unfortunately, solve no problems! Quite apart from the difficulty of deciding what the 'common trunk' of basic education ought to be, and how, when and where it shades off into vocational education, there is, as we have seen, a hiatus between institutionalized schooling (which is compulsory) and post-school learning (which is largely voluntary). What we have to reckon with at the post-school stage are two distinct types of motivation, one of which is vocationally orientated, the other more or less disinterested. This is recognized in the 1944 English Education Act, which classifies further education under two headings: (a) full-time and part-time vocational training; (b) organized leisure-time cultural and recreative activities for those who are able and willing to profit by them. Of these, the first clearly corresponds to the notion of recurrent education, the second to the more informal and less definable aspects of lifelong education. Equally clearly, the first is instigated by motives which are, strictly speaking, economic rather than educational whereas the second is engaged in for reasons of personal satisfaction and to that extent may be called cultural.

Now it may seem obvious that the main drive in the foreseeable future will be to secure the higher professional qualifications and specialist skills which are needed in an advanced industrial society. For many, if not all, recurrent education will mean taking advanced courses, 'going back to school' as the Americans say, in order to keep abreast of developments in specialist fields and to obtain the additional qualifications which will help in gaining promotion. This being so, it is worth asking whether the obtaining of such qualifications is necessarily one and the same as the process of education and whether or not it answers much more closely to a process of training. It is also worth asking how many of these paper qualifications bear little or no relation to the *on-the-job* situation for which they are alleged to be necessary.

In the long run, assuming that current trends towards shorter working hours, holidays with pay and rising standards of living continue, it seems reasonable to suppose that the second type of motivation, the one characterized above as personal and disinterested, will supervene, in which case 'learning for its own sake' will become as meaningful and rewarding for the man in the street as it has been in the past for a handful of scholars and privileged connoisseurs. If this sounds utopian, we should at least take note of the contemporary cult phrase – 'doing one's own thing' – which, whatever else it may imply, means the very reverse of 'going back to school'! It means the rejection of bureaucratic institutions which operate as closed systems in favour of those which are convivial and open.

3 THE TRANSITION FROM WORK TO LEISURE

Incautious as it may be to say that all this spells the onset of a counter-culture, we cannot ignore the turbulence caused by the rising tide of human aspirations and expectations in the sphere of industrial relations as well as in the minds of the young. There is a growing disinclination to place any absolute trust in a nineteenth-century industrial ethic which decreed that *homo faber* must produce or starve. Because man was condemned to live by the sweat of his brow, liberal education was always an unattainable ideal, reserved, of necessity, for the few who were free to lead a life of leisure.

And this is why the prospect opening up before us is at once so exhilarating and so terrifying. Exhilarating because for the first time in history liberal education for all looks like entering the domain of practical politics; terrifying, because the educational services remain subservient to dubious policies of industrial growth which do little or nothing to prepare the masses for a life of leisure. We are all captives, it seems, in the squirrel's cage of production and consumption. To that extent, our thinking is inevitably conditioned by the phenomenon first diagnosed by Marx as *alienation*, by Durkheim as *anomie*, and by sociologists like David Riesman as *other-directedness*. If it is the case, as we have already argued, that henceforward it is not going to be possible to provide schoolchildren with a corpus of knowledge which will serve them for the rest of their lives, we must be prepared to follow the implications of such an argument. In effect, what we are saying is that it is necessary to abandon all hopes of giving the learner a built-in code of values and morality. On the face of it, this is tantamount to saying that the school is in a state of normlessness and that its inmates are *ipso facto* anomic. If so, the problem of filling the existential vacuum created by a disappearing work-based ethic requires far more serious consideration than futurologists have so far given it. More plainly, as Jessup puts it,[8] 'It is a mistake . . . to stress too much the economic significance of lifelong learning. . . . Perhaps a materially poor society must adopt a utilitarian attitude towards education, but a society which has achieved a fair measure of affluence . . . can afford to take a more liberal view and recognize that education is, quite simply, part of the Good Society; "it is a good in itself, an end, not merely a means to an end." '

4 EQUALIZING OPPORTUNITY?

Like deschooling, the campaign for lifelong education may be seen as an ideological movement whose main strength derives from its moral fervour and whose greatest weakness is a tendency to stress what is desirable while ignoring what is feasible. As with deschooling, the danger is that its rhetoric may outrun its rationale. It is easy enough, say its critics, to draw up bold, imaginative plans for the future, but such plans are not worth the paper they are drawn on unless they receive the overwhelming support of public opinion and unless ways and means of implementing them are available at the highest level of policymaking. As things are, neither of these conditions can be satisfied by those who champion the cause of lifelong education: they lack both the popular support and the political power which are needed if planification is to have any chance of being taken seriously. It is true that planification has scarcely begun and that there is no cause for premature pessimism because the progress made so far has been minimal. At the same time, there is no cause for unwarranted optimism either. Since 1965, UNESCO, OECD and the Council of Europe have organized conferences and working parties to explore the possibilities of lifelong education, to consider its long-term implications and to suggest strategies for alternative futures. A number of impressive reports and monographs have been issued which have certainly helped to stimulate interest and discussion – but there are no signs that these have had much, or any, effect. A cynical appraisal of the present state of affairs in the world of discourse about lifelong education might well be that it is mostly *talk*!

In at least two respects the ideology of lifelong education is clearly international: (1) in stressing the urgent need for innovation; (2) in seeking greater equality of opportunity. This general unanimity, however, admits of as many variations and disagreements among its adherents as does any religious or political creed. As an ideology, it is certainly not strong enough to transcend particular national interests. Among the reasons for thinking so are the following:

(a) National systems of education seem to be incorrigibly nationalistic. Each of them is rooted in its own history and traditions, in its own language and culture, its own ethos, and to that extent may be said to be *sui generis*. Thus, in France, *l'éducation permanente* has a strong appeal to those who react against authoritarian regimes – classical *lycée*, Nazi occupation or Gaullism. In England, lifelong learning is seen by many as the means of removing the social inequalities which must remain so long as comprehensive and selective grammar schools continue to operate side by side. But the fact that there is a recognizable kinship between the Frenchman's *après-vente* philosophy and the Englishman's approval of 'second-chance' policies (fair play for the underdog!) cannot obscure the vital intellectual and cultural differences between them. The historic determinants which gave rise to the First Republic were not the same as those which led to the formation of Disraeli's 'Two Nations'. It is a truism to say that a great deal more than twenty miles of sea water separate the French from the English way of life; and as a consequence, despite their geographical proximity, the two education systems have their own distinctive characteristics. The same is true of all the other members of the European Community. Far from having common structures, they resemble rather the pieces of a jigsaw for which an agreed pattern (*la cultura Europea?*) has yet to be found. It

may be thought that this is a typically British and isolationist point of view and that it will change once Britain has had more experience as an active member of the European Community. It is certainly true that enthusiasm for the cause of lifelong education is greater in the countries of the original six members and it is arguable that this is because their experience in making common cause in economic policies has given them a confidence in the efficacy of supranational agencies and institutions which Britain at present lacks. Against this, comparative studies suggest that the forces which preserve the separate identity of a national education system are vastly more potent and more subtle than those which decide its economic and monetary systems.

(b) All education systems are peculiarly resistant to change. By nature, they are essentially conservative. Max Weber's theory of social, political and educational change applies here: according to this, the interplay between the interests and ideas of competing groups results in a process of conflict leading to an alteration of dominance and counter-assertion. Eventually, one status group gains power and establishes its authority over the others. As times goes on, however, this dominance is challenged by rival status groups which seek to overthrow it and eventually succeed in doing so, whereupon the cycle of dominance-assertion is repeated *ad infinitum*. Baldly summarized in this way, Weber's theory may seem crude, but it is helpful in explaining the situation in which advocates of lifelong education currently find themselves. That situation, it has to be recognized, is comparable with that of the opposition in parliamentary democracy, *not* that of the government. Not unnaturally, the establishment tends to see any move which looks like disturbing the equilibrium of the social order as a threat to its authority and imposes its own sanctions on pressure groups which it regards as being in any way potentially disruptive. Innovation may be tolerated in small doses, but radical change is frowned on, and violent change is anathema to it. In this, moreover, the establishment has the support of public opinion. Thus, although forward thinkers may be convinced that the accelerating pace of technological and cultural change has already passed the point at which a drastic reformulation of our ideas on education is demanded, the fact remains that they are in a minority. As a creative minority, they must bide their time until a consensus is arrived at, when, and only when, it will become possible for them to take the

initiative. Advocates of lifelong education, it may be thought, have an irrefutable case, but until it is proved in open court there is little chance of justice being done and, more important, being seen to be done.

(c) National education systems are at different stages of development. The European countries did not all become industrialized at the same time. In the case of Britain, the first industrial nation, it took 100 years to lay the foundations of the first stage of the continuous process – elementary schools for all and universal literacy. It took another fifty years to make 'Free secondary education for all' more than a socialist-inspired slogan. At the moment, the tertiary stage is still

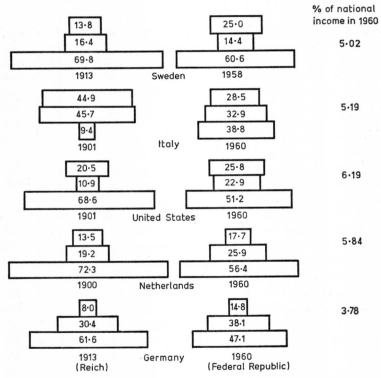

Fig. 5   Educational expenditure at different levels: percentages of total expenditure for primary, secondary and higher education
(From F. Edding, *The Economics of Education*, ed. E. A. Robinson and J. E. Vaizey, 1966)

taking shape. As Fig. 5 shows, educational expenditure in other European countries and in the USA varies considerably according to the stage of development reached by each system at a given time. In the early years of the twentieth century top priority was given to the primary stage – but not in Italy! Seventy years later, the priorities have changed, with a more balanced shareout between the three stages and a bigger allocation being made for higher and further education – again, not in Italy!

In the immediate future it seems probable that increased provision for pre-school services will claim the attention of the planners in several European countries, in which case adjustments will have to be made to the allocations for the rest of the statutory system, or a further increase in the proportion of GNP devoted to education will have to be considered. At the moment, 50 per cent of three year old children and 80 per cent of four year olds receive nursery schooling in France. In Belgium the ratio is 80 per cent and 90 per cent respectively. Italy and Holland provide nursery places for roughly 50 per cent of their young children. Britain provides them for only 5 per cent!

These examples, which could easily be multiplied, serve as reminders that even in advanced industrial societies the education system is still far from being completed. Each system has plenty of unfinished business to contend with. Trying to make ends meet is difficult enough with the limited resources available without engaging in ambitious projects which would swell the already escalating costs. More than one ministry of education is currently wondering whether it can afford to carry the ever-increasing financial burden of maintaining the educational services. Despite the advice of experts who urged the need for a 'systems approach' to the problems of administrative decision-making, the authorities understandably protest that it is only possible to do one thing at a time and that any reforms must be piecemeal. In pressing their claims, advocates of lifelong education render their cause a disservice if they fail to distinguish between policies which are eminently desirable but strictly non-viable.

(d) Since the education system is a subsystem of the social system, any major reforms must await major changes in the latter. In other words, the tail cannot wag the dog! This is one reason why cultural anthropologists are contemptuous of educational theorists – Dewey's instrumentalism and the progressive education movement arising

from it provide one recent example – which seek to ameliorate the social order by means of transforming the curricula, methods of teaching and school organization. Although the interaction between the education system and the society it serves does not entirely rule out the possibility of the one influencing the other, there is little doubt that societal forces are preponderant.

If so, we are faced with the uncomfortable fact that the ideal of lifelong education for all may be unattainable. Both Marxist–Leninist doctrines in the USSR and Jacksonian democracy in the USA have been compelled to come to terms with inequality as an indispensable feature of industrial society. The fact, from which there appears to be no escaping, is that industrial society is essentially meritocratic. Moreover, there are no indications that a post-industrial (i.e. scientific-technological) society will be any different: on the contrary, it looks very much as though such a society will confirm and reinforce present meritocratic tendencies. Certainly, Raymond Aron is not alone in foretelling a future in which the vast majority of human beings will be condemned to a termite-like existence and, which is worse, see nothing wrong with it so long as their creature comforts are catered for by a dominant élite.

Is this just another example of the *1984–Brave New World* type of horror fiction? On the contrary, it represents the considered opinion of many social scientists. Bourdieu's analysis[9] suggests that all education systems, as at present constituted, ensure that the cultural capital of society will remain for ever in the hands of a dominant élite, and that the existing class distinction between bourgeois ('high') and proletarian ('low') culture will become permanent.

Commercial entrepreneurs apparently take the same view, judging by a recent forecast of trends in the leisure market in Britain.[10] According to this, leisure time is expected to increase by 5 per cent between 1973 and 1980, but the total spending on leisure will rise from £6,995 million to £16,024 million during the same period – nearly half of which will be spent on alcoholic drinks! Sales of do-it-yourself kits are expected to show a 181 per cent increase, TV, radio and record/cassettes a 177 per cent increase, with similar increases for air and car travel, holidays and gambling. In short, the whole emphasis is on *entertainment*.

But it would be wrong to conclude from all this that the auguries the problems of organization encountered nowadays in advanced in-future modes of thought and values which are typical of a phase in the evolution of industrial society which, for all we know, may not last very much longer. These modes of thought may be characterized as linear, deterministic, mechanistic and materialistic. Probably the greatest hope for an alternative way of life in which lifelong education for all will become as natural as breathing is to be found in the emergence of a distinctive youth subculture which is in open revolt against the established values and institutions of contemporary society. Commonly shared beliefs – for example, the belief in the necessity for cut-throat competition, and the belief that the good life is epitomized by a white collar job, a house in suburbia, a high-powered car and colour television sets – are increasingly being called in question and rejected by many young people today. More so than their elders, they are not prepared to countenance the inequalities and injustices of a system which bestows *la dolce vita* on a favoured few at the expense of a multitude of laborious poor. Unlike their elders, they need no learned sociological analysis to convince them that the statutory education system is, in many respects, a colossal confidence trick, and that its promises of equality of opportunity are fraudulent. Their diagnosis agrees with Slater's: 'The core of the old culture is scarcity. . . . The key flaw in the old culture is, of course, that the scarcity is spurious, man-made in the case of bodily gratifications and man-allowed or man-maintained in the case of material goods. . . . The new culture is based on the assumption that important human needs are easily satisfied and that the resources for doing so are plentiful.[11] The feeling that modern technology and the machinations of big business have manœuvred the young into a state of impotence and virtual redundancy adds to the deep sense of outrage. 'Who the hell wants to "make it" in America any more?' asks Jerry Rubin, the yippie leader. 'The American economy no longer needs young whites and blacks. We are waste material. We fulfil our destiny in life by rejecting a system which rejects us.'

Admittedly, the revolt of youth cannot be approved of in its uglier manifestations, least of all those which are so psychologically disturbed as to be destructive, but that it heralds the breakdown of the established social order can hardly be doubted. The 'crisis of the school' is also the crisis of our time, in transit from an order which is old and effete to one which seems disorderly and anarchical because it is still in the throes of parturition. In the contemporary state of flux it is possible to discern a number of apparently contradictory phenomena: a vast growth of bureaucratic controls, a significant increase in the arbitrary exercise of power by those in authority and a corresponding narrowing of the scope of political freedom on the one hand, and on the other a growing demand for participatory democracy, for sexual freedom, for co-operative social action and for 'doing one's own thing'.

In asking what the probable outcome of this Weberian conflict between the forces of 'dominance' and 'assertion' is going to be, futurologists who take it upon themselves to plan lifelong education for the year 2000 and thereafter should beware of allying themselves with the former. If ours is an age of protest it is precisely because there is a widespread revulsion against techniques of management and control which affect the life styles of individuals in ways which they are powerless to prevent. As the preceding argument has endeavoured to show, the chances are that the established order, faced with growing dissidence and the threat (as it sees it) of civil disruption, will resort to repressive measures in order to maintain the *status quo*. In that event, any projection of current trends must conclude that the probable, if not the inevitable outcome will be the kind of society which Harman, rightly, calls a garrison state.[12] Only by assuming the advent of a dramatic transformation of values and beliefs is it legitimate to anticipate an alternative future which would be less horrible. So long as forecasting is based on linear modes of thinking it is bound to be deterministic and to that extent will be inclined to see society (and its education system) as subservient to the industrial system, not vice versa. And this is why the revolt of youth, like the genius of the avant-garde artist whose canvases scandalize the public because they are not immediately comprehensible, is charged with significance for anyone who takes the cause of lifelong education seriously. A generation whose motto is 'Trust no one over the age of thirty!' is not likely to be overawed by institutions and by regulations whose authority is patently dubious, nor are they likely to submit easily to a school regimen which keeps them indefinitely in a state of dependence and passivity. These are the youngsters whom Margaret Mead, in *Culture and Commitment* (a study of the generation gap), categorizes as the 'pre-figurative generation' – the unknown children whose outlook on life is fundamentally different from that of their parents. This, presumably, is what McLuhan has in mind when he tells us that the post-TV generation are 'different animals'.

The best hope of avoiding a garrison state in which technocrats rule the roost and the masses are condemned to a termite existence, then, is to be found in the promising lead set by the rising generation. The attitude shifts needed to bring about a person-centred society (Harman's term for an alternative future) have their source in the hearts and minds of the young: they, and only they, are the ones who quite literally have the future in their bones. Theirs is the dynamic which alone can energize the theory of lifelong education.

Such a person-centred society, thinks Harman,

> will be a planned society, but planned in such a way as to deepen, not diminish, the freedom of the individual. Opportunity will be provided for real participation in planning by those for whom the planning is done. Management structures will be such that power flows both ways. . . .
>
> Education will centre on developing self-learning habits and skills, problem-solving and decision-making abilities, individuality, sound valuing capabilities, capability of continuous self-renewal and self-understanding. Education will be much more equated with life, and with the distinction between formal and informal education having become blurred it will be much more a lifetime activity. The significant distinctions will not be work vs education or work vs leisure, but work-education vs 'killing time'.

As a prescription, this sounds fine. Once again, however, a caveat is necessary. If lifelong education is ever to become more than an impossible dream, many of our cherished notions about the process of education in its present institutionalized forms will have to be discarded, and many values whose correctness is now taken for granted will have to be modified. This is why, to begin with, it is necessary to ask, 'What is the difference between education and schooling?' – and why, in the last resort, it is even more necessary to ask Job's question, 'What is Man?', or, as the Greeks preferred to pose it, 'What is Man's *arete*?'

8 Towards a generative theory of education

Each mortal thing does one thing and the same;
Deals out that being indoors each one dwells;
Selves – goes itself; *myself* it speaks and spells,
Crying, 'What I do is me; for that I came'.

Gerard Manley Hopkins

A child's play must always be interpreted as the imaginary, illusory realization of unrealizable desires. At this higher level, play is displaced wish fulfilment often aided by what Vygotsky called a pivot – a prop that embodies a feature of the sought-for state, as a stick serves as a horse to ride. The pivot is the symbolic substitute. So play and aimed intention, while contrasting, seem of the same coin. The one holds the end constant, while varying the means; the other requires ends and means, but changes each to suit the other with a kind of measured zest.[1]

Educational theorists who ride their hobby-horses might do worse than reflect that displaced wish fulfilment lies at the very heart of all their thinking. They are concerned ultimately with what-might-be rather than what-is. The question is whether the elevated and abstruse child's-play they indulge in points the way to adult equestrian skills – to real horses – or whether, in the nature of things, it is destined to remain at the infantile level of fantasy and makebelieve.

SEERS OR CHARLATANS?

Broadly speaking, advocates of lifelong education fall into two classes. For some, it means a further expansion of the existing services and the addition of new ones: compulsory nursery schools, periodical in-service training, more courses for adults and so on. For others, it means something altogether more radical but at the same time a good deal more nebulous, a sought-for state which might be called the disinterested pursuit of personal well-being through cultured leisure activities. As the realists see it, descriptions of this futurological state are so vague that no one could possibly recognize it if it ever arrived. As for its prescriptions, they are written on air – and the air is decidedly foggy. For idealists, on the other hand, the prospect of more and ever lengthier institutionalized schooling is nothing less than horrific. One side pins its faith on a theory which characterizes itself as people-processing – the theory that the learner needs to be subjected to special treatment and placed under the guidance and control of some mentor in order to become fully human. The other, more inclined to a child-is-father-of-the-man philosophy, believes that free self-activity is the indispensable means of achieving 'education' as distinct from 'training' – Curle's point, surely, when he says that 'Men and women become free through their own efforts'. Disputes between the two factions tend to be as wordy and as turgid as those of the medieval schoolmen and in the absence of any resolution of opposed and contradictory theories they are likely to prove equally inconclusive.

Yet whichever way we care to think of lifelong education its ideology shares certain common features: (1) in being future-oriented; (2) in being reformist and activist – i.e. in agreeing with Marx that 'Philosophies have only interpreted the world in different ways. The point is to change it'; (3) in representing a flat denial that the main purpose of education is simply to prepare the young for adult life; and (4) in being markedly egalitarian.

On each of these counts the charge of charlatanism levelled against those who profess the theory of lifelong education needs to be taken seriously. Consider, then, how the case for the prosecution might be stated.

1 Futurology is not to be despised merely because it happens to be fashionable at the moment, but it remains largely an art of conjecture: even in the economic field no great reliance can be placed upon its projections. The current preoccupation with prediction in the social sciences, indeed, may itself be a symptom of the disease of

change. Toffler's diagnosis of it may not be exactly clinical but he is not alone in being

> appalled by how little is actually known about adaptivity, either by those who call for and create vast changes in our society, or by those who supposedly prepare us to cope with those changes. Earnest intellectuals talk bravely about 'educating for change' or 'preparing people for the future'. But we know virtually nothing about how to do it. In the most rapidly changing environment to which man has ever been exposed, we remain pitifully ignorant of how the human animal copes.[2]

In short, the charge is that talk of a 'learning society' and plans for 'alternative futures' are mostly sophistry: a case of the blind leading the blind.

2 More deadly is the accusation that the conspiratorial stance adopted by those who rally to the cause of lifelong learning is explained by the fact that they carry large chips on their shoulders. Outwardly, their motives may appear to be entirely praiseworthy. Inwardly, their idealism is rooted in a dissent which is basically irrational. On the one hand, says Lucien Morin, *l'éducation de masse* (the term loosely used to cover a whole range of obscure notions including 'schooling for all', 'popular culture', 'education for leisure', etc.) implies a fight to the death against the élite, the later being seen as the monstrous oppressor: on the other, it must be seen in the political context of the class war, dedicated to the improvement of the conditions of employment (and the wages!) of the workers. 'D'abord, il faut se débarrasser de l'élite. L'élite, enseigne le charlatan éducateur de masse, c'est le patron, c'est le pouvoir.'[3]

A somewhat less prejudiced critic draws attention to the hidden persuaders in the language of discourse used by advocates of lifelong learning. *Learning to Be*, incidentally, is full of them. As Kenneth Minogue points out, the crucial distinction between a description and a prescription is that while the former may be more or less conclusively supported by evidence, the latter remains eternally powerless against the obdurate. The trick is to pass off what-might-be for what-can-be.

> An ideologist may immediately be identified as a political writer who seeks to make his arguments appear entirely academic, and who must gain all his political effects by an apparatus of selective description.

The simplest way of understanding this technical innovation is to consider one of the simplest attributes of language. In everyday discourse, we all use easily and fluently words which simply point to objects in the world, or to aspects of those objects (hat, tree, house, green, hard, etc.); and words which indicate our attitude to things (good, bad, horrible, disgusting); and words which combine these two functions (blackguard, tyrant, terrorist, rebel). Now it is obvious that the first class of words may be useful in describing the world, but will never guide us in action; and that the second class of words will guide our attitudes but will not tell us very much. If we are to solve the ideologist's problem, which is to construct a body of knowledge which will also guide us in action, then we must make use of the third class of words, which simultaneously describe and guide our emotions. But in academic terms, such words are recognized as dangerous to the understanding. To talk academically is, very strictly, to purge one's discourse of words of this very kind. The trick of constructing a successful ideology is to coin new technical terms which operate as logical amphibians in this third manner.

Hence it is that the categories of ideology – such as 'revolution', 'proletariat', 'imperialist', 'class war', 'race', 'decadence', 'progress', 'reaction' and the rest – are categories of practice. They betray a bastard parentage: the mother is a thought, sometimes a respectably academic thought, but the father is a passion, and often one of the nastier passions – hatred, greed, envy or revenge.[4]

(The obvious comment here must be that Minogue seems to have fallen into the very same error that he is denouncing. If this last sentence of his is not typical of ideological writing, what is? It is an illusion to suppose that human knowledge or the language in which it is expressed can ever be entirely objective; and there is no justification – other than an ideological one! – for pretending that 'thought' is respectably academic whereas 'passion' is somehow disreputable. The necessary union between the two is emphatically *not* a bastard parentage, a point which Michael Polanyi was at pains to demonstrate in *Personal Knowledge* and one which need not be laboured at this stage of the argument.)

3 To reject a school first/life later theory of education is to fly in the face of immemorial practice. Such a rejection must expect to run the gauntlet of public derision just as Rousseau's *Émile* did or, more

recently, Illich's *De-Schooling Society*. These periodic outbursts may cause temporary shocks and tremors but invariably the education system absorbs them and reverts to its steady state. In the natural sciences the rebel genius may succeed fairly quickly in converting his colleagues because the validity of his theory can be demonstrated. Not so in the field of education. It has taken more than 200 years for the essential truths of *'l'éducation négative'* to win partial and grudging recognition in some of our primary schools. How long it will take before there is general assent to D. J. O'Connor's view that the term 'theory of education' is no better than a courtesy title is anybody's guess. In the meantime the charge of charlatanism is certain to stick.

(But the charge of charlatanism is a two-edged sword. The defence will immediately raise the objection that all that the prosecution is trying to prove is that it is only a matter of time before a new and seemingly outrageous theory ousts an old established one. The history of education is full of examples. At the time of its publication, Froebel's *Education of Man* must have seemed the most pitiful mumbo-jumbo, an open-and-shut case of charlatanism at its worst, yet it is arguable that in the long run Froebelian methodology has been more wholesome in its effects than that of Herbartianism. This being so, who is to say that proponents of lifelong learning, for all their woolly-mindedness, are false prophets? Objection sustained.)

4 There remains the charge that in so far as its appeal is to the cause of equal opportunity and social justice lifelong learning represents a fool's paradise. Its advocates are crying for the moon. Plato's 'deliberate lie' in *The Republic* in fact contains a historical truth: *all* civilized societies have a pyramidal structure, headed by a minority which provides the leadership and having a large majority of third-class citizens. Arnold Toynbee's verdict, at any rate, is that 'To him that hath shall be given: this is not just, but it is one of the facts of life. . . . A society enters on the process of civilization as soon as it can afford a minority, however small, whose time and energy is not wholly taken up in producing food and the other necessities of life.'[5] Certainly, all the evidence suggests that not more than a third of the individuals in any age group are capable of serious intellectual studies and that it is from this segment of the population that nearly all our creative artists, scientists, politicians and inventors are drawn.

But the evidence is deceptive. It is one of the ironies of history that, apart from its literature, most of the artefacts which today evoke our admiration for 'the glory that was Greece' were the work of slave craftsmen. The identification of social status with literacy and the sharing of political power is of comparatively recent origin. A theory of education which ascribed the impotence of a 'multitude of laborious poor' to the natural incompetence of three-quarters of the population may have seemed reasonable in a society in which three-quarters of the population spent most of their time and energies in mind-destroying labour, but such a theory is clearly untenable today. Just as the eighteenth century's conviction that 'The poor have no need of education' gave way to the nineteenth's that the most that could be conceded was elementary schooling for the masses, so the late twentieth century's outlook envisages yet more liberal concepts of education as a continuous process.

Traditional theory, relying as it did on the assumed helplessness, not to say viciousness, of human nature, found its typical expression in the Owenite dogma, 'The character of man is without exception formed for him, not by him.' It resulted in that Herbartian pedagogy which kept the instructor firmly in command and the pupil in a submissive role, the effects of which are still with us, renewed and reinforced, indeed, in Skinnerian techniques. In its original form, both theory and practice underestimated the capabilities and capacities of the great majority of children, and while it has to be acknowledged that the same cannot be said of Skinner's operant conditioning or Bloom's 'mastery learning', it is fair to say that their approach, no less than Herbart's, presupposes the learner's inability to fend for himself. In general, the old pedagogy and the new are based on a theory which is essentially deterministic.

By contrast, a generative theory begins from the premise that from birth onwards human beings can and do 'make something of their lives', that life is ongoing, endowed with intentionality, and that in greater or lesser degree, as Herbert Read never tired of saying, 'We are all artists.'

BACK TO INNATE PRINCIPLES IN THE MIND

What are persons really like, asks Rom Harré? Should we think of them as sitting ducks and stationary billiard balls or as loaded guns and sticks of dynamite?

On the whole, the tendency of educational theory and practice alike has been to treat them as if they *were* billiard balls, inert objects which needed to be pushed around in order to get them moving and steer them into the right pockets. In the natural sciences this billiard ball syndrome, i.e. the habit of mechanistic thinking in terms of linear causality, has been abandoned ever since it reached a dead end in quantum theory, but the habit still lingers on in many classrooms. Pussyfooting didacticism, as we have called it, may no longer be the order of the day, but the belief that most learning takes place at the teacher's instigation and under his supervision takes singularly long to die.

Biologically, human beings are the least programmed of animals in the sense that they are deficient in rigid, readymade instinctive behaviour patterns: they belong to a species that is open-ended – 'unfinished beings' as the Faure Commission rightly styled them. At the same time, they are born with a feed-forward capacity which is quite independent of external stimuli, an inner potential for expected outcomes. Like sticks of dynamite – not the aptest of similes, certainly – they need only a bare minimum of priming before they go off on their own accord.

It might be better for us all if we had an educational theory which envisaged human nature as explosive, dangerous stuff that needed to be handled gently, not something that could be pushed around with impunity. As it is, formal schooling is a game which can only be played safely so long as the teacher wields, if not the big stick, his professional cue. The trouble is that no matter how he manipulates it there is never any certainty that the behaviour of the 'billiard balls' will follow the predicted paths: as often as not, if they do not actually backfire in his face, they have a disconcerting knack of shooting off in directions of their own. In a word, they possess volition.

All of which is not to deny that human beings are constrained by genetic and environmental forces, nor that they can do without care and protection and a modicum of priming, but simply to assert that their course of action is never entirely determined. If the single cell *paramecium* can find its way around in a hostile universe we must credit *homo sapiens* with infinitely greater powers of self-direction. Robin Hodgkin makes the point more graphically when he observes that, to begin with, the young kingfisher on first emerging from its nesting burrow has one chance in twenty of catching a fish for itself, yet within a few days its chances improve sevenfold. If avian evolution has been going on for 500 million years, why has a higher hereditary success rate not been achieved? he asks.

The kingfisher does not inherit the power to live by fishing; it inherits the *power of learning quickly how* to fish. We inherit the power of learning language and this involves the right brain circuitry which the linguists and biologists may some day unravel, *and* it involves the inheritance of a lot of play and looseness. Compared with computers we are not only incredibly complex, but also remarkably slack. We inherit specific information through the genetic language of DNA, but we also inherit an open-ness which makes vast subsequent enrichment of the system possible through language and other symbol systems. The result is a system which is both open and directional.[6]

If only because it is based on love, the mother-child relationship which makes possible the 'miraculous birth of language' must be the paradigm for any humane learning theory. As an example of that 'minimum of priming' which enables the educative process to become self-directing, it cannot be bettered: by comparison, a paternalistic theory which purports to shape behaviour as if it were composed of bits and pieces of a jigsaw which needed to be put together by someone – parent, teacher, any except the learner himself – is made to appear not so much Procrustean as absurd. How else to explain the fact that the most difficult feat of human learning, articulate speech, is performed during the first two years of life?

In a very real sense the infant invents his own language. The baby plays with gurgles which eventually turn into vocables in the same way as he does with his thumb or his big toe. The noises uttered mean whatever he chooses them to mean, and when they become intelligible as words they usually cover a wide range of referents. It is true that language is a cultural universal with its own complex rule structures which have to be acquired before the child can use them effectively. It is equally true that the culture is itself a support system which, at any rate in the context of the mother-child relationship, enables the learner to discover the rules of the language game more or less unaided. As Bruner notes, very little is yet known of rule learning: as he says, 'A most tempting way of conceiving culture is as a limited body of generative rules which, once learned, permits one to act, to anticipate, to predict in a wide variety of situations.'[7]

The assumption on which a generative theory rests is that the 'power of learning quickly how to' is inherited, in other words, that it is built into the human organism. So far as language is concerned, this, broadly, is Chomsky's position, and however controversial his model of a generative grammar may be, there is no denying the force of his argument nor resisting the conclusion that all the other linguistic theories are inadequate, at least in so far as they are incapable of explaining how the subtleties of rule learning are acquired in the absence of anything resembling formal instruction. In learning his mother tongue, the child has to make do with very inadequate data (rather like a scientist who can perform no experiments other than thought-experiments but nonetheless contrives to formulate laws about the world) despite which the child rapidly develops a highly complex and articulated theory of enormous predictive scope. In the hackneyed examples of sentence formation, 'John is easy to please', 'John is eager to please', no rule that can be taught will explain just why in the first case the middle word (adjectival) refers back to the subject whereas in the second the middle word (also adjectival) points to other people. The inference is that the child generates the rules himself. Only someone initially informed of the underlying 'laws' of language, pre-set, as it were, could possibly do this. The existence of innate principles in the mind, consistently played down by educationists ever since Locke's *Essay concerning Human Understanding*, is due for a major comeback.

Not that Locke ever doubted their existence, for all his efforts to disprove it in the first two books of the *Essay*. Immediately following the famous *tabula rasa* passage ('Let us then suppose the mind to be, as we say, white paper, void of all characters, without any ideas; how comes it to be furnished? . . . To this, I answer, in one word, From experience') there is an admission which admirers of the apostle of commonsense have always tended to play down or to overlook:

> The other fountain from which experience furnisheth the understanding with ideas is the perception of the operations of our own minds within us, as it is employed about the ideas it has got; which operations, when the soul comes to reflect and consider, do furnish the understanding with another set of ideas which could not be had from things without; and such are perception, thinking, doubting, believing, reasoning, knowing, willing, and all the different actions of our minds; which we, being conscious of, and observing in ourselves, do from them receive into our understanding as distinct ideas, as we do from bodies affecting our senses. *This source of ideas every man has wholly in himself*; and though it be not sense,

as having nothing to do with external objects, yet it is very like it, and might properly enough be called 'internal sense'. But as I call the other 'sensation', so I call this 'reflection'.[8]

Despite this, the whole trend of empirical investigation in psychology and in educational studies until recent times has been biased in favour of the methods used in the physical sciences and to that extent much more concerned with 'external objects' than with the 'operations of our own minds within us'. Phenomena which could not be directly observed, measured, tested or manipulated were, almost by definition, excluded from its terms of reference. The more that educational theory sought to emulate the scientific method in dealing with the black box problems of learning, the more preoccupied it became with inputs and outputs and the less inclined to have any truck with the unseen goings-on inside the box itself. Its evaluations stressed the importance of *products* – post-test scores, examination results, etc. – at the expense of *processes*. Its leading psychology became behaviourism. Its epistemology exalted the symbolic forms of 'public' knowledge while ignoring, when it did not actually go out of its way to disparage, the essential privacy of personal knowledge. It placed a heavy premium on concept formation – where 'formation' implied the need to build in (human engineering) as distinct from the act of conceiving. Its learning theory concentrated on the '*structure*' of systems while remaining largely indifferent to their '*states*'. Its philosophy became increasingly analytical, more interested in the logic of propositions than in existential issues, which accounts for its glacial, sterile character in recent years – likened by more than one critic to a diet of disinfectant.

The reaction against all this which is now taking place in the life sciences, in organismic and phenomenological thought, as well as in the counter-culture, must be seen as a revolt against dead nature, against mechanical models of behaviour. As Marjorie Grene says, 'The Cartesian-Newtonian world was, in the last analysis, a world without life. That simple fact had, and still has, disastrous consequences for the conception both of the object of knowledge and the subject who knows.'[9]

No good purpose is served, of course, by pretending that the effects of pedagogy, Herbartian or otherwise, have invariably been to treat children as if they were inert objects, 'void of all characters'. Even so, the belief that a great deal more than a minimum of priming was needed, that pupils could not be trusted to act responsibily and that it was essential to keep them under a tight rein has long been, and remains, deep-rooted in professional and public opinion alike. By contrast, a child-centred approach has made relatively little headway beyond the primary stage, and suggestions like R. F. Mager's that 'If you give them the objectives there may not be much else for you to do' have been received for the most part with sheer disbelief. Even among research-minded educationists the mass of evidence which shows that sound learning does *not* depend upon efficient instruction is stubbornly contested – or conveniently ignored because it arouses a crisis of confidence too unpleasant to be entertained. In the educational game the teacher's skill in handling the cue is still regarded as the only safe and sure way of steering billiard balls into their appropriate pockets. Moreover, as Roy Nash's study of how the game is played in *Classrooms Observed* demonstrates, the teacher's influence in deciding which balls are cued for success, and which for failure, is so paramount as to serve as a self-fulfilling prophecy.

In short, the post-Comenian tradition has consistently approved of an educational theory and practice which battened on the helplessness of the learner and subjected him to external discipline and controls. It makes little difference whether we label the underlying philosophy of that tradition behaviourism, determinism, structuralism or reductionism. *Any* theory of education as people-processing is ultimately nihilistic because it seeks to explain human nature in terms of nothing-but-ness, and denies the no-thingness of man. It rests on what Koestler has called the four pillars of unwisdom: (1) the belief that biological evolution is the result of nothing but random mutations preserved by natural selection; (2) that mental evolution is nothing but random tries preserved by reinforcements; (3) that all organisms, including man, are nothing but passive automata controlled by the environment, whose sole purpose in life is the reduction of tensions by adaptive responses; and (4) that the only scientific method worth the name is quantitative measurement; and consequently that complex phenomena must be reduced to simple elements accessible to such treatment without undue worry about whether specific characteristics of a complex phenomenon – for instance, man – may be lost in the process.[10]

But surely, the exasperated reader may protest at this point, none of us can be accused of being parties to beliefs of this sort. Why paint the vices of traditional theory blacker than they deserve? Was it ever anything like so bad as this, and if so, how to explain the fact that it has survived so long and for the most part unchallenged? An argument which stigmatizes the normal classroom set-up as if it were still back in the age of Dickens can only blame itself if it is counter-productive. Any teacher worth his salt knows better than to treat children as if they were billiard balls. Good teachers the world over recognize the need to cater for individual differences, the need for caring.

So they do. So, one hopes, do nurses in lunatic asylums. To say this is not to caricature the school as a kind of madhouse, simply to make the point that the two institutions are analogous. Both answer to the description of detention centres whose inmates are removed willynilly from the rest of society and kept under restraint and close supervision for their own safety and their own good. And if this reads like a scurrilous view of the learning situation as it affects the rank and file of teenagers, how does it come about that in the typical secondary school,

> The musical chairs timetable is based on the assumption of a norm of pupil passivity and recalcitrance. Pupils have to be told what to do; they cannot be trusted; they do not want to learn: this involves imposed discipline; they don't like discipline and are liable to rebel: they therefore need constant supervision. Professing to cope with this situation, the timetable exacerbates it. Sustained concentration, rhythmic development of learning to a natural climax, is impossible. At the sound of a bell everything must change – the room, the subject, the teacher, sometimes the group. Half the energy of every lesson is taken up by the attempt to establish borders, procedures, norms for an arbitrary unit which will be abandoned again in a few moments. The overriding criterion of timetable planning is to make sure that all classes are occupied in all contract hours. The effect of adjacent lessons on each other, the effect of the cumulative sequence of lessons, is not considered. The need for balance between different types of concentration, between absorbing and creating, between accommodation and assimilation, is unconsidered. The overall effect is an imposed superficiality, a self-fulfilling prophecy of pupil passivity, uninvolvement, restlessness and all that follows.[11]

Granted, the fragmented and compartmentalized character of a collection curriculum and the rigid egg-crate structure of school organization show signs of falling into disfavour. Along with other

inherent defects of formal schooling, they stemmed from the traditional theory which held that pupils were incapable of finding out
what they needed to learn without firm direction, without having
things done for them and, above all, *to* them. So long as information
was in short supply there was some justification for a system that was
school-based and teacher-based. While this does not mean that it
should necessarily be immediately overthrown, it has to be said that
traditional theory and the practice to which it gave rise were fundamentally mechanistic.

How, then, would a generative theory differ from the one which
has given us the concept of education as people-processing? In order
to see what the argument is driving at, it is instructive to note the
difference between a generative process as understood in mechanical
terms by, say, an engineer and in organismic terms by a farmer. A
mechanical generator transforms one source of energy – coal, oil or
whatever – into another – electricity – invariably with some slight loss
of energy in the input-output process being incurred. It is a process of
production. By contrast, organic generation is a process of *reproduction*, a matter of creation rather than of transformation. Seed or
germ-cell feeds on its environment and grows by division, so that far
from any loss of energy being involved the outcome is an entirely
new and ongoing organism. The theory and practice behind a
mechanical generator can be applied successfully to the making of
material goods but are misapplied, and break down, in the making
of mice or men.

The transition currently taking place from an educational theory
modelled on a theory of manufacturing, a transition which manifests
itself variously as 'child-centredness', a 'developmental approach' and
as a 'continuous process', is also a transition from a practice which
endeavoured to shape behaviour according to a predetermined pattern
to one which allows greater scope for self-activity. The onus for
learning is clearly shifting from the teacher as kingpin and prime
mover to the learner himself as an autonomous agent. Enablement,
not formation – or transformation – is the true business of education.

Play and interplay are of the essence in any generative theory and
practice, the indispensable means for the enablement of human goal-
seeking at all levels and all ages. If it is true that 'A child's play must
always be interpreted as the imaginary, illusory realization of unrealizable desires' then, as we have already argued, there is a sense in
which educational theory itself must be seen as a higher form of

displaced wish fulfilment. For a long time, educators have stressed the intimate connection between play and learning as the key to child development. Psychologists have emphasized its importance as pre-purposeful activity engaged in by young animals in encounters with their physical and social environment. The point about play, we are told, is not so much that it serves as a breathing space in which the realization of mature purposes is deferred, as that it is completely self-absorbing. As D. H. Lawrence said, 'Everyone individually and spontaneously busy, like a bird that builds its own nest, busy about its own business, alone and unaware.'

But the notion of 'play' and 'interplay' carries with it implications which go far beyond those concerning child study and child development. In this connection, it is interesting to remind ourselves of some of the variant usages of the two words:

1 'Slack' – the word for play in a machine.
2 'Openness' – the word for play in any system animate or inanimate.
3 'Interplay' – the word for play between the components of a mechanical system, between human beings or animals in a society, in the case of human beings between vital ideas, usually mediated symbolically in language, ritual, art, etc.
4 'Interface' – the word for the locus of play as defined in (3). Colloquially, 'Where the action is', 'The space between the words', McLuhan's 'resonant interval', etc.
5 'Sex' – normally, the word for loving play between male and female.

Such a thesaurus might easily be extended, but only at the risk of allowing excessive latitude – play! – in language usage. Thus, 'freedom' itself might be taken as meaning play when perceived existentially as scope for 'making sense', 'making love', 'making something of one's own life', 'doing one's own thing'.

Looked at in this way, it becomes possible to see how, in a technological society that is rich in resources for learning and study aids, education may once again interpret itself as 'leisure' (the original Greek word for school) and as a game (Roman *ludus*). When learning can no more be separated from living than can breathing, any hard and fast distinctions between 'spontaneous' and 'artificial' or 'cultivated' knowledge, 'commonsense' and 'uncommonsense', learning virtually disappears. In other words, while a completely instructor-less education system, like a classless society, may be a delusive ideal, some withering away of the present unwieldly apparatus has to be anticipated.

Nor is the dualism in the forms of knowledge which has given rise to the 'divorce of school from life' the only one that a generative theory would help to resolve. No less troublesome is the dualism which is referred to by educationists and psychologists as affective and cognitive learning – 'heart' and 'head' in popular parlance – as if the two were different sides of the same coin.

That intellect and emotion, sensation and reflection, thinking and feeling, are mutually interrelated has of course been recognized from time immemorial – not least by the ancient Greeks, for whom rationality (*nous*) implied the necessity for balance (*sophrosyne*). The nature of this relationship, however, remains a mystery. Only if one thinks of this inner dialogue and its dynamics in terms of interplay between different brain centres does a plausible hypothesis concerning the genesis of all mental processes become comprehensible.

Where and how, after all, do ideas, moods, flights of fancy and humdrum cogitations originate? There is a passage in *The School Curriculum* which hazards a guess – it can hardly be called an answer – to that question:

> Intellectualism presupposes a well-developed roof brain, and modern educational thought agrees with that of ancient Greece in insisting that this is *the* attribute by virtue of which man is man. This Platonic homage to the ideal of the severed head finds its clearest expression in the *Phaedo* – 'thought is best when the mind is gathered into herself and none of these things trouble her, neither sights nor sounds nor pain nor any pleasure, when she takes leave of the body and has as little as possible to do with it' – is largely responsible for that class of peculiar people who call themselves educated.
>
> Uneasy lies the head that wears an intellectual crown, however. For beneath the newly evolved roof brain lurks the ancestral cerebral core, seat of the passions of the old Adam. This core cannot decode messages couched in intellectual forms, but is acutely sensitive in terms of auditory, visual and sensory-motor perception. Normally, its activities are monitored and censored by the roof brain. Circumstances may arise, however, in which disturbance in the central nervous system causes an uncontrollable spasm, almost as if a quiescent volcano had erupted.[12]

Some skating on thin ice here, admittedly. This idea of cerebral structure as the source and centre of a mental conflict situation or, rather, a dynamic inner dialogue, was suggested by Sir Charles Sherrington's accounts of vivisection experiments on animals whose forebrain had been removed and by the striking resemblance between the weird behaviour of these wretched creatures under electric stimulus and the no less weird antics of pop-group drummers, not to mention the jiggings and jivings of hysterical teenyboppers when 'turned on' ('possessed' used to be the word for it) by a supergroup concert. McLuhan's theory of a 'distortion of sense ratios' induced by exposure to the all-at-onceness of the new electronic audiovisual media had something to do with it also.

Bastard parentage, no doubt, yet this idea, and the hypothesis which goes with it, finds a good deal of support from physiological and neurological research, enough, at any rate, to provide a tentative starting point for a generative theory of learning. Put simply, the hypothesis is that all mental processes arise from the interplay between the neo-cortex and the cerebral limbic system: alternatively, if a mechanical analogy is allowable, that the brain functions like a battery which generates an electrical charge from positive and negative terminals.

It may be objected and with good reason that the connection between brain and mind is elusive enough without introducing a further complication which presupposes a dualism in the operations of the brain itself. Despite some notable advances in surgical and physiological knowledge more remains to be discovered about those operations and their infinitely complicated circuitry than is yet known for certain. The parts played by the frontal lobes and by one of the twin hemispheres which control speech and the 'higher' thought processes have been ascertained with a fair degree of accuracy, but there are large areas of cerebral 'geography' which remain uncharted, *terra incognita* marked 'Here be dragons'. Nevertheless, the basic facts, such as they are, are not in dispute and can easily, if crudely, be summarized.

In the first place, although the brain functions as a unitary system, it consists of three main components, each of which may be regarded as a subsystem: (1) the *neo-cortex* (sometimes referred to as the fore-brain or roof brain, phylogenetically the latest to be superimposed and by far the most highly developed in human beings); (2) the *meso-cortex* (or mid-brain, corresponding to a more primitive stage of mammalian development); and (3) the *arche-cortex* (a relic from the reptilian-amphibian stage of evolution). Between the first subsystem and the other two (i.e. the limbic system) there is, apparently, relatively poor co-ordination. In tissue and structure the cells composing the limbic system are quite different from those of the neo-cortex. It is as though the couplings and feedback loops between new and old textures of 'grey matter' were tenuous and slightly insecure. While it would be a dangerous oversimplification to say that there is a well-defined division of labour with the 'old brain' in charge of sensory and emotional experience and the 'new' responsible for cognition, it looks very much as though we have to reckon with what Koestler calls a schizophysiology in brain functioning which is built into the species. *Homo sapiens*, he suggests, is a man riding a horse with an alligator at its tail. Nature, he thinks, has let us down: man's brain is an evolutionary mistake for there is a serious mismatch between the centres which control the higher thought processes – 'the things of the mind' – and those which control the animal passions and appetites. Thus, intellect can never free itself from the downdrag of the archaic influence of the 'old' brain: taste, smell, touch and viscera still dominate the affective life to an extent which renders pure rationality impossible. He quotes one of the leading neurological authorities, Dr Paul MacLean, as saying that 'The old brain is characterized by its capacity for learning new approaches and solutions to problems on the basis of immediate experience. But . . . it does not have the ability to put its feelings into words.'[13]

This view of human nature as a three-level hierarchy – appetitive, spirited and intellectual – merely updates the views put forward by thinkers like Plato and Aristotle more than 2,000 years ago. It finds its contemporary expression as educational theory in Bruner's 'spiral curriculum', in which learning begins at the 'enactive' level and ascends by way of the 'iconic' to the 'symbolic' level of concept formation. Implicit in these ancient and modern views is the assumption that the workings of the 'old' brain are necessarily inferior, sub-human and somehow indecent – and that every advance in civilization and culture must be attributed to man's increasing sophistication in the use of second-signal symbolic skills. Hence the kind of pedagogy which sees the ribbon development of the forebrain as the main business of education and awards pre-eminence to intellectual prowess.

But in exalting the 'things of the mind' it is worth asking what becomes of the 'gut reaction' and the 'bowels of compassion' without which there could be no 'finer feelings'. Instead of thinking of the neo-cortex and the limbic system as belonging to higher and lower orders of mental organization it makes better sense to regard them as partners.

As things are, the axiom which holds that man is man by virtue of his mastery of verbal language is difficult to question, let alone reject. Thought that does not involve the use of words, we say, is practically inconceivable. 'Whereof one cannot speak, thereof one must be silent' is the sum of our educational philosophy. For the literate-minded, it comes naturally to ask, 'How do I know what I think until I see what I say': 'Je ne suis jamais plus moi-même que plume en main et dans le silence du cabinet', as Sainte-Beuve observed. This heavy emphasis on literacy, and the long and arduous training in reading, writing and number skills, have always been regarded as indispensable for any education worth the name, certainly long before industrialism made the acquisition of such skills universally necessary. As a consequence, the conviction that verbal language represents the supreme form of human expression remains deeply entrenched in our thinking; which explains, for example, why any signs of deterioration in reading standards in schools or of passive resistance to book learning occasion public disquiet. Despite broadening and modernization, the school curriculum still takes its values from a tradition of literary intellectual scholarship.

A point which tends to be overlooked in all this is the one noted by Vygotsky, i.e. that thought and speech have different generic roots, and that the two functions develop along different lines and independently of each other. All communication takes place at the interface between the tacit and the explicit. Speech is one way in which messages are encoded, but not the only one. There are other 'languages'. The artist's design, the musical composer's theme, like the speaker's words, well up from a formless underworld, only taking shape when expressed in their appropriate codes. Appropriate, because the message cannot be communicated in any other way. In each case, understanding the message depends upon the ability to decode second-signal symbols – words, notation, visual composition – but at the same time there are messages which are not so dependent. In daily life there are many occasions when we are forced to admit that words fail us, when a nod is as good as a wink. It is not simply that 'high' culture finds its expression in non-verbal codes – Beethoven's

Ninth, Michelangelo's *Moses*, Rembrandt's *Night Watch* and the rest – the fact is that most of the information which provides the stuff of learning, quite apart from its being non-verbal, comes to us through the immediacy of *signs*, not symbols. Normally, we call it 'experience' to distinguish it from the kind of understanding derived from the decoding of second-signal symbolic languages which we call 'knowledge'. This, arguably, is the kind of information which is secreted in the old brain and remains tacit there because, as MacLean puts it, 'it does not have the ability to put its feelings into words'.

It may well be that the processing of this kind of information is necessarily subsidiary to the decoding of verbal language. As one psycholinguist sees it,

> The meaning and significance of decoding ability is widened and deepened by its being referred today to a large and growing variety of codes and messages. Reading into and out of the new media implies new decoding abilities. The new man of the Seventies must be able to read not only printed messages but those of oral discourse and radio, and the audiovisual messages of cinema and television. However, inasmuch as all information as such is transformed into conceptual knowledge via language, book-literacy remains, and probably will remain, prominent in human culture, as a lasting asset to be eventually integrated with other forms of communication.[14]

The question is whether *all* information has to be mediated in this way, and whether conceptualizing is impossible without the mastery of verbal language. Most people, one imagines, would say yes. In that case what are we to make of the contention that thought and speech have different generic roots and how do we account for the non-verbal 'capacity for learning new approaches and solutions to problems on the basis of immediate experience'? Are there not songs without words, silent languages, *lacrimae rerum*, intimations, sympathies, intuitions, indications and a host of experiences every bit as significant as those we receive through the medium of verbal language?

Whatever form the dualism takes – Locke's 'sensation' and 'reflection', Polanyi's tacit knowing and explicit knowing, Freud's conscious and unconscious, verbal and non-verbal communication, or the physiological dualism of the neo-cortex and the limbic system – the dualism can only be resolved by invoking some principle of interplay. If the brain is the powerhouse of the mind – womb is a better metaphor – it is because vital ideas are instinct with a life of their own, begot, as babies are, in the intimacy of a flesh and blood discharge.

That the heart has reasons which the head knows nothing of is a hoary maxim, to be sure; and it may seem that the argument so far amounts to little more than a longwinded way of saying just that. As yet, neurophysiologists are still groping for an adequate explanation of how a generative theory of learning 'works' but already they have provided some valuable clues. 'Characteristically', says Bruner,

> an overt movement in an organism is triggered by a neural discharge to relevant effectors, but its coming is widely signalled to many other parts of the nervous system by a corollary discharge of 'feedforward'. Close analysis of motor activity indicates that there is considerable information condensed into the corollary discharge or feedforward to assure adequate and widespread information in the nervous system about action about to occur or in process. Corollary discharge contains specifications concerning the act's intended course. Correction can therefore be effected on the basis of a discrepancy between the act as executed and the act as originally specified – what the neurophysiologist Bernstein (1967) has referred to as an *Istwert* and a *Sollwert*.[15]

Back, then, to what-is and what-might-be! At the neural level, at the level of the newly born's encounter with the world and at the level of educational theory alike, we are left with the idea of play and interplay as aimed intention. This constant exchange, two-way flow of information, inner dialogue – call it what we will – is the *fons et origo* of mental growth as it is of physical. Just as the cambium (the layer of cells which separates the bark from the wood) regulates the flow of sap in a tree and generates its growth, so the apparent separation of act-as-specified from act-as-executed regulates the flow of information and generates 'the force that drives the green fuse through the flower' of the mind. Admittedly, the biological analogy cannot be pressed too closely:

It is not growing like a tree
In bulk, doth make men better be;

but it provides the necessary growth point for commonsense learning if only because, as Locke observed, 'this source every man had wholly in himself'. Only a generative theory can rightly claim to take its stand on the basis of our common humanity. Which is what D. H. Lawrence had in mind when he said that 'Me alive ends at my finger tips'.

But is not this generative theory another name for the one we are accustomed to refer to as child-centred? In a sense, yes: the difference is, first, that its rationale is more realistic than romantic; second, that it applies to learning in all its forms and throughout the life cycle, not just to its institutionalized forms and in early youth. That the trend is towards a generative theory and practice cannot be doubted. Between them, three contending metaphors have guided educational thought in the modern era. Their typology, as represented by Professor Philip Taylor in Table II, is only too familiar to students and teachers. Until fairly recent times, whenever a controversial issue was raised, say, streaming versus non-streaming, supporters of the teacher- and subject-centred faction usually contrived to have the better of the argument. As metaphors went, the 'lump of soft wax' was generally preferred to the 'seed in the garden', while any suggestion that 'The child is the discoverer of his own world' tended to be dismissed as unconvincing and less than helpful.

TABLE II TYPOLOGY OF EDUCATIONAL METAPHORS[16]

Category	Indicators	Advocate	Epistemological basis
Child-centred	growth, harmony unfolding,	Plato, Augustine Rousseau	Insight
	discovery assimilation, readiness	Pestalozzi Freud	Naturalism
Knowledge-centred	store, foundation, stock, bricks, structure	Descartes, Wm. James, Dewey Bruner	Rationalism Pragmatism
Teacher-centred	guiding, shaping moulding, directing, imparting	Locke Herbart	Empiricism

In an attempt to apply the quantitative methods of educational research to trends in educational theory, Professor Taylor analysed four official publications dealing with primary schools in England: *The Handbook of Suggestions for Teachers* (1905), the Hadow Report on *The Primary School* (1931), *The Handbook of Suggestions for Teachers* (1944 edition), and the Plowden Report, *Children and their Primary Schools* (1968). The results, summarized in Table III and Fig. 6 bear out his conclusion:

> There has been a general decline in the favourable employment of teacher- and knowledge-centred metaphors, and a corresponding increase in favourable child-centred metaphors. These trends are entirely supported by the unfavourable use of the different metaphors. The child-centred metaphor today stands as high and as much in favour as did the teacher-centred metaphor at the turn of the century.[17]

TABLE III TRENDS IN TYPES OF METAPHOR (%)

		1905	1931	1944	1968
Child-centred	Fav.	5.0	32.0	51.0	54.0
	Unf.	10.0	3.5	0.0	0.0
Knowledge-centred	Fav.	30.0	39.0	3.5	3.5
	Unf.	0.0	14.0	28.0	17.5
Teacher-centred	Fav.	55.0	11.5	17.5	7.0
	Unf.	0.0	0.0	0.0	17.5
		100.0	100.0	100.0	100.0

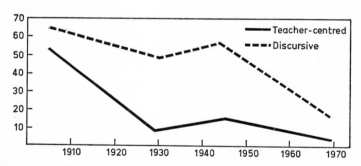

Fig. 6 Distribution of teacher-centred (favourable) and discursive metaphors in four official publications

It would be jumping to conclusions to infer that this shift in the centre of educational theory and practice is other than local and partial: after all, it refers only to developments which have occurred at the primary stage. A similar investigation carried out at the secondary stage would almost certainly reveal considerable resistance to the trend in favour of a child-centred approach. For that matter, there is no guarantee that recent trends in the primary school will not be reversed – there are people in high places who would be only too glad to see that happen! Any doubts on this score can be set aside, however, by recalling that when it comes to the tertiary stage independent study has always been regarded as the beau idéal. For 'child-centred' read 'learner-centred' and the case for a generative theory is as near to being proved as it needs to be or is ever likely to be.

Anyone who asks what the practical applications and implications of such a theory are to be has only to look around him. Current developments in fields as diverse as voluntary nursery playgroups, integrated day curricula in primary schools, community service projects and the numberless non-formal common interest groups which are springing up outside – or alongside – the statutory education system strongly suggest that the practice is well in advance of the theory. The shape of things to come is already discernible.

As yet, the underlying principles of the theory can only be stated in the broadest terms:

1 Any policy resulting from a theory of education as 'enablement' must be to give people access to resources and the tools of learning and wherever possible to leave them to get on with the job. In an age of technology these resources and tools are readily available and can be made more freely accessible to all than they are at present. The Open University in Britain and the Deutsches Institut für Fernstudien in West Germany provide two examples of support systems which afford greater opportunities for independent study and which, to some extent, allow of freedom to study where, when and how the individual finds it most convenient. With more sophisticated multimedia systems on the way there is nothing to prevent their use being extended downwards into the secondary school age groups. Not only are they becoming economically viable, but provision can be made for the idiosyncrasies of different cognitive styles and for the control of learning strategies by the learner – something which has never been, and never can be, possible in the lockstep procedures of the conventional classroom or lecture theatre. This, presumably, is what Ivan Illich has in mind when he writes:

Our analysis of schooling suggests the shape of a deschooled society. This renewed society would rely on the autonomous and self-adjusting use of components and tools. It would encourage trust in personal experience and the rise of dispersed associations in which decisions were made by those directly affected, and in which common purpose frequently emerges only in the very instance of its achievement. Access to information and tools must be random if new connections are to be discovered. . . . The only alternative to the present educational system is a return of each man's present to him and to the members of the informal group emerging around him. This is admittedly a surprising proposition but without surprise there is no hope.[18]

2 A generative theory credits the learner, be he infant or adult, with an inborn capacity for decision-making and problem-solving. As a statement of principle, obviously, this needs to be qualified. No one is so foolish as to deny that the very young are in need of care, protection, guidance and a measure of formal instruction. 'Give them the tools' is a poor prescription for the acquisition of most skills! That some prompting and priming is necessary – taking the horse to the water, so to speak – cannot be denied: all that the principle asserts is that a pedagogy which puts the teacher in charge of the learning situation has always been ineffective and must now be reckoned largely unnecessary. The emphasis on things-shown-and-done-to-the-children has been overdone. The outcome is an over-schooled society. It has been said with some justification that if the same methods which are used in teaching children to read and write were to be employed in teaching them to speak the world would be full of dumb people and stutterers. As it is, most of us learn to become what we are more in spite of formal instruction than because of it.

3 A generative theory assumes the existence of latent capabilities – 'talents' – which formal schooling too often fails to foster if it does not actually suppress them. The recent interest shown in creativity may be seen as a tentative breakthrough in this direction – though the research findings indicate that the divergent pupil is more than likely to find himself at a disadvantage in the normal classroom setting. The recognition of 'intelligence of another kind' not only enhances prospects for equal chances of success, but, more important, serves to promote that permanent taste for learning which formal schooling too often discourages.

4 A practice based on a generative theory would remove the age-old distinction between *labor* and *opus*. It would open the way for a society in which work is play and play is life.

5 A generative theory would also remove the distinction between those forms of knowledge whose validity is sanctioned by the academic community and those which at present receive neither recognition nor reward because they do not fall within the frames and classifications of school-bound learning. This is not to say that pushpin is as good as poetry. Washing an elephant may not be in the same category intellectually as solving quadratic equations, but as a learning experience it has its place. If it is the case that the impact of non-verbal media is increasingly affecting the outlook of the young, some weakening of the all-out claims on behalf of literacy and numeracy has to be bargained for. Under the existing arrangements, theirs alone are the values which determine success or failure. Inevitably, a system which gives pride of place to 'cultivated' and 'uncommonsense' learning is a system in which many are called but few are chosen. Many of the young are thereby condemned to lead a marginal existence, outsiders looking out at life through the classroom windows. Raring to go, frustrated, at a loose end, they seek their satisfactions anywhere except in school.

Not entirely without success, it seems. If Frank Musgrove's investigation in the Manchester area are anything to go by,

> The counter-culture is the most significant contemporary experiment in lifelong learning. It is not 'youth culture', except on a very generous definition of youth. . . . It is impossible to put a tidy structure on the behaviour and beliefs which characterize the counter-culture, but its adherents are almost certainly low on what Adam Curle calls 'belonging-identity' and correspondingly high on 'awareness-identity'. They have a weak sense of groups and grids; they seek the dissolution of traditional social, intellectual and perceptual boundaries. They embrace ecstasy, madness, chaos and disorder. They reject rationality for mystery, calculation for spontaneity, scepticism for awe. In a world which apparently 'needs' Apollonians systematically fashioned in the *Grandes Écoles*, Dionysus is the child of tomorrow.[19]

As a shorthand account of current trends this is scarcely reassuring, the kind of futuristic nightmare which causes eyebrows to be raised in common rooms and snorts of disgust from university dons. (A. L.

Rowse, for one, is on record as saying that 'Ordinary human beings are incapable of behaving without direction'.) A recipe for anarchy, say the defenders of the established order.

On the face of it, the generation gap seems unbridgeable with the middle-aged and the old upholding the conventional wisdom on one side and its assailants crying, 'Garbage!' on the other. Whatever it turns out to be, the emergent answer to the question, 'What knowledge is of most worth?', is as unlikely to meet with the approval of the elders of the tribe as Herbert Spencer's was in the middle of the nineteenth century – and for the same reasons. And for the same reasons its ascendancy has to be anticipated. Musgrove, certainly, is not alone in discerning the elements of an entirely new curriculum. In the 'cognitive domain' he notes the growing interest displayed by young people below the age of thirty-five in biological-physiological knowledge (with special reference to foodstuffs, additives, drugs, etc.), in environmental knowledge (ecology, pollution), in psychology, in political philosophy (mainly Leftist), in Eastern mysticism, comparative religion, anthropology and even astrology. In the 'affective domain' there is a motley array of activities which includes, among others, beadwork, leatherwork, poetry, chanting, music contemplation, tactile communication (!), body movement and postures. 'And the values it promotes,' adds Musgrove, 'are compassion, sincerity, courage, sharing, self-denial, frugality, joy and spontaneity, and tolerance of dirt. At its heart is an acceptance of disorder, shifting and uncertain boundaries.'[20]

Values, it may be thought, which are conspicuously absent from the *grandes écoles*. Head-shrinking or mind-expanding: which is it to be? If it comes to a choice, only a generative theory can help to compose our difficulties.

6 A generative theory would rationalize the deployment of resources for learning. In practice it would operate as an open system through informal networks and voluntary agencies rather than through the closed-shop institutions of the statutory system, whose legitimacy would to some extent be curtailed as a consequence. Under its auspices, the provision of alternative forms of education, currently exemplified in such breakaway movements as 'free schools' and 'schools without walls', would cease to be looked upon as abnormal and would be extended. If we are prepared to accept the evidence which indicates that formal schooling plays a relatively unimportant part in the young person's upbringing, not to mention

the evidence of steady escalation of costs, the inference is inescapable. 7 A generative theory supplies the dynamic for education as a continuous process in which all the members of a society are engaged at all times and in all places. In doing so, it avoids the charge levelled by cultural anthropologists and other critics against the futility of social reforms based on school reform alone.

So outlined, the theory cannot but be sketchy. While it does not proclaim, as Helvétius did, that, 'L'éducation peut tout', it agrees with Olivier Giscard d'Estaing that, 'Tout est éducation'.[21] To that extent at least it envisages the advent of a learning society (as adumbrated by Faure and Husén) in which responsible action (as advocated by Coleman, Etzioni *et al.*) and a more convivial way of life (as understood by Polanyi as well as Illich) are given freer rein.

9 The two cultures and the information revolution

Revolutions which change the course of history – *bloody* revolutions – tend to be nasty, brutish and short: it is only when they cease to be red in tooth and claw and become long drawn out affairs that we can safely confine them within quotation marks. Ever since the publication of that minor classic *The Silent Social Revolution* the literature of education has been replete with 'revolutions'. With so many to choose from, is there any point in adding to this doubtful progeny? The cry of 'wolf' has been heard so often before that few are disposed to heed its warning.

In *The Structure of Scientific Revolutions* Thomas Kuhn argued that developments in any branch of science are not linear, i.e. not a steady, uninterrupted progression from absolute ignorance to final truth, but characterized instead by a succession of stages, some of which are later seen to have been false starts and blind alleys.[1] Stable periods of what he called 'normal science' are punctuated in turn by periods of stagnation ('shoddy science'), by controversy ('crisis') and eventually by a breakthrough ('revolutionary science') in which old, established theories are overthrown and abandoned in favour of entirely new ones. Among the historical examples he quotes are the transition from a geocentric to a heliocentric theory in astronomy –

the 'Copernican Revolution' – the phlogiston controversy and the discovery of the structure of NDA. There are obvious analogies, if not exact parallels, in the field of fine art where styles of painting, sculpture and architecture answering to the canons of good taste are from time to time eclipsed by quite different styles.

Each school of thought, Kuhn suggested, is associated with a particular paradigm which determines the ambit of its theorizing and its philosophical world view. The paradigm prescribes the problems for investigation, the research methods and their standards of reliability and validity for members of the academic community who embrace it. Studies which fall outside the limits defined by the paradigm are looked upon as suspect or, at best, as peripheral. Until a major breakthrough occurs, innovations in science are treated as unscientific just as those of the early Impressionists who were driven to exhibit their works in the Salon des Refusés were held to be inartistic. Disagreement between rival schools of thought is symptomatic of a 'crisis', the birth pangs of a new paradigm and a new orthodoxy.

In deliberately aping the title of Snow's famous Rede Lecture on *The Two Cultures and the Scientific Revolution* the purpose is not to revive a controversy which generated more heat than light in academic circles and which frankly deserved no better than the decent burial it has since been given, but to draw attention to an altogether more fundamental division in contemporary life and learning than the one that marks the hazy boundaries between 'arts' and 'sciences'. The 'information revolution' referred to in the title represents the latest phase in the process of cultural change which began with the onset of industrialism. It should not be regarded either as a fancy name for the 'knowledge explosion' – a phenomenon which is only too familiar – or as a technical term to denote developments in information and communication theory, cybernetics and all that. What is at issue is not the staggering amount and variety of information made available by modern technologies – radio, film, TV, recordings, data processing, computers, satellites and the rest – but the dramatic change in its *quality*. That the change goes largely undetected is not surprising in view of our ignorance of the laws of the media to which we are daily exposed: after all, the first industrial revolution took place more or less unnoticed by the governments of the day although its disruption of the *status quo* was plainly visible in the restructuring of the new urban society – much more visible, certainly, than the subtle psychic effects with which we are concerned.

For the moment, any attempted analysis of the reasons for the change in the quality of information and its effects on our ideas about learning and on quality of life itself must be deferred. First it is necessary to describe the change. In the first place it goes without saying that a great deal of the information now being disseminated is essentially non-verbal. In the second, it makes its impact through immediate signals – images and sounds – and to that extent bypasses the decoding skills which are necessary for the acquisition of literacy and numeracy. It is the difference between following instructions step by step from a manual and knowing what to do instanter from watching a set of traffic lights. Third, and most important, this information has an appeal which somehow transcends linguistic, intellectual and ideological barriers to interpersonal communication. This universality of appeal can be illustrated in homely ways without mystifying it with phoney talk about the 'global village'. Thus, the learned professor and his six year old son laugh equally heartily while watching a programme like *The Goodies*, say, something they can hardly be said to do quite so unaffectedly when putting their heads together to read even the best of children's books. Thus, too, young people behind the Iron Curtain respond uninhibitedly to the same popular songs and dance rhythms as their opposite numbers in the West, although in other respects they are poles apart; and if this illustration is disliked, how about the fact that the latest No. 1 in the charts is likely to be as well received in the snootiest discothèque as it is in the slummiest. As information goes, we may not think much of the intellectual content of a pop recording, but at least its ability to cut across social class differences has to be acknowledged. Even a Solzhenitsyn cannot reach so wide an audience: for better or worse, a Bob Dylan can!

Without jumping to conclusions and inferring that what is in store for us is a changeover to a post-literate culture, a psychedelic nightmare if ever there was one, it is as well to bear in mind the fact that the 'great divide' is not the one between arts and sciences but between those learners who are perfectly satisfied to find self-fulfilment through the educational services provided for them and those who either reject, or feel rejected by, these services. The roots of this division lie deeper than the ones usually adduced, namely social class influences. In a schooled society there are satisfied and dissatisfied customers. Whether the former or the latter are in a majority is immaterial: the significant thing is that both meet on the common ground of information which falls outside the scope of formal learning.

EDUCATION AND THE QUALITY OF LIFE

Yet the conviction that education is the indispensable means of achieving the good life goes back to the age of Pericles and beyond. It is a conviction which may be queried, but never seriously contested. Again, the knowledge that standards of living have risen steadily ever since mass schooling was first introduced in modern industrial societies admits of no dispute. Why, then, the furtive sense of disillusion which apparently goes with affluence and which nowadays increasingly finds its expression in intellectual circles – though rarely elsewhere – in talk of an imagined threat to the 'quality of life'? That education has not succeeded in bringing about the greatest happiness of the greatest number is evident enough, but the fact that most people would agree with T. S. Eliot that it is a fallacy to suppose that education makes people happy is no reason for agreeing with him that it is also a fallacy to suppose that education is what everybody wants. As a goal-seeking creature, the human learner's desire to fulfil himself has to be assumed. Learning to be *what*? is the crucial question which nags those who are otherwise satisfied with formal schooling as well as those who are not. To be the proud possessor of two cars, a colour television and all the trimmings of material success – is this really all there is to it?

Rather than engage in discussions which can all too easily be made to circle around a philosophical non-problem, it seems advisable to begin with two self-evidently true propositions: (1) questions about the quality of life necessarily involve a value judgement; (2) questions concerning the nature of human life are basically metaphysical. It follows that neither type of question can be settled by empirical evidence alone. This is not to say that such questions are not amenable to scientific investigation, simply that any evidence obtained in this way cannot provide the kind of answers that are needed.

Now, almost the only definition of education on which universal agreement can be expected is that it is a process of bringing about changes in human beings. As regards the nature of *homo sapiens*, however, there is a wide spectrum of philosophic theories (mechanistic, organismic, intellectual and spiritual) which in turn give rise to various psychological and pedagogical theories (deterministic, behaviouristic, biological-developmental, rational-humanistic and religious), each of which offers its own explanations as to how changes in human beings can be, and are, brought about. Without necessarily implying that all the others are essentially reductivist, it is fair to point out that only the spiritual-religious approach to the problem of the quality of life insists upon its sacred character and seeks its criteria in other than purely natural causes.

In the modern era, and more particularly since the rise of the schooled society, there has undoubtedly been a marked decline in religious belief and a corresponding trend in favour of theories based on the kind of prediction and control which has proved serviceable in the natural sciences, in industry and technology. Its origins are epitomized in the chapter heading of *The Great Didactic*: 'If a man is to be produced it is necessary that he be formed by education' – the same principle that was endorsed and reinforced in the sociology of Durkheim: 'The object of education is to superimpose on the individual and asocial being that we are at birth an entirely new being. It must bring us to overcome our initial nature: it is on this condition that the child will become a man.' In short, man was to be man-made.

On this reckoning, as we have seen, the identification of education with formal schooling came to be, if not legitimized, at least taken for granted. As a side effect, educational research was strongly influenced from the start by E. L. Thorndike's axiom, 'Whatever is exists in some amount.' Techniques of assessment modelled on those which had produced spectacular advances in the physical sciences stressed the need for rigorous experimental design and statistical analysis of data. Increasing sophistication in the use of tests of various types fostered the conviction that ultimately any distinction between quality and quantity could be broken down, in other words that it involved only a difference of degree, not one of kind. According to this view, the same accuracy of measurement which made prediction and control possible in the laboratory was applicable to the conduct of human affairs. Quality checks, consequently, have come to be accepted as being as much a part of the educational as they are of the industrial scene.

It is no part of the argument to deny that techniques of educational assessment have their uses and their place: certainly, they are vastly

more refined and searching than they were, say, thirty years ago
when the so-called IQ test was administered more or less indis-
criminately as an all-purpose dipstick which could reliably assess an
individual's worth. What *is* being asserted is that any approach to the
problem of the quality of life must take the form of a critical
appraisal, not of a measurement, for the question we are concerned
with is one of criteria, not of any norms that can be scaled.

Before deciding what these criteria are it is helpful to take a look at
some historical examples of centres of excellence in which human
genius has flourished and see whether they have anything in
common. The Athenian city-state has already been put forward as
one prototype of an educative society. The courts of the Medici family
during the heyday of the Florentine Renaissance might well be taken
as another example. A third, nearer home, might be William of
Wykeham's twin foundations of Winchester College and New College, Oxford. Granted these are not the examples which everyone
would choose, but for the immediate purpose they will serve as well
as any. Belonging as they do to different phases of European civilization, all three exhibit the characteristic features of an aristocracy –
small, enclosed communities, educative in the sense that merely to
belong to them conferred a privilege and a sense of well-being which
brought out the best in their members. Quite apart from the fact that
the upbringing of the *ephebos*, the young Michelangelo and the
chorister-scholar took place in surroundings which reflected the best
that had been thought and said and done in their world, with the
result that their influence was assimilated unconsciously, there
was the self-enhancing awareness that they were heirs to good
fortune.

Why so? One short answer might be that their learning environment brought out the best in them because it was free, active and
convivial; which suggests that where one or other of these three
conditions is not observed the effect is disabling and that where none
of them is granted the effect is to bring out the worst in the learner.
This, arguably, is precisely what is happening in many classrooms.
Far from conferring any sense of privilege or of glorious opportunities for exploits and personal service, compulsory attendance
virtually rules these out, with the result that in the eyes of some
pupils at least schooling seems to be conducted in a bleak atmosphere. Learning itself is degraded to a joyless, loveless exercise.
Recognizing this, the authorities have sought to counter it by means

of extracurricular activities, games, social functions and other morale boosters, all of which have helped to promote a more closely knit community life within the school organization and a friendlier, more relaxed pupil-teacher relationship.

But when all is said and done, if one asks what it feels like to be *in statu pupillari* the only honest answer must be that more often than not it is anything but free, active or convivial.

CONVIVIALITY AND THE ACTIVE LIFE

To be sure, the idea-ideal of conviviality has been at the heart of educational thought since the Socratic dialogues of Plato and the epistles of St Paul. Throughout the chequered history of education, theorists have never failed to pay lip service to the belief that learning should be pleasant and that education is nothing if not a social process. In modern times this quasi-religious belief in the need for shared experience was the mainspring for Dewey's 'progressive' education. Latterly it has been revived and popularized by Ivan Illich, but for a more sober exposition of the rationale of conviviality the one offered by Michael Polanyi is probably to be preferred.

To begin with, says Polanyi, all shared experience is essentially tacit. The fellow feeling which enables society to cohere rests on attitudes, values and beliefs that are formed below the level of conscious thought, as unaware of their own existence as breathing or digestion are. This invisible network of mutual interaction is the dynamic infrastructure from which the intellectual passions are launched on their various courses. Normally, it becomes explicit in the first instance through the medium of speech, but conversation is by no means the only way in which it can be communicated: as he points out, companionship among men and women, children too, for that matter, is often best enjoyed in silence.

At the primordial level, as when the infant learns its mother tongue, pure conviviality is the common experience of human beings and animals alike. People pack bingo halls just as partridge coveys huddle together for the sake of warmth and security. But this low level of shared experience is sheeplike unless it leads to participation in joint activities of a more purposeful nature. Polanyi distinguishes four 'coefficients' of societal organization: (1) sharing of convictions; (2) fellowship; (3) co-operation; and (4) the exercise of authority. Without the first two, co-operation of any kind would be impossible.

Such co-operation is usually incidental to a purpose jointly aimed at, but it becomes purely convivial in the joint performance of a ritual. By fully participating in a ritual, the members of a group affirm the community of their existence, and at the same time identify the life of their group with that of antecedent groups from which the ritual has descended to them. Every ritual act of a group is to this extent a reconciliation within the group and a re-establishment of continuity with its own history as a group. It affirms the convivial existence of the group as transcending the individual, both in the present and through times past.[2]

According to this, such ceremonial occasions as graduation, prize-givings, acts of corporate worship – even schooling itself – serve a necessary sentimental function and it is only to members of the out-group that they appear to be a meaningless charade. Before denouncing the forces of inertia in the education system, therefore, it may as well be conceded that they are the source of its greatest strength. If shared experience and the pursuit of common interests are to enjoy a continued existence it can only be through the establishment of permanent institutions.

In the last resort, thinks Polanyi, co-operation must rely on the authority exercised by a handful of acknowledged experts. In science, for example, no single individual is competent to judge at first hand more than a hundredth of the total output of research and it is only because the authorities in particular branches of science share common standards and tests for truth that those who are left to make second-hand judgements are able to do so with any assurance that they are not being deceived. Although the authority vested in the natural sciences is not so easily achieved in politics, religion or philosophy, there is, he believes, a measure of consensus which accords recognition and merit to the intellectual leaders in any society – statesmen, divines, authors, composers, etc. Authoritative institutions, therefore, provide the indispensable framework for a free society. Just as artistic genius flourished under the patronage and protection of a Maecenas or a Lorenzo de' Medici, so Everyman can only learn to become wholly and truly himself by owning allegiance to the traditional mores.

Can we face the fact that, no matter how liberal a free society may be, it is also profoundly conservative?

For this is the fact. The recognition granted in a free society to the independent growth of science, art and morality, involves a dedication of society to the fostering of a specific tradition of thought, transmitted and cultivated by a particular group of authoritative specialists, perpetuating themselves by cooption. To uphold the independence of thought implemented by such a society is to subscribe to a kind of orthodoxy which, though it specifies no fixed article of faith, is virtually unassailable within the limits imposed on the process of innovation by the cultural leadership of a free society. . . . Must this institutional framework be accepted as the civic home of a free society? Is it true that the absolute right of moral self-determination, on which political liberty was founded, can be upheld only by refraining from any radical action towards the establishment of justice and brotherhood? That, indeed, unless we agree that within our lifetime we must no more than loosen the ties of a free society, however iniquitous they may be, we shall inevitably precipitate men into abject servitude?

For my part, I would say: Yes.[3]

For their part, activists would say no. To their way of thinking, to accept freedom on these conditions is to take things lying down. In a throwaway culture in which nothing remains unchanged for very long, respect for the permanence of institutions is not so forthcoming. Besides, to submit to the rulings of a cultural leadership in a society which is characterized by mutual distrust is to condone a state of affairs which is itself best described as abject servitude. On these terms, 'freedom' and 'conviviality' are reduced to a mockery: they deny the individual's right to act responsibly.

If distrust and disillusion are rife at all levels in contemporary society it is because its established institutions – political and religious as well as educational – are perceived as inauthentic: their appearance of give-and-take masks a genuine 'take' and a non-existent, or at best a token, 'give'. This, at any rate, is Etzioni's thesis in *The Active Society*: 'A relationship, institution, or society is inauthentic if it provides the appearance of responsiveness while the underlying condition is alienating.'[4]

Inauthentic institutions invariably resort to manipulative devices in order to beguile and assuage those who come under their influence; for example, TV commercials and advertising generally, or compulsory schooling. The subtler these devices are the more effective they become, so that in the end large-scale organized insincerity becomes the rule. In advertising the hidden lie, in education the hidden curriculum, is glossed over and tricked out so attractively that eventually the pseudo shades off imperceptibly into an alternative for the genuine article. It becomes next to impossible for the victims – there is no other word for them – to tell margarine from best butter. In this way, inauthentic institutions foster inauthentic personalities. The latter suffer from a schizophrenic frame of mind because of the inescapable demands of role-playing. On the one hand, they have to preserve the surface appearance of a community life which is 'free' and 'democratic', on the other to recognize in private that the underlying realities of that life are subservient and bureaucratic. Thanks to this, inauthentic institutions never succeed in mobilizing all the energies and aspirations of their members – they are either bottled up or allowed to run to waste.

Inauthenticity is one aspect of alienation, a term which suffers from being bandied about far too loosely in the literature of dissent. As defined by Etzioni,

> Alienation . . . is not only a feeling of resentment and disaffection but also an expression of the objective conditions which subject a person to forces beyond his understanding and control. Hence, even if a person is only vaguely aware of his own deprivation, dependency and manipulation, he is still alienated so long as he is unable to participate authentically in the processes that shape his social being. Alienation, thus, has structural bases and psychological consequences . . . the roots of alienation are not in interpersonal relations and intrapsychic processes but in the societal and political structure.[5]

Ultimately, then, it is not a question of whether this or that institution is inauthentic: it is a question of the quality of life in society as a whole. That there is something rotten in the state of an advanced industrial society, and that it is in some way connected with historical developments in which man's relation to nature has increasingly been determined by science and technology, is a proposition which few would now care to refute. The very thought that these developments may be irreversible and that their connection with the 'something rotten' refuses to be pinned down only adds to the individual's sense of baffled impotence. What irks him most is not the fact that he cannot do as he pleases but the realization that he is constantly prevented from doing things which could be done and need to be done. It is the admission that certain questions must never be asked, certain innovations never entertained – because the show must go on even though everyone knows that it is a sham performance. 'Toe the line' is the instruction given to those who are admitted to the grace and favour of inauthentic institutions (as happens, of course, in every in-group which has its own agreed rules of membership and its honoured rituals). The trouble is that in a highly complex society common interest groups – trade unions, business corporations, the academic community among others – tend to develop into large-scale, impersonal associations, each of which erects barriers to protect itself from outsiders. In this situation, the individual inhabits a world run by faceless men and full of locked doors and 'Keep out' notices. In this way, C. H. Waddington observes, 'the present social intellectual system of the West actually does suppress the search for meaning.'[6]

The inhibiting of personal initiative in the education system affects those who are in charge of it quite as much as it does the pupils and students who are subjected to it. Most teachers, for example, are only too aware of the restraints imposed upon them, which accounts not only for their low morale but for their contempt for the glaring discrepancies between theory and practice. In theory, in England at least, they are *said* to be free to teach whatever they think necessary and, within reason, to do so as they see fit – one of those carefully cherished myths which is near to becoming a sick joke: in practice, they know, the reality is very different. Or consider the case of the Open University. From its inception, any prospects of genuine innovation have been checked by a contradiction that was written into the Royal Charter in 1969 which proclaimed on the one hand that the objective was 'to provide education of university and professional standards' while professing on the other 'to promote the educational well-being of the community generally'. This last objective, like electioneering promises which are made without any serious intention of their ever being kept, may be taken as a fair specimen of inauthenticity. To put it bluntly, so long as it calls itself a university, the new institution must abide by the same kind of regulations as govern its predecessors: it must be a degree-awarding body – or else!

Consider, again, the restraints placed upon educational research. It is confined almost exclusively to organized learning in schools, colleges and universities. Informal learning of the kind which takes place in the home, the peer group, the neighbourhood, in occupational settings, in public libraries, through the mass media, etc. is really none of its business, or only peripherally so. Almost without exception, those who engage in educational research are specialists in school-based learning. Together, they form a circumlocution society, conferring in a jargon of terminological exactitudes which is incomprehensible to anyone outside their magic circle, peppering their learned papers with back-up references to the work of fellow workers in their restricted field. These, says David Mitchell,

> are the people who have devoted their lives to education and have learned, in effect, that organizational structures must be maintained at all costs, as the saying is. To be sure, they will urge improvements and nominal changes will be introduced – team teaching, curriculum reform, non-grading, open plan, etc. – but the traditional system is so robust that the chances are that it will survive, at least temporarily, without undergoing any fundamental revision.[7]

Too harsh a stricture, it may be thought. Nevertheless, there is some excuse for suspecting that, for the most part, educational research is engaged in as a painstaking enterprise for its own sake, one which discourages any inclination to ask awkward questions or to think adventurously, simply because it *is* so painstaking. It is no accident that the recent demand for action research has come from outside its ranks.

If Etzioni is right, the grassroots growth now proliferating in the innumerable voluntary agencies and associations – community service projects, student action groups, task forces, tenants' associations, protest marches, women's lib and all the other 'movements' springing up all over the place – are to be seen as a reaction against a way of life that is suddenly felt to be stifling, empty and inept. Constraints which have long been accepted as necessary now tend to be seen as arbitrary restraints and rejected accordingly. It is as though ours is an age of *makers* – people in whom the urge to 'make sense' to 'make music' and 'to do something about it' is steadily growing stronger. So far as the mobilization of human aspirations is concerned, it may seem that we have a long way to go before the take-off point is reached and an active society (and hence a learning society) becomes a reality. Nevertheless, the signs are encouraging.

Historically, the process of cultural change which began with the first industrial revolution reached its second stage in the scientific-technological revolution and is now entering its third (final?) stage in the information revolution. Stage 1 saw the mechanization of work and the relegation of the masses to the role of machine-minders. It created cities and societies in the image of the machine. Like the towers of San Gimignano, its institutions were originally erected for defensive purposes. Inside these strongholds, the inmates were virtual prisoners with little or no chance of communicating with the outside world or with their fellows in other towers inside the city walls.

Stage 2, by comparison, sees the beginning of automative control of machines and the emancipation of the workers from the treadmill of mass production. One by one, the towers are crumbling and although the desire to maintain them for reasons of prestige remains strong, many of them begin to look like picturesque survivals. Inter-institutional, interdisciplinary, interpersonal and international barriers and boundaries are dissolving. Networks are 'in' and walls are 'out'. While it is easy to exaggerate the extent and the rate of these changes the emergence of a more open society in which freedom of access and lateral communication is coming to be the rule is plainly discernible. Resources for learning and other assets which make for the good life are less unequally distributed than they used to be – which is not to say that they are anywhere near to being as equally distributed as they might be. Above all, more people than ever before are sufficiently well informed to feel capable of managing their own affairs. It is fitting, therefore, that Etzioni's forecast should agree almost word for word with that of the Faure Commission in *Learning to Be*:

> The post-industrial world will be marked, in addition to the con-tinued increase in the potency of instruments available and an exponential growth of knowledge, by man's ability to control both. An active society, one which realises this potential, would differ from most modern societies in this key way: it would be a society in charge of itself rather than unstructured or restructured to suit the logic of instruments and the interplay of forces they generate.[8]

EDUCATION AS TRAINING: THE GREAT CONFIDENCE TRICK

But the fact that more people than ever before are sufficiently well informed to feel capable of managing their own affairs is no guarantee that they *are* capable. If it is true that formal education has not suc-ceeded in making people happier (and as we shall see there is evidence to show that in some cases it makes them positively discontented with their lot), it is no less true that increasing knowledge has brought no corresponding increase in human wisdom. If anything, the growth of demand for more and more educational services must be seen as conducive to a decline in the quality of life, *not* because the effect is to spread 'high' culture widely and thinly, *not* because it turns out, as J. S. Mill feared it would, to be 'a mere contrivance for moulding everyone to be like one another', but because the desire which prompts it is chimerical.

Since the point is a trifle obscure it can best be elucidated by examining the course of events in the USA. A similar course is observable in Britain and other European countries though in their case it has not as yet led to quite the same excesses. That it will sooner or later do so unless present expansionist policies are discontinued seems obvious enough. Common to all these policies is the assumption that education is the key to economic prosperity, that investment in 'human capital' yields handsome dividends. For governments, for individuals, and until quite recently for most economists, the conviction that education *pays* is so unshakeable that no amount of disproof is likely to dislodge it. Happiness, wisdom – these can be dispensed with; but to suggest that the time and effort spent on education do not necessarily bring a bonus in the form of hard cash is the unkindest cut of all. If *this* conviction is ill founded what else is there to believe in?

Not surprisingly, the 'investment in human capital' approach has always had a strong appeal in the USA. Much more so than other advanced industrial nations, the American belief that 'Education pays: stay in school' and that 'Everyone must go to college' has backed a massive expansion of higher education which now consumes roughly 3 per cent of the gross national product, very nearly the same proportion as that spent on the state schools system. Not only have the standards of academic qualifications of teachers been forced up, but the numbers of teachers increased by almost 50 per cent in a single decade (1950–60) – against a growth rate of only 15 per cent for the rest of the labour force. After analysing the statistical evidence, Professor Ivar Berg is driven to the conclusion that this mounting demand for education feeds to a great extent upon itself. As regards occupations other than teaching, which now accounts for three-quarters of all jobs for which a college degree is demanded, he finds that blue collar (textile) workers' productivity is inversely related to length of schooling and level of general education. The same is true of bank clerks (tellers): indeed, those with the worst 'performance on the job' records are the keen ones who are attending evening classes. Job satisfaction, apparently, declines as formal education increases.[9]

In a way, this is what might be expected. The fact that many jobs are dull and boring is no excuse for arguing that those who occupy them could do with less education than they have received. It is, however, a good reason for thinking that it is an error to suppose that the number of years of schooling gives any significant prognosis for occupational competence. To that extent, employers are deceiving themselves in calling for paper qualifications which are strictly unnecessary, and students are being duped into taking longer and stiffer courses of training in order to gain credentials which have little relevance to the work they will be doing. The danger is not simply that of producing more graduates than can be absorbed, real as the danger is: much more serious is the thought that, in the name of 'education', young adults are being blackmailed by a glorified protection racket. The spectacle of unemployable PhDs left high and dry on social security is only one aspect of the tragic consequences of over-schooling. It is true that cases of this sort rarely occur in the teaching profession, thanks to an alleged 'shortage' of entrants and need for smaller classes; nevertheless, Berg's findings and criticisms hold good here as they do for other occupations. They are borne out, moreover, by the International Educational Achievement investigations which lend no support to the belief that high qualifications assure high professional performance. All that is certain is that high qualifications raise the student's self-evaluation, which is good *per se,* though it may be the source of a divine discontent which eventually results in his quitting the classroom for a more lucrative appointment in administration or in teacher training itself. Adam Curle may be wrong in thinking that of all forms of education teacher training is probably the worst, but he is within his rights in insisting that it *is* training, not so narrow as to unfit students for anything but a career in the schools, but still narrow.

If individuals can be carried beyond the point of no return, committed during their formative years to this or that specialist expertise – expertise they will probably never utilize – when they might otherwise spend the time in pursuing interests of their own choice, where is this over-schooled society heading? Should the fact that the educational establishment is growing by leaps and bounds be regarded as a cause for congratulation or for dismay? Is the growth cancerous?

This speaks to the point that many young people seek to make when they protest about government contracts with universities and the irrelevance of contemporary education. They charge that education focuses on vocational placement in a society of buttondown personalities and grey-flannel mouths, competing to breathe the technicians' polluted air, to drive the engineers' beached whales on crowded cement ribbons that choke the planners' cities. Education mirrors a society, they argue, in which liberation is confused with 'upward mobility', and in which human relationships are confounded with the ritual behaviour of the polite middle class. One may conjure up an image of an educated community in which the inanities of the cocktail-party patter regularly pass for conversation, in which clam dip serves as social cement, in which work is a job and not labour . . . spiritual values are high-proof, neutral and pure grain, and suburban husbands are handymen with sex privileges.

These charges are not lightly dismissed as educable teachers realize and as most parents of teenagers are obliged to learn. It is the adult culture, especially its educated culture, the young argue that has most truly gone to pot.[10]

It is a telling indictment, not to be brushed aside by those of us who belong to an 'educated culture' because we cannot bring ourselves to admit that we have been taken in. If Berg's analysis of the situation fails to convince, any remaining doubts are likely to be removed by reading the Rand report *How Effective is Schooling?* This impressive document was prepared for the President's Commission on School Finance (March 1972) and involved sifting through thousands of educational research studies with a view to making policy recommendations in the light of the available knowledge about the effectiveness of schools. As a critical review of the research literature, the report was nothing if not exhaustive and its findings, unwelcome as they are, can only be described as devastating.

The commission organized the vast array of evidence with which it was confronted into five basic types of investigation which it classified as:

1 the input-output approach
2 the process approach

3 the organizational approach
4 the evaluation approach
5 the experiential approach.

In each case they looked at individual studies, examined the methods used and their internal validity, their consistency with other studies following the same approach, and discarded those which failed to meet the criteria of rigorous research. Finally, they correlated the results of all five approaches in order to find out if any general conclusions or policy implications could be drawn from this mass of evidence. While they had reservations about the limitations of each of the five approaches and the trustworthiness of their findings – as they noted, educational research is seriously deficient in its scope and focus and hence tends to be horribly inconclusive – the commission had no hesitation in pronouncing that the results 'provide little reason to be sanguine'.

1 As regards the input-output approach (i.e. studies of the resources available in schools) the conclusion seemed to be that resources are not consistently important but that background factors – learning outside the classroom – certainly are. There was nothing to indicate that massive increases or *decreases* in resources would make any significant difference to the effectiveness of schools.

2 As regards the process approach (i.e. studies of how resources are deployed) the conclusion seemed to be that teacher qualifications, methods, size of classes, etc., revealed no consistent effect on pupils' achievement.

3 As regards the organizational approach (i.e. studies of the effects of the school's structure, regulations and procedures), it was found that there was a positive correlation between system size and centralization: the bigger the bureaucracy the lesser the opportunities for innovation and adaptation.

4 As regards the evaluation approach (i.e. studies which are policy-orientated in the sense that they are concerned to find out what happens when reforms are introduced) the conclusion seemed to be that almost without exception none of the major projects had so far achieved any beneficial results. Attempts to compensate pupils from disadvantaged backgrounds – Head Start in the USA, EPAs in the UK – had shown some initial gains but these appeared quickly to fade unless continuously reinforced.

5 As regards the experiential approach (i.e. studies of what actually

happens to pupils in schools either by way of participant observation
or by 'straight' reporting) the conclusion was that schools are on the
whole authoritarian and make little allowance for individual differences. Their methods stress the rightness and wrongness of answers
to questions which are found to be ambiguous in the world outside
their walls. They inhibit the spirit of free inquiry and the zest for
creativity. They impose a set of social, cultural and ethical values,
which serve to create feelings of inadequacy among pupils who for
one reason or other are incapable of sharing them. 'Schools are mindless in that they fail, in any operationally useful way, to question
either the assumptions on which they operate or the relevance of their
approach to their pupils' needs.'

After every allowance had been made for the shortcomings, incon-
sistencies and general inconclusiveness of the research evidence
which was, after all, the best available and certainly not the kind
which informed academics can easily reject, the Rand Report felt
obliged to make a number of drastic recommendations for any future
policymaking. First and foremost, it was obviously necessary to
abandon the traditional practice of pouring more and more money
and more and more highly trained personnel into the school system
in the hope that the system would thereby become more effective.
Increasing expenditure and the award of top priority to such things
as raising teachers' qualifications, salary scales and conditions of
work and reducing the size of classes make relatively little difference
to educational outcomes. 'The best information that we have, regardless of the deficiencies we have noted, is that schools do not have a
tremendous impact on the achievement that does occur.' In short, if
the answer to the question, 'How effective is schooling?', is 'Not
very', it seems evident that the time has come when a significant
redirection of expenditure to agencies outside the school system can
be made without risking any serious deterioration in educational outcomes. In other words, if some of the money, time and effort now
being spent on formal schooling were to be siphoned off and used to
finance and encourage the growth of learning networks in the community the results could hardly be worse than those obtained so far.
Any significant improvement can only come through sweeping
changes in the organization and structure of the established system.[11]

On this last point, the report was adamant. Non-school factors are
more influential than school factors, so much so that they swamp the
effects of variations in formal educational practice. The logical

inference, therefore, is that the whole area of non-school learning deserves much more attention – and recognition – than it has received in the past.

THE INFORMATION REVOLUTION

In the current flux of opinion, it was said earlier, issue is joined between those who are satisfied with the equation of formal schooling with education and those who are not. Were it not for the open dissent now being expressed within the academic community it might be tempting to say that the clash is between that community – 'the pedagogical juggernaut' – and the non-academic world at large. Essentially, however, what is at stake is the predominance of literate-mindedness and the emergence of life styles in revolt against it.

Like all generalizations, this last statement is neither very meaningful nor helpful as it stands. By way of clarification, suppose that we take as our starting point one of the popular aphorisms of our time, 'The medium is the message'. As starting points go, many would say that this one is more offputting than promising, the kind of saying that has become so hackneyed as to be no better than an empty cliché – a bit of a joke, really, and a tiresome one at that. Its meaning, admittedly, remains enigmatic, none the less so when its author construes it as 'The user is the content', but at least it serves its purpose in reminding us that, of all the commandments in the educationist's credo, 'Thou shalt understand media' is by far the hardest to obey.

For McLuhan enthusiasts, of course, *The Gutenberg Galaxy* remains a classic work of reference, yielding insights into the subtle effects of one medium – print – on human modes of thought and perception. By comparison, *Understanding Media*, full of inspired hunches and *jeux d'esprit* as it is, chances its arm too often to be entirely convincing: not so much a mosaic as a display of pyrotechnics presented by a master of discontinuous prose. The wry puns which delight and offend simultaneously, the never-failing assurance of oracular utterance, the sudden switches of thought which either dazzle or leave the average reader in the dark – these and other mannerisms are apt to deter any willing suspension of disbelief. No doubt because of this, and because his later writings are so little known on this side of the Atlantic, the impression that McLuhan is a spent force, no longer worthy of serious consideration, has been gaining ground. Not so long ago his *obiter dicta* were headline news, picked up and parroted by students, journalists and trendy academics the world over. While the waning of a cult which thrived on obfuscation and cheap publicity is not to be regretted it would be wrong to conclude that it was a case of much ado about nothing. If its originator's reputation is temporarily in eclipse – the fate suffered by all nine days' wonders – the fact remains that he *is* an originator, a genius with a flair for starting hares which stay-at-home minds are too slow and too lazy to follow.

Latterly, McLuhan has modified and systematized his earlier, impressionistic attempts to formulate the 'laws of the media'. The ways in which the human learning situation is affected by exposure to old and new media can, he maintains, be observed and studied under four aspects: amplification, obsolescence, retrieval and reversal. Just what each of these terms implies may not be immediately apparent but may be summarized as follows:

1 All media amplify human faculties or attributes.
2 All media displace (or obsolesce) some faculty or function by extending the environment of services available to human beings.
3 All media retrieve older forms of service and communication.
4 All media when pushed to their limits tend to flip over into some opposite form.

So compressed, these general 'laws' are too cryptic to be readily intelligible, let alone capable of being implemented. Let us begin with the first one, whose concept of man as a tool-using creature is familiar enough. When Kohler's chimpanzees first hit upon the knack of using a stick in order to reach bananas outside their cage they were initiating, however dimly, the same process which has brought about the civilization of mankind. Every schoolboy knows that Mechanical Advantage is calculated by dividing the amount of the Load by the amount of Effort required to lift it. The notion of a medium as an extension of some bodily function is perfectly acceptable, as is the notion that the long-term effects of such extension are psychological as well as physiological. Advantageous mutation led to changes in the bone structure of the hands and the enlargement of the brain centres for fingertip control. The use of hand tools enabled the user to perform tasks which would otherwise have been impossible, literally beyond his reach: above all, they opened the way for other inventions

– skins for clothing, wheels for transport, eventually, of course, for alphabetic writing – and in so doing enlarged the learning environment and the mental horizons. In each case, however, the adoption of a new medium involves a certain loss of functions which have previously been relied upon, as happened, for example, when man's concentration on hand-and-eye skills brought about a lessened reliance on the sense of smell.

So far so good, then, as regards 'amplification' and 'obsolescence'. 'Retrieval' and 'reversal', on the other hand, are a good deal harder to grasp and seeing that a clear understanding of their implications for the 'information revolution' is vital – if only because the implications are that our ideas about what constitutes 'learning' are undergoing a sea-change – they call for further explanation.

Before going on, however, some reference has to be made to the distinction drawn by McLuhan between so-called 'hot' and 'cool' media. (The choice of adjectives was unfortunate, more calculated to bamboozle than to enlighten, but let them pass for the moment.) In general, 'hot' media are characterized as those which (1) amplify isolated senses or faculties; (2) displace or suppress most of the other senses or faculties; (3) retrieve the usage of some sense or faculty suppressed by a preceding medium; and (4) end by reversing into a 'cool' (i.e. less specialized) sensory mode. Against this, 'cool' media involve the use of diverse senses and functions and displace specialized sensory modes. On this reckoning, cold print is a 'hot' medium (all eyes!), as is sound broadcasting (all ears!), whereas film and television, appealing as they do to more than a single sense, may be rated as 'cool' ones.

The concepts of retrieval and reversal become clearer once it is recognized that all new media, and particularly 'hot' ones, tend to specialize in so far as they amplify one or other of the bodily functions; and that in greater or lesser degree they displace (obsolesce) functions which had previously been dominant under the influence of an older medium. In the process of amplifying one function and obsolescing others there typically occurs a return to modes of perception and action which have fallen into abeyance – in other words, a *retrieval* of an earlier media usage. When, however, the amplification of the overall media situation ceases to be specialized and becomes all-involving the effect is to bring about an entirely new outlook – a *reversal* of the total life situation.

Under the heading of ' Gadget lover: Narcissus as narcosis',

McLuhan summarizes his structural approach to the 'laws' of the media as follows:

1 Each amplification of human functions by translation into other matter is a kind of 'fission' that entails a chain reaction both in psyche and society.

2 Each fission of a human faculty or function absorbs much energy in the task of achieving a new equilibrium among the total components of the situation. The sudden drain of energy acts to numb overall awareness.

3 The retrieval of older functions with each innovation may occur as a result of altered echo or resonance. Each new extension of man as a new service environment presents itself subliminally as a narcissistic image of himself in the mirror of the new situation.

4 The well-adjusted user of any new service becomes a servo-mechanical robot of that service. (It is the role of art to liberate man from this servitude by 'le déréglement de tous les sens'.)[12]

As Eric McLuhan says, 'These statements are intended to be construed as tentative and not as final. By virtue of the nature of the subject, indeed, it is doubtful if any final statement is possible. For example, three different "sets" are obtained for the medium of Print if one considers it in the context of the sixteenth, eighteenth and twentieth centuries. The same is true of film before and after television, etc.'[13]

McLuhan himself affords as nice an illustration as any of the tension created by the action and counteraction of 'amplification' and 'obsolescence', 'retrieval' and 'reversal'. By training an academic and bookman, he has achieved notoriety as the spokesman and prophet of a post-literate, post-industrial society – a reversal of roles if ever there was one. At the same time he has revived (retrieved) the Renaissance belief that 'truth can be apprehended in images', a belief shared by all pre-Gutenberg thinkers and incidentally one which explains why even Shakespeare showed little interest in the publication of his plays. (Had it not been for the enterprise of his executors we should never have had the First Folio.)

Even if his stance appears to be that of a Mr Facing-Four-Ways, McLuhan cannot be accused of inconsistency. Thanks largely to him, in the case of the one medium – print – which has had a powerful influence on modes of thought, not least educational thought, during the last four centuries, it is now possible to begin to understand how the laws of the media operate. Print *amplified* the importance attached to the written word and visual-symbolic information, while simultaneously *obsolescing* the spoken word, oracy and interpersonal dialogue: simultaneously, too, it *retrieved* the privacy of individual learning while *reversing* into a collective experience in which the information communicated was the same for all. Under the impact of the new electronic media these long-term, gradual changes in modes of thought and perception have not only been speeded up, but the switch from the static display of information mediated by literacy to the dynamic multimedia learning situation in which we find ourselves today has induced a state akin to cultural shock.

There are, in effect, two cultures. On the one hand, there is the world of discourse which upholds the supremacy of verbal language and formal, institutionalized learning: on the other, an as yet unaccredited world of experience which derives its inspiration and satisfactions from the immediacy of non-verbal media and non-formal learning. Caught between these two worlds, the predicament of professors of education who are so disenchanted with the established system that they feel impelled to vacate their chairs and that of the drop-out who refuses to go along with school regulations – 'What a bloody way to grow up', as the boy from Marburton[14] put it – are strictly comparable. The interesting thing is that the defection from the ranks of the young and disadvantaged – the dissatisfied customers in the education system – is today spreading to the upper echelons of the academic community itself. It is symptomatic of a reversal of outlook as total and as far-reaching as that witnessed in the changeover from medieval to Renaissance man. To account for it solely in terms of media exposure would, of course, be simplistic. Still, the influence of television, with its all-at-onceness, its action replays, split-screen images, flickering mosaic and hypnosis of eyes and ears, provides as telling a clue as any to what is happening. Whether we think of it as turbulence in the nervous system or as disruption in the education system there is little doubt that a steady state in our life and affairs has somehow been altered – some would say thrown into disequilibrium – by the non-stop electronic bombardment to which we are now exposed; a disturbance in psyche and society, as McLuhan says. It is the contrast between the patient, slow decoding of messages in silent reading and the jolting charge of power-packed images and emotive soundtracks in a psychedelic floorshow. The contrast, and the effects of moving from a settled to an unsettling life style, can easily be exaggerated. They cannot be overlooked since they are the stigmata of a culture in transition.

It is no accident that addiction to transistors, muzak, television and all the other manifestations of electronic communication is much stronger among the ranks of non-academic youth than it is among those who see formal schooling as the royal road to social status and membership of a cultural élite. For the disadvantaged, the new media offer a welcome escape from a learning situation which does not speak to their condition and therefore leaves them cold. It makes little difference whether we ascribe this failure to respond to the fare provided for them in school to a sense of alienation, to social class factors, to the generation gap, to the secular trend towards earlier physical maturity or to innate dumb insolence – underlying all of these is a profound shift in the nature of information itself. This is why curriculum theorists like Holly are saying that the content of courses needs to be revolutionized, not merely reformed; why the Rand Report recommends cutting back on expenditure devoted to the maintenance of an ineffective school system; and why the main issues and problems in education are losing their pedagogical character and defining themselves more and more in terms of lifelong learning.

This shift reverses literate-minded traits of thought which have been uppermost since the invention of printing and returns us to the kind of experience in which the most heartfelt meanings – beyond the reach of words – are irradiated and stirred by a type of communication that is enactive and iconic rather than symbolic. What is communicated cannot be fitted into any of the frames and classifications of school-bound learning or the forms of knowledge at present recognized as 'educational'. It is the *lingua franca* of the marginal man.

It may be thought that the distinction drawn earlier between the immediacy of the new media and the second-signal symbolic codes to which we are accustomed in literacy and numeracy is a false one. St Augustine did not think so. In *De Magistro* he outlined a theory of communication which, for all its simplicity, has yet to be bettered. According to this, the intended message (*significabilia*) could be transmitted via the spoken word (sign) or at second hand by the written word (second-signal symbol). So long as information was in short supply, teachers and libraries provided the main resources for formal learning; and training in the decoding of verbal language was the main business of schools from the start. St Augustine, however, stressed that the message was never contained within the words themselves, spoken or written: they were merely the medium for an inner dialogue which enabled the learner to perceive eternal truths. Just as the eye was capable of seeing physical objects through the medium of light rays proceeding from the sun, so the human mind was capable of grasping metaphysical meanings through the medium of 'Divine Illumination'. (In passing, it may be noted that this theory finds its secular counterpart nowadays in the conversational models of learning systems developed by cyberneticists like Gordon Pask.) This capability was not entirely dependent upon the ability to decode verbal language and hence not a *sine qua non* for everyone. In a pre-literate culture there were sound reasons for believing that 'There are two ways leading to wisdom. One is the way of education, the other the way of Faith. Faith is for the many. Education is for the few.'

If, by 'education' we mean 'schooling', the same may be true in a post-literate culture. If the slogan 'Secondary education for all' no longer carries quite the same conviction that it did at the turn of the century, it is because it offers something that many pupils have no great desire for, on terms which they find increasingly irksome. For them, learning is not to be restricted within the walls of even the best-equipped classroom. It does not have to be worked for under the constant threat of sanctions or the fear of failure. Its values have little to do with those of the learned disciplines. Not primarily cognitive at all, such learning craves opportunities for moral self-determination and finds them, not at second hand – 'I hate books, they only teach us to talk about things we know nothing about', as Rousseau said – but in the free-for-all media of an age of technology.

Contemporary culture the world over appears to be divided: on the one hand there are those who abide by the values of an age-old, established order whose institutions are prestigious and secure; on the other, those who champion a way of life that often seems less than respectable because it is less than articulate. Are the former 'techno-logical idiots in terms of the new situation', as McLuhan thinks, and are the latter 'different animals'?

To speak of one culture as 'literate' and the other as 'post-literate' is not to say that we are faced with an either-or choice, nor to imply that the legitimacy of the first is in any way to be impugned. But at least those of us who are literate-minded owe it to ourselves to ask whether or not verbal language necessarily marks the final stage of human communication.

10 Beyond schooling: the search for a new paradigm

Whether or not the information revolution heralds the breakthrough which Kuhn saw as the necessary *coup de grâce* for 'shoddy science', the contemporary situation in education is clearly one of 'crisis'. A theory of people-processing which has prevailed for centuries and which restricts the most formative developments to the learner's school life is now being called in question. The practices derived from it bear little or no relation to the theory and are increasingly seen to be ineffective. If 'crisis' is thought to be too strong a word for the situation in which we find ourselves, we may as well acknowledge that there is scarcely a single issue in the educational field today that does not arouse fierce controversy. As Julia Evetts observes:

> The world of education presents the spectacle of a battlefield of warring parties, conflicting doctrines and alternative models. Not only does each conflicting faction have its own set of interests and purposes, but each has its own picture of the world in which the same objects are given quite different values or meanings. In such a situation, the possibilities of communication and agreement are minimal. In addition, a further obstacle to the achievement of any sort of consensus in education is the obstinacy of the various

partisans who refuse even to consider or take seriously the theories of their opponents, simply because they belong to another intellectual or political camp. This state of affairs is made even more complex by the fact that the educational world is far from free from the struggle for personal distinctions and power.[1]

The state of deadlock which exists between contending parties who are equally well informed but cannot compose their differences is aggravated by the curious unwillingness of research-minded educationists to face up to the mounting evidence that formal schooling is in many respects a waste of time and money. Some of that evidence has already been summarized and nothing would be easier than to go on adding to it. Comparative studies of teacher training in England, France and West Germany, for instance, show that 'there is no more glaring gap than the failure to equip the teaching profession for its altered contemporary functions'[2] – yet the only consensus which admits of no serious disagreement is that the school system must carry on as before, getting bigger and bigger as the years go by in spite of the likelihood of its getting worse and worse. By the end of the century it is estimated that we shall have 10 million boys and girls in our schools and half a million teachers. It is, of course, possible to query the figures in the numbers game played by the planners, but no one doubts that their projections are tolerably accurate. 'Wider still and wider' . . . the old imperialist refrain may ring a trifle hollow nowadays, but the melody lingers on in our psychology. As for considering, let alone taking seriously, any suggestion that the pedagogical juggernaut has become a mega-machine which needs to be slowed down here and now – or the even wilder suggestion that its gears ought to be thrown into reverse – the common attitude is to dismiss such ideas. Neither the authorities who are responsible for the smooth running of the education system, nor the hordes of employees whose livelihood depends upon servicing it, nor the mass of people who look to it to supply their needs, are inclined to regard favourably any move which may threaten the conventional wisdom.

The fact that the best available research evidence has so little impact on current practice is proof that it is distrusted. Among the reasons usually adduced for this distrust are (1) the uncritical adoption of models borrowed from the physical sciences; (2) the tendency of research to become an end in itself; and (3) a reliance on statistical techniques which, for all their superficial sophistication, are incapable of coping with the complexities of the human equation. A further and more fundamental reason, we have argued, is the unquestioning acceptance of a theory of learning which requires all educational knowledge to be transmitted and translated in verbal terms.

This *concordia discors*, conceivably, marks the breakdown of one stage in the evolution of educational theory – a stage which has existed long enough to be regarded as stable and therefore 'normal' – and the onset of a state of uncertainty. But a breakdown, supposing that there is one, is not the same as a breakthrough. The paradigm that will transform our outlook as totally as Copernicus transformed that of the flat-earthers or as the Fauves transformed that of the Académie française is still awaited. In the current ferment of ideas and opinions, what pointers to its possible formulation can leading forward thinkers give?

As a tailpiece to *Education and Schooling*, the following account of a project in which the author was personally involved may shed some light on that question. How far it goes towards providing a paradigm is, of course, another matter. Finding a theory, as Gilbert Ryle has remarked, means creating paths where none as yet exist; a chancy business at the best of times, but there is always the hope that the way ahead will lead to a clearer and more wholesome view of education than the one we have.

THE AGNELLI SYMPOSIUM

1 Prologue: 'such stuff as dreams are made on'

One night, half-awake, half-asleep in the small hours, I wondered what would happen if some of the most eminent figures in the world of education were to be brought together in a setting similar to that of Plato's *Symposium*. Like a child who finds a box of assorted toy soldiers at his bedside on Christmas morning, I found the game that followed instantly and totally absorbing. Supposing, for the sake of argument, that it *were* possible for them to sit down together, freed from every constraint, would any marriage of minds occur? For that matter what would they talk about? In what language? By the time I had dropped off again, the question of the topic which these world-renowned men would discuss had pretty well settled itself. The theme of the symposium, I had decided, was to be 'Lifelong learning in an age of technology'.

What followed is best construed as a fairy tale. Much of it reads like pure fiction – Cinderella and the magic ballroom all over again. Thanks to the intervention of a fairy godmother in the person of Signora Clerici de Marchi, the Fondazione Agnelli agreed to sponsor an international symposium on the theme of 'Lifelong learning in an age of technology'. It was agreed moreover that what was wanted was not just another conference, still less a think-tank, but a free interchange of views among some of the most seminal minds in the field of educational studies. The opening and closing sessions would be held in Turin, but to ensure an informal atmosphere for discussion the three intervening days would be spent in a mountain retreat at Entrèves close to the foot of Mont Blanc. Each of the participants was to be invited to present a paper outlining his personal viewpoint, all the papers being circulated well in advance of the meeting.

Even in fairy tales, three wishes is the usual quota allotted, but the largesse of the Fondazione Agnelli far outran my original hope of inviting a mere seven or eight guests. In the event, one or two had to cry off because of previous commitments, but the list of names of those who attended is enough to indicate that this was no ordinary gathering, and that it lived up to its stated intention of being both interdisciplinary and international. In alphabetical order, those present included:

1 Günther Dohmen, Director, Deutches Institut für Fernstudien, Tübingen
2 Olivier Giscard d'Estaing, Director-Founder, Institut Européen d'Administration des Affaires, Fontainebleau, and Deputé des Alpes-Maritimes in the French National Assembly
3 Giovanni Gozzer, Director, Centro Europeo dell'Educazione, Frascati
4 Michael Huberman, Co-Director, School of Psychology and Educational Sciences, Geneva
5 Ivan Illich, Centro Intercultural de Documentacion, Guernavaca
6 Walter James, Dean of Educational Studies, The Open University, Milton Keynes
7 Eric McLuhan (representing Marshall McLuhan), Center for Culture and Technology, Toronto.
8 David Mitchell, Professor of Educational Technology, Sir George Williams University, Montreal
9 Wolfgang Mitter, Director, Deutches Institut für Internationale Pädogogishe Forschung, Frankfurt am Main

10 Frank Musgrove, Sarah Fielden Professor of Education, Manchester
11 Gordon Pask, Director, System Research Ltd, Richmond, Surrey
12 myself
13 Bertrand Schwartz, Conseiller a l'Éducation Permanente, Ministère de l'Éducation Nationale, Paris.

In addition, papers were received from Torsten Husén, Dr R. H. Dave and Professor Mauro Laeng, all of whom had been helpful in the preliminary planning, but were unfortunately not able to join the company during the five days concerned (23–8 September 1973).

2 *Plenary session*

Ostensibly, the symposium had two objectives: (1) to decide whether the 'master concept' of lifelong education as adumbrated in the Faure Commission's report *Learning to Be* was merely rhetorical and, if not, to examine its practical implications; (2) to consider how far, if at all, modern technologies of communication provide the ways and means of realizing the idea-ideal of a 'learning society'.

'Learning to be what?' seemed to be one of the questions in need of further clarification. Another concerned the nature of learning itself. In view of the current information revolution, could learning any longer be confined within the pedagogical frames and classifications imposed upon it in the past? Had schooling assumed so exaggerated an importance that, for many, it had come to be thought of as one and the same as 'education'? Above all, bearing in mind the changes now taking place in the human life cycle in post-industrial societies – in particular the steady erosion of an age-old work ethic, greater leisure, rising expectations and aspirations – how was one to conceive of an all-encompassing theory and practice of education beginning at the moment of birth and ending nowhere short of the grave?

With these objectives in mind, where was one to begin? It had been agreed that there was to be no chairman, no leader, only a host. This being so, the discussions inevitably tended to be unstructured, with the result that at times the ensuing mêlée came near to being incoherent. Or was it because the questions posed admitted of no clearcut answers? Were we all engaged in doublespeak in using words like 'education', 'schooling' or even 'learning' and to that extent fated to be at cross-purposes?

At any rate, from the moment the travel-weary guests assembled in the marbled foyer of the Hotel Excelsior Principi di Piemonte a simmer of disputation began. Scarcely were the introductions over than we fell to haggling about the procedures to be adopted on the morrow. One was all for drawing lots to decide the order of speakers. Others objected to anything like a fixed agenda. In the end, for the sake of compromise and to ensure that each was given the opportunity of saying what he wanted to say, it was agreed that during the opening session no one would take longer than thirty minutes to summarize his particular point of view. Even on this meagre allowance it would take six or seven hours for everyone to have their say, so that, of necessity, any preliminary discussion had to be cut to the barest minimum. There would be plenty of time for a free for all during the three days at Entrèves, they were reminded.

So at last the symposium settled down to a long, hard day of round-table expositions – long for obvious reasons, hard because some of the participants found it irksome to condense the contents of their papers in this summary fashion, irksome, too, to have to hold their peace while listening to speakers with whom they were in strong, even violent, disagreement. As might have been anticipated, there was an underlying conflict between those who envisaged lifelong learning in terms of a further expansion of the existing educational services – more nursery schools, more in-service training, more courses for adults, more everything – and those who were openly contemptuous of the established order and all it stood for. One side, it seemed, was concerned to press the claims of vocational and industrial training, *recyclage* and all that; the other voted for an uninhibited personal culture. More than once during that first day, and the days that followed, our deliberations bore an uncanny resemblance to those of the medieval schoolmen – nominalists and realists facing each other across the table with ill-concealed dislike. Prophets or charlatans? Radicals or diehards? – I kept asking myself as, one by one, the idealists floated their *ballons d'essai* and, one by one, the hard-headed realists brought them down to earth. Caught in this crossfire of argument and counter-argument, a Mercutio might have been forgiven for crying, 'A plague o' both your houses'. Instead, as a privileged observer, it was not for me to reconcile blacks and whites, simply to record – and how tricky a task that is – their yeas and nays as impartially and faithfully as possible. In each case, the following headings are taken from the titles of the papers submitted by the various participants.

1 *On the necessity to deschool society* Ivan Illich started off the proceedings in impetuous fashion, like a centre forward determined to boot the ball clean out of the stadium straight from the kick off. 'I have not modified the views presented in *De-Schooling Society* because I now realize that I was wrong', he declared, a disconcerting opening gambit which caused some puckering of eyebrows. Every one of the papers he had read needed challenging. The time had come to renounce fixed ways of thinking, to affirm that 'I no longer believe in education'. Why so? Because education had become the reproductive organ of a stillborn society, a society which had committed its resources to satisfy the inhuman demands of an industrial production system. Schooling had become the measure of men and of nations, the world polarized between the haves and the have-nots. Learning itself had become a commodity, packaged and marketed by the education industry. Informal learning and self-initiated activity had been demeaned.

By its very nature, an education system which was capital-intensive could not be other than divisive and inequitable, he went on. Only a reversal of present trends, and the adoption of a 'transparent' technology which enabled people to shape and control their own lives, could save us. As things were, any plans for so-called lifelong education should be rejected as future-oriented programming. 'To hell with the future!', he said vehemently, a double-entendre which was not lost on his listeners. It would be better for all of us, he ended, if the vast and ever-increasing sums of money consumed by the education system were cancelled here and now.

'Oh, what a blow that phantom gave me!' As a speaker, Illich commands attention not so much by the inexorable logic of argument as by the sheer force and passionate intensity of its delivery. Fired by a smouldering anger at the manifest ills of an imperfect world, by a profound disgust for what he regards as its Gadarene rush to destruction, his concern is self-evident, eloquent and vibrant to the fingertips.

2 *East–West perspectives on schooling* After the explosiveness of Illich's theory, the still small voice of Wolfgang Mitter helped to lower the temperature somewhat. As a comparative educationist, he called in the existing old world to redress the balance of the new.

During the past decade, expansionist policies in the German Laender, based on the slogan, 'More high school graduates', had, he believed, been misguided. Thanks to them, a surplus of academically trained youth was left all dressed up with nowhere to go: this, despite a massive increase in the number of university entrants. As a consequence, growing uneasiness about current developments had led to demands for total or partial deschooling becoming topical. It should be noted, however, that these demands sprang from conflicting ideologies: on the one hand, from liberals who saw deschooling as a means of emancipating the individual, on the other, from Marxists who supported deschooling as part of a general campaign for the overthrow of capitalistic institutions.

In *theory*, the need to devise alternatives to formal schooling was now widely recognized. Outside the field of recurrent education, however, few systematic experiments had been conducted and, to date, empirical analyses of their effectiveness were still lacking. In short, viable alternatives had yet to be found. In *practice*, the authorities responsible for the maintenance of the education system were in a dilemma whenever they sought to free themselves from the unrelenting pressure of demand for more and more expansionist policies. 'If they don't adopt them, others will', Mitter thought. It was as well to remember that the West's dissatisfaction with formal schooling was by no means shared by the East. The latest law of education ratified by the Supreme Soviet on 19 July 1973 had as its first priority the provision of general education and vocational training for all young people – and it was clear that throughout the Communist bloc as a whole the intention was to retain and reinforce a rigidly controlled, hierarchically structured and bureaucratically regulated system of schooling.

3 *Centres and margins: a world fit for outsiders to live in*   Next, Frank Musgrove started a few hares of his own which showed a fair turn of speed as they galloped off towards the Promised Land. Not for the first time, some of us were left breathless and trailing far behind.

'Our subject is holiness', he began. Were we discussing a non-problem, he asked? Historically, organized schooling was a form of mass production, but it now began to look like a curious aberration. The wonder was that it had succeeded in hoodwinking us for so long. If lifelong learning meant recurrent education – adjusting people, updating them to keep abreast of change, retreads for middle-aged workers, etc. – then so far as he was concerned it was not worth talking about. What was at issue was the rephasing of the human life cycle in a post-industrial world. Demographic trends – longer life expectation, marriages which lasted for forty-five years compared with an average of fifteen years as formerly – were staring us in the face; and anyone who studied them was bound to realize that we were living on the hinge of history. For centuries the education system had been designed so as to classify the young for their future roles as workers. The present mismatch between supply and demand was caused by this same determination to place and fix people in their proper categories. In the past, this process of classification and fixation had met with little resistance. The working man – Apollonian man in Musgrove's terminology – was obedient, reliable, frugal, content to live within the boundaries set for him.

But now the boundaries were dissolving. In order to understand what was happening we needed to look to the misfits, the rejects, the outsiders and outcasts in contemporary society. Far from being a lunatic fringe, these were the creative minority. Not so small a minority, either – in the Manchester conurbation he estimated that as many as 40 per cent of young people below the age of thirty-five were now, as he put it, 'refusing to make bastards of themselves' by submitting to the deadening influence of a lifetime of routine in office or factory. This refusal to conform was trenchantly expressed by one of his interviewees: 'Work fucks your mind.'

Accordingly, the counter-culture was to be seen as the most significant experiment in lifelong learning. What we were witnessing was the birth of a new type of man, a worshipper at the shrine of Dionysus, one who embraced disorder, frenzy, ecstasy. *Ek-stasis* – literally 'standing apart' – was the stance of the individual who had thrown off the shackles of convention, the complete outsider. By contrast, the 'well educated' man was the insider, the lawmaker-engineer who was rapidly becoming obsolescent. In the world of the future, as in medieval times, education would be for the few, a process of rigorous training reserved for a janissary class of technocrats; for the many, a life of ease and go-as-you-please.

'This is what lifelong education in a cybernetic revolution is all about: the rebirth of a Dionysiac culture,' he insisted. 'It is not about updating engineers.'

4 *Multi-media distant study as a starting point for structural reform in scientific learning and continuing education in an age of lifelong*

learning After the divine afflatus, Günther Dohmen brought us back to the gritty rockface. As Director of the Deutsches Institut für Fernstudien, which caters for as many as 130,000 students in West Germany, it was not his custom to indulge in flights of fancy. As he saw it, the problem facing us was to build bridges between high-flown theories and the sordid realities of everyday practice. It was relatively easy to formulate new ideas, infinitely harder for those who had to implement them. The trouble with schools and universities was that they had always been playgrounds for speculative theorists.

No improvement in the established system could be expected until scientific, academic and educational research ceased to remain as secluded and withdrawn as they usually were. The urgent need was for action research, for research and development. The credibility gap between theory and practice, and especially the gap between a school life spent in academic learning and the experiences encountered in the world of work, left many students in a state of 'practice shock'. Some never recovered from it, others plunged headlong into political radicalism or joined protest movements which were counter-productive or simply abortive. For this and other reasons, the relationship between students and their teachers nowadays was peculiarly tense. The personality cult fostered by the traditional German universities was no longer relevant or practicable. The days of the learned professor surrounded by a handful of worshipful disciples were long past. Increasingly, the teacher's role defined itself as that of an *animateur*, not an instructor. Today, resources for learning could be placed at the student's disposal with a fair degree of spatial and temporal flexibility. The large-scale use of aids to study in the form of self-contained modules which enabled students to learn what they needed at their own convenience might well be seen as the first step on the road to lifelong learning. Far from being depersonalizing, as was often feared, modern media could be the means of revitalizing the education system. How to find the right media mix, then? Between them, radio, television and film did not provide an adequate answer, helpful as they were in boosting motivation or arousing interest. Indeed, printed materials differing little, if at all, from the kinds used in old-fashioned correspondence courses were still the most economic and reliable vehicle for the promotion of Fernstudien. In any case, dissemination of learning materials was only half the battle: the other half, yet to be fought and won, concerned the organization of human relationships in these new, extra-institutional settings. As the teacher-as-instructor gradually receded into the background, there was a growing demand for closer personal contacts, discussion and co-operation among the students themselves.

As for the long-term prospects, Dohmen was not prepared to hazard a guess. For the moment, the point he wished to emphasize was that the construction, testing and distribution of flexible multi-media learning systems called for special skills, not to mention a great deal of time and effort; and that in the present state of the art purely speculative theories were more of a hindrance than a help for those engaged in that task.

5 *The laws of the media: a structural approach.* Talk of media seemed to be the appropriate cue for Eric McLuhan. He began by explaining that 'The medium is the message' meant that the user was the content. No less tantalizingly, he went on to say that we must shed our preconceived notions of linear causality: invariably, the effects *preceded* the cause – witness the saying, 'The time was ripe'.

In this sense, lifelong learning was already a *fait accompli*. In effect, the experience of living for three or four centuries was now being packed into the space of a single lifetime or less. In other words, we should not be thinking in terms of 'education' at all: to do so was rather like saying to a man, 'Last year was a good one for you: you get a B rating for that.'

Since Graeco-Roman times Western man had been visually oriented, so much so that the transportation theory of communication, i.e. moving data from point to point in time and space, was the only one he was capable of understanding. By contrast, non-literate man (and, by inference, post-literate man?) found it easier to think of communication in terms of transformation rather than transportation.

A structural approach to the laws of the media focused attention on the new life styles arising from the creation of new modes of perception and the realignment of old ones. However subliminally, all media were manipulators of men. For the social scientist, and especially for those who controlled the mass media, therefore, it was imperative to consider and, so far as was possible, anticipate their effects on whole populations whose lives were certain to be disturbed, if not actually disrupted, by being exposed to their influence. Each technological innovation could be seen as the introduction, as it were, of a new musical key: it transposed all the other instruments of communication in the orchestra.

By the same token, literate man's antennae were being transposed from a dominant visual 'key' to one which might be described as auditory-tactile. T. S. Eliot's 'auditory imagination' penetrated far below the conscious levels of thought and feeling. Similarly, the idea of *interface*, popularly expressed as 'where the action is', was implicit in all structures, whether physical, chemical, psychic or social, because it involved the factor of *touch*. Touch, as the frontier of change, was indispensable to the study of structures. Basic to it was the notion of 'play' – the resonant interval or 'slack' between wheel and axle without which movement would be impossible.

Western man now found himself at a cultural interface (Musgrove's 'hinge of history'?), caught between the claims of a visual, print-dominated tradition and the counter-claims of the new electronic communication media. Much of the confusion and stress in contemporary life, psychic and social as well as intellectual, were occasioned by this changeover from a static, step-by-step learning situation to one best characterized as a dynamic, simultaneous, acoustic mosaic. Systematic investigation of the laws of the media was still in its infancy. But just as Lamarck had been led to formulate his laws of evolution by observing the effects of different natural environments on animals, so, it was hoped, the McLuhan approach would eventually throw light on our adaptive reactions to manmade environments.

6 *The future of the Open University* Walter James, who followed, would certainly resent being called a media man. Far from extolling the Open University as a triumphant example of a multimedia learning system in the grand manner, he seemed disposed to regard it as a missed opportunity, an example of what happens when there is too naïve a faith in the ability of the technologies to change the system to which they are applied. Its achievements so far were, he thought, limited, and as for its future he was troubled in case it was too far gone to change. In so far as the Open University functioned as a degree-awarding body of the traditional kind, it obviously *had* a future, at any rate for those of the underprivileged and the dispossessed who were only too eager to pick up the crumbs which fell from the academic community's high table. But even on this reckoning, the pabulum offered by the Open University consisted of 'plastic

packages and soggy bread' (his own words). In short, it was serving essentially the same purpose as any of the other institutions engaged in the mass production of higher education, making essentially the same product more available.

Of the objectives laid down in the Open University's Royal Charter of 1969 only the last – 'to promote the educational well-being of the community generally' – offered any prospect of significant change. This objective, unfortunately, was nullified by the prior requirement, which was 'to provide education of university and professional standards', i.e. to serve the *status quo*. Admittedly, availability of higher education had been substantially increased, and at a fraction of the normal cost; students had to some extent been liberated from the constraints of age, space and time which had shackled them in the past: and the feedback obtained from the use of radio, TV and packaged learning materials had helped to make course of instruction more efficient. Indeed, the speed with which the Open University had gained recognition had led to its acquiring an aura of prestige with the result that other countries were now seeking, mistakenly in his opinion, to imitate it. The danger was that by providing cut-price higher education that was at once efficient and widely available an essentially élite system would simply be reinforced and perpetuated. If *that* was to be the future of the Open University the sooner it was changed the better.

In the meantime, he continued, the hungry sheep looked up and were not fed. A more worthwhile objective, in his judgement, would have been 'to promote the educational well-being of the human being'. 'Man cannot himself be fully human if he diminishes the capacity of others to be so', he affirmed (Illich's sentiment precisely). In the final analysis, what mattered most was the capacity to belong to others, to care for others, to share with others, and in so doing to *become*.

Education in this sense was best understood as community service. As such, its morality abjured the self-seeking values which passed for virtues in academic circles, and the purely cognitive curriculum which denied the value of human relationships. In the existing climate of social, economic and political opinion it might well be impossible for the Open University or any other institution of higher education to promote the well-being of the human being by devising a curriculum capable of developing genuinely humane qualities and dispositions which disclosed themselves in action. Before that could be attempted there would have to be a general change of heart and a wholesale reversal of existing policies. But at least James left his listeners in no doubt that against all the odds the attempt ought to be made.

7 *Comment favoriser l'égalité des chances?*   Just what Bertrand Schwartz was thinking about this omnium gatherum of opinions was anybody's guess. Shrewd, impassive apart from the merry twinkle in his eyes, he had bided his time patiently. As a ministry official, no doubt, he was less free than some of the others to speak out boldly against bureaucratic imperialism. Even so, he was suitably scathing about the labour-intensiveness of the teaching profession and critical of the folly of educational policies which were content to see costs escalating while productivity declined. Critical, too, of the steady lengthening of the learner's school life. The average age for taking the baccalaureate examination had risen from 17 to 19·3 years in recent decades. Going over to the blackboard, he worked out an arithmetical sum using the equation:

$$\frac{\text{Number of pupils}}{\text{Number of teachers}} \times \frac{\text{Average number per class}}{\text{Average number of hours work}}$$

and proved to everyone's satisfaction that the yearly 10 per cent increase in the French educational budget was yielding a nil return. Schwartz prefaced his remarks by making the point that any educational enterprise only made sense if its defined objectives and the means of achieving them were congruent. If the aim was to form a human being who was fulfilled (*épanoui*), creative, free (*autonome*) and social, it followed that education must satisfy two conditions: (*a*) it would be continuous (*permanente*); (*b*) it would do everything possible to guarantee equality of opportunity.

L'éducation permanente and equality of opportunity were, in fact, only two of the seven principles on which the educational 'Plan Europe 2000' outlined in Schwartz's book *L'Éducation demain* (Une étude de la Fondation Européenne de la Culture, Aubier Montaigne, Paris 1973) had been based. The others were: *orientation* (guidance), *autoformation* (i.e. exercise of individual responsibility), *cogestion* (i.e. devolution of decision-making), comprehensiveness (i.e. no discrimination by sex, race, social class, etc.) and mobility (i.e. releasing studies and students from the restrictions of time and space). All seven principles were interrelated, of course, but for the moment he wished to concentrate on these first two.

It was an illusion to imagine that educational reform alone would ever solve the problem of equality of opportunity. As a first step towards greater social justice, nevertheless, his own inclination was to lower the age when compulsory school attendance should begin to two and a half or three years. But if compulsory schooling allowed every child to develop according to his natural rhythm the traditional classroom set-up was bound to disappear sooner or later. The sooner pupils were given opportunities for acting responsibly, the better. Towards the end of the secondary stage, however, this led to a contradiction between individual freedom of choice and the manpower needs of a society which, rightly or wrongly, retained a high regard for paper qualifications.

So far as the school was concerned, the only hope of achieving equality of opportunity was by providing basic training (*formation de base*) and by developing some kind of common course (*tronc commun*). For adults, inequalities of opportunity could be compensated for to some extent in two ways: first, by a system of recurrent education which enabled them to pursue professional-vocational studies at any time during their working careers without financial sacrifice and without putting their own or their promotion prospects at risk; second, by local community services which allowed people to learn what they wanted in their own time and in their own way.

In brief, the French approach to *l'éducation permanente*, bureaucratic and meritocratic as it might seem, was also an approach to structural reforms which would have profound and far-reaching consequences, not least in qualifying some of our fixed ideas about schooling. One advantage of lowering the age of compulsory attendance would be to leave more time for the growth of self-discipline and the exercise of individual responsibility through less formal agencies – essential if the ideals of social justice and participatory democracy were ever to be realized. As a realist, nevertheless, it was necessary to add the caveat that wishing to achieve such objectives was one thing, willing the means quite another.

8 *The nature and nurture of learning in a social educational system*
By now the afternoon was wearing on and the end of the marathon still nowhere in sight. (Presumably we must have had a break for lunch, but, if so, I had been so heavily preoccupied trying to keep

track of the various speakers that it was lost without trace in my memory.) After a brief adjournment during which the simmer of talk continued unabated, the hearings were resumed.

To Gordon Pask fell the invidious task of condensing the contents of a lengthy, abstruse paper which few of his listeners had had time to read, let alone assimilate. He set about it with all the panache of a master magician. But, then, Gordon *is* a master magician. Armed with a formidable array of charts and diagrams, each of them a sort of Ordnance Survey of a domain of knowables, this cybernetic Puck quickly put a girdle round our intellectual earth and conjured up our willing suspension of disbelief.

Miracles *were* possible, he began. Catalytic agents, seemingly insignificant in themselves, could bring about dramatic, large-scale organizational changes. One such agent was educational technology, for him a branch of practical epistemology, and he made it plain that before he had finished none of us would be in any doubt that educational technology was the proper study for mystics.

Tuition, he believed, was not the appropriate paradigm. The mismatch between conventional methods of instruction and individual cognitive styles was grossly improvident, ineffective, and usually frustrating for student and teacher alike. Most lessons and lectures degenerated into a pedagogical speaking tube. According to the cybernetic model, on the other hand, learning resulted from an internal dialogue, i.e. the brain was seen as having a 'teacher' part and a 'learner' part. Most learning theories, and particularly those popularized by B. F. Skinner and other behaviourists, were inadequate.

'What I *know* is essentially a *relationship*', Pask explained. Similarly, a *concept* (usually thought of as a classification) is a *reproducer of relationships*. Memory, in turn, is a *reproducer of concepts*. He went on to distinguish between two main types of learner: serialist (linear step-by-step) and holist (*Gestalt?*). It was also necessary to distinguish between 'operation' and 'comprehension' types of learning, the existence of which had been empirically confirmed. The former relied heavily on deductive inference, the latter on the abduction of morphisms – isomorphisms, homomorphisms, analogies. The typology was never clearcut – needless to say, both components played a part in normal learning – but it was expedient to take note of the differences between them. Failure to do so would inevitably confirm a preference for imposed strategies of learning (in which the student had to follow and obey instructions) as opposed to strategies conceived by the student of his own accord. Hence the all too frequent mismatch between cognitive styles and the different requirements of 'operation' and 'comprehension' learning.

Hitherto, the objection had always been that the costs of replacing the 'flesh and blood' teacher were prohibitive. This objection was no longer valid. As proof of this assertion, he described a conversational operational system, CASTE (Course Assembly System and Tutorial Environment), which enabled the student to set his own goals and control his own learning strategies. Far from being a dehumanizing device, as was commonly supposed, the machine was a vehicle for driving through the maze of tracks in the infinite realm of the knowable. Just as the body was the vehicle men used for walking, so the brain's capacity for mental space travel could be augmented and enhanced by using more versatile, sophisticated vehicles. 'Learning how to learn effectively' was no longer an idle dream: experiences in the conversational mode of CASTE had shown that it could be done. There was no limit to individual awareness.

9 *Learning, democratizing and deschooling*   As a booster rocket for flagging morale, Pask's intervention was nothing if not timely. Any euphoria was short-lived, nevertheless. Michael Huberman, Piaget's youthful American collaborator at Geneva, struck a more captious note to begin with.

Equality of educational opportunity was a myth, its theory vitiated by the practice of granting only differentiated opportunity. Preferential treatment for the few was the rule. All the sociological evidence proved conclusively that the education system was designed to favour middle class families and their children. Its basic premise was that since resources were scarce there was not enough schooling to go around, hence the necessity for distributing it unevenly. Broadly, the argument was that since scientists, directors, administrators, etc., held the key positions in society, these were the kind of people on whom resources should be concentrated, the ones who needed to be identified as early as possible so that they could be given the lengthiest and most expensive training. Since this scarcity model postulated the impossibility of giving the same amount of education to everyone, schools were left to treat unequal children as if they were somehow equal.

Psychological tests, in purporting to be 'culture-free', only served to mask this pretence: almost invariably, they concealed a built-in prejudice in favour of academic performance. Thanks to them, the 'intelligence' of children from working class backgrounds had been consistently underrated. The norms for such tests were largely decided in accordance with the symbolic skills and conceptualizations of a dominant middle class culture. Because of this, many pupils were alienated and frustrated, the rejectees of the education system. In effect, full educational opportunity for a minority was being subsidized by the majority.

Granted that the established system was in many respects inequitable, even anti-democratic, how could it be reformed? So-called compensatory education was no answer ('cultural fascism', he called it). Schematically, there were three possibilities, he thought:

1 To change the present mode of functioning in primary and secondary schools. This could be done by specifying norms of attainment and allowing pupils to achieve them at their own pace and according to individual cognitive styles – rather than requiring them to do so by a given age. This more flexible organization was a good deal less utopian than it might appear: it was already operating in many enlightened primary schools, and the research findings indicated that it was more successful than the kind of organization which retained standardized instructional periods, 'class' groupings, uniform materials and lockstep methods.

2 To equalize the resources available to the early leavers as well as those who continue on to higher education. Crudely, this meant giving the drop-outs the money that would otherwise have been spent on their education and letting them use it as and when they pleased. Less crudely, this equalization fund might take the form of a post-school credit or voucher. As things were, the early leaver's share of public educational expenditure represented only a small fraction of that of a boy or girl who stayed on to take a university degree. A voucher scheme would be difficult to operate, certainly, but there were good reasons for wishing to canvass it.

3 To abolish compulsory schooling altogether.

In Huberman's judgement, however, there were serious, practical objections to the theory of deschooling. If it were acted upon, the effect, almost inevitably, would be to play into the hands of the haves at the expense of the have-nots. In any case, schools were semi-religious institutions which could not be dismantled like factories.

Children were too precious a property for their welfare to be discussed dispassionately. Few children, besides, were self-motivated before they attended school. Societies did not voluntarily give parents full control over the development of children, at any rate up to the age of puberty.

Technologically, the 'global village' of McLuhan and the 'new primitivism' of Illich might be possible, but socially and culturally we were not yet ready for either. With all their faults and shortcomings, schools were probably a wiser, and certainly a safer, investment than any of the alternatives so far proposed. In the long run, he believed, we should come round to the sensible conclusion that a youth of fifteen or sixteen had as much right to work as to study, and that the adult at any age had as much right to study as to work. The practice of squeezing education into the period of childhood and adolescence stemmed from a historical context in which the average life expectancy was forty to fifty years. A more intelligent way of spacing events in our life cycle was now essential.

10 *Practical applications of educational technology* If, at this late hour, Giovanni Gozzer was inclined to take a poor view of the proceedings, he could hardly have been blamed. To have to sit through hour after hour of expositions in an alien tongue was bad enough, but for one who was daily faced with intractable practical problems the whole tenor of the discussion must have seemed (as he confided later) 'incapace di planare verso la realtá'. Too high-falutin' by half.

He spoke guardedly and briefly. Politically, the contemporary state of affairs in Italy was potentially explosive, virtually a 'Chilean situation'. Any attempt to adapt the education system to avant-gardist theories could very easily prove to be catastrophic.

Educational technology for practical purposes could be thought of as consisting of didactic and learning systems which fell into three categories:

1 Supportive systems – e.g. audio-visual aids
2 Self-instructional systems – e.g. programmed learning, computer-assisted instruction
3 Mixed systems – ETV, video cassettes, etc.

A basic problem, common to all three and as yet unsolved, concerned the 'logic' of the languages used in the dissemination of information. Even in the classroom, with a teacher in charge, uncertainty, ambiguity and redundancy were regularly to be found in everyday speech. If, as seemed probable, the video-media were destined to play an increasingly important role alongside programmed learning it was essential to establish closer rapport between expression (*lingua e linguistica*) and transmission (*informatica*).

Another problem facing the educational technologist arose from the stiff resistance, particularly in Latin cultures, to innovations in any shape or form. Yet another raised the question of who was to control the production and marketing of hardware and software: commercial entrepreneurs or those who were their customers? Makers or users? Obviously teachers were ill prepared to assume control. That being the case, how to ensure that industrial managerial agencies would be socially responsible?

11 *Educational technology for lifelong education* To close the innings – already it had lasted longer than his flight from Montreal – David Mitchell wielded his bat to good effect, scoring boundaries to off and on sides of the field, Not Out to the end.

Misunderstanding of the fundamental nature of educational technology, he was sure, engendered widespread and needless fears that it would prove to be a dehumanizing influence. In reality, educational technology manifested itself at five different, ascending levels:

Ed Tech 1 – instructional technology, perhaps best typified by programmed learning
Ed Tech 2 – the selection, processing and storage of information, production and testing of learning materials, etc.
Ed Tech 3 – the management of resources
Ed Tech 4 – systems technology dealing with problems of design, construction and evaluation
Ed Tech 5 – high-level educational planning.

Conceived in this hierarchical manner, educational technology might well be destined to emerge as *the* humane discipline of the future.

From this perspective, Mitchell developed a three-dimensional conceptual model of lifelong education. According to this, learning at all stages was seen as part of an integrated system consisting of four sectors: (1) schooling – learning in the classroom; (2) occupation – learning on the job; (3) social life – learning in the family, in the peer group, in church, through travel, etc.; (4) community resources – learning through the mass media, museums, libraries, theatres, etc.

Lifelong learning was a coalescence of all four sectors. The trouble was that schooling monopolized not only the resources but also the sense of importance attached to education by public opinion. Research into the system as a whole was apparently nobody's business. Academics, administrators and for that matter most educational technologists had not given anything like sufficient attention to the devisal of alternative institutional arrangements. 'We ignore the non-school sectors at our peril', he warned them.

The great virtue of a systems approach was that it cut formal schooling down to size, revealing it as a subsystem – and an overrated one – in the educational enterprise. Given the skills and the know-how that were now available, the prospect of a life of continuous learning was less a hope for the future than a present reality.

For this relief, much thanks. And so to dinner. It spoke well for their stamina after these sessions of plain sitting and high thinking that the buzz of animated conversation among the participants continued far into the night. All in all, though, taking the rough with the smooth, it had not been such a bad day. Hard, yes, but necessarily so. At least the major ingredients of the symposium had been pooled and given a preliminary stirring. Plenty to think about and no mistake. What would the outcome be, – panacea or half-baked witches' brew? It remained to be seen. Tomorrow to fresh fields and alpine pastures, a change of scene which could hardly fail to be exhilarating.

3 *Private retreat*

Io non posso ritrar di tutti a pieno
peró che si mi caccia il lungo tema
che molte volte al fatto il dir vien meno.
Dante, *L'Inferno*, Canto IV, 145–8
Nay, but I tell not all that I saw then;
The long theme drives me hard, and everywhere
The wondrous truth outstrips my staggering pen.
Translated by Dorothy L. Sayers

Jovial as children on a Sunday school excursion or a rugger team bound for an important away match, the party boarded the specially chartered bus for Entrèves.

It was a golden morning and a golden journey: first to Ivrea across the plains of Piedmont – maize fields, poplars and vineyards, with the snows of the Gran Paradiso spectral above the scarves of cloud that wreathed the distant foothills, then through the walled-in crags and castles of the Valle d'Aosta, tunnel after tunnel opening up on new surprise views, new splendours. To travel hopefully *may* be better than to arrive, but when we stepped out at the road's end, to be greeted by the sight of Mont Blanc arrayed in all its glory, the idea seemed positively ridiculous. Ahead, the Brenva glacier looked to be only a stone's throw from the hotel door, backed by the sinister spires of the Aiguille Noire de Peuteret. On the right, the alpine meadows and pine-dark slopes of Val Ferret huddled beneath the serried flanks of Europe's grandest massif, their spidery arêtes climbing up to the gashed skyline and the monstrous horn of the Dent du Géant.

An idyllic setting for lofty thinking. Or was it? At times during those glorious, hectic three days it seemed as if the mountain air had gone to our heads: we were all 'marginal' men taking a holiday from the dreary routines of normal cogitation. It was as though a dozen symposia were taking place simultaneously. Not so much a teach-in as a series of happenings. Even for a peripatetic host, trying to keep track of them all was out of the question. It was, you may say, a totally unmanageable situation – and maybe all the better for being so. Individuals who had earlier failed to see eye to eye across a table struck up friendships 12,000 feet up on the Aiguille du Midi or with their feet up in the hotel lounge. Conversation rather than formal discussion seemed to be preferred by all concerned. As 'an assembly of learned men met together for the sake of intellectual peace' a Newman might have found it all disconcerting, lacking the composure of the original *symposium* – but to have recaptured *that* was more than anyone could have hoped for or expected.

CONCLUSIONS

Returning to Turin for the closing public session felt rather like being summoned to a court martial, beset with Monday morning blues and misgivings. Had we done our homework? Were we ready to face the firing squad? The lucky ones had planes to catch and left early. The less lucky, most of whom resented any suggestion of a consensus having been reached, now had to put their thoughts into some sort of order. No chance of fending off inquiries with a terse No Comment, the tactic so often adopted by spokesmen emerging from conference halls where collective bargaining is still deadlocked. No good muttering platitudes about 'useful talks'. Disclaimers would never satisfy an expectant audience. How to tell the waiting world that we had wrestled with questions for which we could find no clear answers – except *one*, and that answer so hard to take as to be virtually incommunicable?

Presumably this was the predicament of Plato's philosopher-king when the time came for him to re-enter the Cave and explain to his fellows that reality was not what they took it to be.

Had we arrived at any conclusions, it was asked? Without risk of serious dissent, it seemed honest to say that we *had* and that there was broad agreement on the following points:

1 that policies of educational expansion cannot safely continue indefinitely or, indeed, much longer along the present lines,

2 that it is vitally necessary to de-emphasize the importance attached to formal schooling (of all the points listed, this was the one which most needed to be impressed upon public opinion and the authorities),

3 that if lifelong learning were to be interpreted as continuous schooling, or even as recurrent vocational training, none of us was really in favour of it,

4 that the significant growth points in contemporary society are to be found in the proliferation of non-formal associations and community service networks,

5 that some of the resources, human as well as financial, now devoted to (and in our judgement wasted on) the statutory education system might more justly and profitably be allocated as grants in aid for these non-formal associations and services,

6 that there is a law of diminishing returns in compulsory school attendance after the age of twelve to thirteen years,

7 that the immediate task is to build bridgeheads between the formal (institutionalized) and the non-formal (associational) organization of learning by creating networks of communication which guarantee free access to the necessary facilities and resources for young and old alike,

8 that resources for learning in the community, as distinct from those made available through the statutory education system, need to be more fully exploited than they are at present,

9 that learning can no longer be contained within the frames and classifications hitherto imposed upon it by the academic community,

10 that the existential problem which has to be faced, and which the

'youthquake' will solve if nothing else does, concerns a society that is information-rich and action-poor,

11 that the information revolution, as evidenced by the new, essentially non-verbal media of communication, necessitates modes of thought and language whose 'logic' and 'grammar' are quite different from those which hold good for literate-mindedness,

12 that despite its inherent dangers, educational technology *is* capable of providing ways and means of realizing the ideal of a learning society; and that this is now possible without in any way infringing the individual's self-control and freedom of choice.

References

CHAPTER ONE

1 A. Curle, *Education for Liberation* (Tavistock Publications, 1973).
2 J. S. Bruner, *The Relevance of Education* (Allen and Unwin, 1972).
3 The National Children's Bureau Report, *Born to Fail?* (ed. Peter Wedge and Hilary Prosser) (Arrow Books, 1974).
4 J. S. Bruner, *Patterns of Growth*, Inaugural Lecture (Oxford at the Clarendon Press, 1974), p. 20.
5 J. Coleman, *How do the Young Become Adults?* (Center for the Social Organization of Schools).
6 T. Husén, *The Learning Society* (Methuen, 1974).
7 D. Wardle, *The Rise of the Schooled Society* (Routledge and Kegan Paul, 1974).
8 T. Husén, op. cit., Preface.

CHAPTER TWO

1 R. S. Peters (ed.), *The Philosophy of Education* (Oxford University Press, 1973), p. 238.
2 S. Cohen, 'New perspectives in the history of American education', *History of Education*, Volume II, ed. M. Seaborne (David and Charles, 1973), p. 82.
3 P. Hirst and R. S. Peters, *The Logic of Education* (Routledge and Kegan Paul, 1970), p. 21.

4 M. Polanyi, *Personal Knowledge* (Chicago University Press, 1958), p. 251.
5 I. Illich, *On the Necessity to De-school Society* (New York, UNESCO International Commission on the Development of Education, Series B : Opinions, 1971).
6 C. Bereiter, 'Schools without education', *Harvard Educational Review* (September 1972).
7 R. S. Peters, *Ethics and Education* (Allen and Unwin, 1966), p. 32.
8 M. Braham, 'The grounding of the technologist', paper presented to the Association of Programmed Learning and Educational Technology Conference, Falmer, 1973.
9 R. S. Peters, *Ethics and Education*, p. 39.
10 L. C. Taylor, *Resources for Learning* (2nd ed., Penguin Books, 1972), p. 247.
11 School of Barbiana, *Letter to a Teacher* (Penguin Books, 1970).
12 Cf. chapter 8 below.
13 See chapter 4, 'The knowledge market'.
14 R. S. Peters, *Ethics and Education*, p. 30.
15 Ibid., p. 38.

CHAPTER THREE

1 I. Illich *et. al.*, *After Deschooling, What?*, ed. Alan Gartner, Colin Greer and Frank Riessman (New York, Harper and Row, 1973), p. 1.
2 Ibid., p. 137.
3 Ibid., p. 147.
4 Doxiadis is the author of *Between Dystopia and Utopia*, *The Future of Human Settlements*, *Ekistics, the Science of Human Settlements* and numerous other publications on problems of town planning and urban development.
5 Alberto Granesi, an analytical philosopher, is the author of *G. E. Moore e la Filosofia Analitica Inglese* (Nuova Italia, 1970), *Il Giovane Dewey* (1966), *Che Cosa ha veramente detto Russell?* (Astrolabio-Ubaldine Editore, 1971) and other books. His reply to question 1 took the form of a lengthy essay, 'Educazione e scolarizzazione', from which this extract has been translated.
6 See chapter 10.

CHAPTER FOUR

1 T. Husén, 'Does more time in school make a difference?', *Saturday Review*, 29 April 1972.
2 Ibid.
3 D. Holly, *Beyond Curriculum* (Hart-Davis, MacGibbon, 1974), p. 165.

4 Ibid., p. 134.
5 *De Republica*, Book II.
6 W. Ong, *Ramus: method and the decay of dialogue* (New York, Octagon Books, 1972), p. 150.
7 Ibid., p. 152.
8 Ibid., p. 154.
9 B. Bernstein, 'Classification and framing of education knowledge' in *Readings in the Theory of Educational Systems,* ed. Earl Hopper (Hutchinson, 1971), p. 197.
10 W. Ong, op. cit., p. 156.
11 Ibid., p. 161.
12 B. Bernstein, op. cit., pp. 196–7.
13 E. Hopper, 'A typology for the classification of educational systems' in *Readings in the Theory of Educational Systems,* ed. Earl Hopper (Hutchinson, 1971), pp. 91–110.
14 M. McLuhan, *The Gutenberg Galaxy* (Routledge and Kegan Paul, 1962), p. 215.
15 E. Hopper, 'A typology for the classification of educational systems', p. 92.
16 P. Bourdieu, 'Cultural reproduction and social reproduction' in *Knowledge, Education, and Cultural Change,* ed. Richard Brown (Tavistock Publications, 1973), p. 73.
17 Ibid., pp. 96–7.
18 School of Barbiana, *Letter to a Teacher* (Penguin Books, 1970), p. 41.
19 R. Aron, *Progress and Disillusion* (Pall Mall Press, 1968), p. 114.
20 Ibid., p. 133.
21 A. Visalberghi, 'Political and economic problems concerning some models of educational growth in post-secondary education', background paper for Plan Europe 2000 (Berlin, December 1972).
22 B. Bernstein, loc. cit.
23 Ibid., p. 197.
24 In a shrewd analysis of the politics of educational knowledge, Michael F. D. Young notes that the projects sponsored by the Schools Council fall into two broad classes, those based on 'academic expertise' and those based on 'good practice'. The former follow the advice of academic experts who start with an explicit idea of what ought to be learnt and define the structure of the subject; the latter largely rely on the Inspectorate's notions of what counts as 'good practice'. Either way, projects must fit into a traditional pedagogical frame:

> The 'academic expertise' style takes for granted the basic structure of academic 'subjects' while the 'good practice' style does not

question the practice of 'good' teachers. Thus each makes implicit assumptions about the autonomy of educational knowledge from the society of which the educational institutions are a part. In this way both project styles may contribute to maintaining for educators the 'reality' of 'something that really *is* education' and the 'non-political' character of education. (Michael F. D. Young, 'On the politics of educational knowledge' in *Education in Great Britain and Ireland*, ed. R. Bell, G. Fowler and K. Little (Open University Set Book, 1973), pp. 77–8.

25 E. Durkheim, *Education and Sociology* (New York, Free Press, 1956), p. 71.
26 Ibid., p. 29.
27 Ibid., p. 82.
28 Ibid., p. 86.
29 Ibid., p. 87.
30 Ibid., p. 88.
31 *Observer*, 4 February 1973.
32 Durkheim, op. cit., p. 123.
33 P. Clyne, *The Disadvantaged Adult* (Longman, 1972), p. 49.
34 E. C. Lindeman, *The Meaning of Adult Education* (Montreal, Harvest House, 1961).
35 J. Le Veugle, *Initiation a l'éducation permante* (Paris, Privat, 1968), p. 9.
36 J. Dumazedier, *Toward a Society of Leisure* (New York, Free Press, 1967), pp. 16–17.
37 E. Leach. 'Education for what?', *Roscoe Review* (Department of Extra-Mural Studies, Manchester University, 1969).
38 A. S. Neill, *Neill! Neill! Orange Peel!* (Weidenfeld and Nicolson, 1973), p. 192.

CHAPTER FIVE
1 C. Bereiter, 'Schools without education', *Harvard Educational Review* (September 1972).
2 Ibid.
3 Ibid.

CHAPTER SIX
1 *Learning to Be* (UNESCO/Harrap, 1973), p. xxvi.
2 Ibid., p. 105.
3 Ibid., p. xxiii.
4 Ibid., p. 23.
5 *Daily Telegraph*, 6 September 1973.
6 Cf. chapter 9, 'The two cultures and the information revolution'.

7 *Learning to Be*, p. 72.
8 Ibid., p. 71.
9 Ibid., p. 144.
10 Ibid., p. 209.
11 Ibid., p. 233.

CHAPTER SEVEN

1 Cf. D. Dolci, *Chissá se i Pesce Piangono* (Einaudi, 1974).
2 F. W. Mitchell, *Sir Fred Clarke: Master-Teacher 1880–1952* (Longman, 1967), pp. 129–30.
3 J. S. Bruner, *Patterns of Growth*, Inaugural Lecture (Oxford at the Clarendon Press, 1974).
4 *Daily Telegraph*, 6 February 1974.
5 F. W. Jessup, *Lifelong Learning* (Pergamon Press, 1969).
6 *The Times Educational Supplement*, 27 October 1972.
7 From *Permanent Education. A Compendium of Studies* (Strasburg, 1970).
8 F. W. Jessup, op. cit.
9 P. Bourdieu, 'Cultural reproduction and social reproduction' in *Knowledge, Education and Cultural Change*, ed. R. Brown (Tavistock Publications, 1973).
10 W. Martin, *The Leisure Market to 1980* (James Morrell and Associates, Economic Research Consultants, London, 1973).
11 P. Slater, *The Leisure of Loneliness* (Beacon Press, 1970).
12 W. Harman, 'Changing United States society: implications for schools', Part 4 in *Alternative Educational Futures in the United States and Europe* (Paris, OECD, 1972).

CHAPTER EIGHT

1 J. S. Bruner, *Patterns of Growth*, Inaugural Lecture (Oxford at the Clarendon Press, 1974).
2 A. Toffler, *Future Shock* (Pan Books, 1971), p. 12.
3 L. Morin, *Les Charlatans de la nouvelle pedagogie* (Presses Universitaires de France, 1973), p. 92.
4 K. Minogue, *The Concept of a University* (Weidenfeld and Nicolson, 1973), pp. 144–5.
5 A. Toynbee, 'Education: the long view', in *American Education Today*, ed. P. Woodring and J. Seanbon (New York, McGraw-Hill, 1964), p. 272.
6 Unpublished manuscript.
7 J. S. Bruner, *Patterns of Growth*.
8 J. Locke, *Essay on Human Understanding*, Book II, chapter 1, paras 2 and 4.

9 M. Grene, *The Knower and the Known* (Faber, 1964), p. 14.
10 A. Koestler and J. R. Smythies (eds.), *Beyond Reductionism* (Hutchinson, 1969).
11 G. Chanan and L. Gilchrist, *What School is For* (Methuen, 1974), p. 16.
12 W. K. Richmond, *The School Curriculum* (Methuen, 1971).
13 A. Koestler, 'Is man's brain an evolutionary mistake?', *Horizon* (spring 1968).
14 R. Titone, 'The information revolution', paper presented at the Agnelli Symposium, Turin, September 1973.
15 J. S. Bruner, *Patterns of Growth*.
16 P. H. Taylor, 'New frontiers in educational research' in *Guidance and Assessment in European Education* (Paedogogica Europaea, Malmberg/Westermann, 1973), p. 27.
17 Ibid.
18 I. Illich, *On the Necessity to De-school Society* (New York, UNESCO International Commission on the Development of Education, Series B : Opinions, 1971).
19 F. Musgrove, 'Centres and margins: a world fit for outsiders to live in', paper presented at the Agnelli Symposium, Turin, September 1973).
20 Ibid.
21 O. Giscard d'Estaing, *Éducation et civilization* (Paris, Fayard, 1971).

CHAPTER NINE

1 T. S. Kuhn, *The Structure of Scientific Revolutions* (Harvard University Press, 1963).
2 M. Polanyi, *Personal Knowledge* (University of Chicago Press, 1958), p. 211.
3 Ibid., p. 245.
4 A. Etzioni, *The Active Society* (Collier-Macmillan, 1968).
5 Ibid.
6 C. H. Waddington, *Beyond Reductionism*, ed. A. Koestler and J. R. Smythies (Hutchinson, 1969).
7 D. Mitchell, 'Educational technology for lifelong education', paper presented at the Agnelli Symposium, Turin, September 1973.
8 A. Etzioni, op. cit., p. 618.
9 I. Berg, *Education and Jobs: the great training robbery* (Penguin Books, 1973), pp. 96–101.
10 Ibid., p. 182.
11 Rand Report, prepared for the President's Commission on School Finance (March 1972).

12 E. McLuhan, 'The laws of the media : a structural approach', paper presented at the Agnelli Symposium, Turin, September 1973.
13 In litt.
14 B. Jackson and D. Marsden, *Education and the Working Class* (Routledge and Kegan Paul, 1962).

CHAPTER TEN
1 J. Evetts, *The Sociology of Educational Ideas* (Routledge and Kegan Paul, 1973), p. 142.
2 J. Lynch and H. Dudley Plunkett, *Teacher Education and Cultural Change* (Allen and Unwin, 1973), p. 14.

Index of Authors' Names